Adorno and the Ban on Images

Also Available from Bloomsbury

Adorno and Neoliberalism: The Critique of Exchange Society,
Charles A. Prusik
Understanding Adorno, Understanding Modernism,
ed. Robin Truth Goodman
Aesthetic Marx, ed. Samir Gandesha and Johan F. Hartle
From Marx to Hegel and Back: Capitalism, Critique, and Utopia,
ed. Victoria Fareld and Hannes Kuch
Modernism between Benjamin and Goethe, Matthew Charles
Red Kant: Aesthetics, Marxism and the Third Critique, Michael Wayne

Adorno and the Ban on Images

Sebastian Truskolaski

BLOOMSBURY ACADEMIC
LONDON • NEW YORK • OXFORD • NEW DELHI • SYDNEY

BLOOMSBURY ACADEMIC
Bloomsbury Publishing Plc
50 Bedford Square, London, WC1B 3DP, UK
1385 Broadway, New York, NY 10018, USA
29 Earlsfort Terrace, Dublin 2, Ireland

BLOOMSBURY, BLOOMSBURY ACADEMIC and the Diana logo
are trademarks of Bloomsbury Publishing Plc

First published in Great Britain 2021
This paperback edition published in 2022

Copyright © Sebastian Truskolaski, 2021

Sebastian Truskolaski has asserted his right under the Copyright,
Designs and Patents Act, 1988, to be identified as Author of this work.

For legal purposes the Acknowledgements on p. viii constitute an
extension of this copyright page.

Cover design by Charlotte Daniels

All rights reserved. No part of this publication may be reproduced or
transmitted in any form or by any means, electronic or mechanical,
including photocopying, recording, or any information storage or retrieval
system, without prior permission in writing from the publishers.

Bloomsbury Publishing Plc does not have any control over, or responsibility for,
any thirdparty websites referred to or in this book. All internet addresses given
in this book were correct at the time of going to press. The author and publisher
regret any inconvenience caused if addresses have changed or sites have
ceased to exist, but can accept no responsibility for any such changes.

A catalogue record for this book is available from the British Library.

Library of Congress Cataloging-in-Publication Data

Names: Truskolaski, Sebastian, author.
Title: Adorno and the ban on images / Sebastian Truskolaski.
Description: London; New York: Bloomsbury Academic, [2021] |
Includes bibliographical references and index.
Identifiers: LCCN 2020032039 (print) | LCCN 2020032040 (ebook) |
ISBN 9781350129207 (hb) | ISBN 9781350196766 (paperback) |
ISBN 9781350129214 (epdf) | ISBN 9781350129221 (ebook)
Subjects: LCSH: Adorno, Theodor W., 1903-1969.
Classification: LCC B3199.A34 T78 2021 (print) |
LCC B3199.A34 (ebook) | DDC 193–dc23
LC record available at https://lccn.loc.gov/2020032039
LC ebook record available at https://lccn.loc.gov/2020032040

ISBN: HB: 978-1-3501-2920-7
PB: 978-1-3501-9676-6
ePDF: 978-1-3501-2921-4
eBook: 978-1-3501-2922-1

Typeset by Deanta Global Publishing Services, Chennai, India

To find out more about our authors and books visit
www.bloomsbury.com and sign up for our newsletters.

*Dedicated to my parents, Magda and Paweł, for the years of
love and support – dziękuję.*

Contents

Acknowledgements	viii
Prelude: *Adorno and the Ban on Images*	1
1 Imageless materialism	9
Part I: Materialism	13
Part II: Imagelessness	34
2 Inverse theology	53
Part I: Theology	57
Part II: Inversion	94
3 Aesthetic negativity	105
Part I: Aesthetics	107
Part II: Natural beauty	133
Reprise: 'Zum Ende'	149
Notes	155
Bibliography	199
Index	213

Acknowledgements

This book began life as a doctoral dissertation at Goldsmiths College, University of London. As such, I owe a debt of gratitude to my supervisors, Alberto Toscano and Brendan Prendeville, for their rigour and generosity, as well as Alexander García Düttmann for his encouragement during the early stages of this project. I would further like to thank my examiners, Andrew Benjamin and Frederic Schwartz, for their generous feedback, which I drew on while revising the manuscript for publication. There are too many friends whose input has shaped my thinking on Adorno to list them all. However, I would like to express my special thanks to the following people: Cat Moir and Johan Siebers; Sami Khatib and Jan Sieber; Jacob Bard-Rosenberg, Rose Anne Gush and Tom Allen; Esther Leslie and Sam Dolbear; Phil Homburg and Chris O'Kane; Matt Ellison and Katja Riegler; Tom Vandeputte, Nassima Sahraoui and Stefano Marchesoni; Jon Catlin and Geoffrey Wildanger. Finally, I would like to thank Caterina Zanelli for her patience and support over the years. The same goes for my sister Anna, and – above all – my parents Magda and Paweł, without whom none of this would have been possible. *Thank you/ dziękuję/dankeschön/grazie.*

An earlier version of Chapter 1 (Part II) has been previously published as: Sebastian Truskolaski, 'Materialism', in *The SAGE Handbook of Frankfurt School Critical Theory*, eds. Werner Bonefeld, Beverley Best and Chris O'Kane (2018), pp. 661–77. An earlier version of Chapter 2 (Part II) has been previously published as Sebastian Truskolaski, 'Inverse Theology: Adorno, Benjamin, Kafka', in *German Life and Letters*, Vol. 70, No. 2 (April 2017): 192–210.

A note on translations: For the most part, I have opted to use existing, English-language translations of major works cited throughout; on occasion, I deemed it necessary to alter these translations. In such cases, I noted this fact in the corresponding endnote.

Prelude

Adorno and the Ban on Images

Die Kinder haben keine Zukunft. Sie fürchten sich vor der ganzen Welt. Sie machen sich kein Bild von ihr, nur von dem Hüben und Drüben, denn es läßt sich mit Kreidestrichen begrenzen.[1]

Ingeborg Bachmann

In an essay titled 'Sacred Fragment' (1963), Theodor W. Adorno gestures towards an irreducible iconoclasm at the heart of Arnold Schoenberg's unfinished opera *Moses und Aron* (1932).[2] Schoenberg's Exodus adaptation 'is in pieces', we are told; it is 'fragmentary, like the tables of the law which Moses smashed'.[3] This sense of fragmentation is thematized in act 2, scene 4 of Schoenberg's libretto – an episode that has been memorably committed to film by the French directors Jean-Marie Straub and Danièle Huillet.[4] It portrays Moses's descent from Mount Sinai where he had received the tables with the Ten Commandments 'written with the finger of God'.[5] Upon returning, Moses finds that the Israelites had grown restless during his forty-day absence. They had urged his brother Aron to reinstate their old religious ways: 'Give us back our Gods to worship; let them bring us order.'[6] Under the threat of death, Aron had relented: 'O Israel, I return your gods to you, and also give you to them, just as you have demanded.'[7] Famously, Aron had proceeded to fashion an effigy in the form of a golden calf, 'common and visible, *imaged* in gold'.[8] The Israelites, in turn, had frenziedly worshipped this idol. Schoenberg's stage notes laconically sum up the action: '*Burnt offerings are brought to the altar*';[9] '*wild drunkenness overtakes everyone*';[10] '*extravagant dancing*';[11] '*blood off'rings*';[12] '*Destruction and Suicide*';[13] '*Erotic Orgy*'.[14] Upon witnessing the Israelites' idolatrous excesses, Moses furiously smashes the tables with the law:

> And it came to pass, as soon as he came nigh unto the camp, that he saw the calf, and the dancing: and Moses' anger waxed hot, and he cast the tables out

of his hands, and brake them beneath the mount. And he took the calf which they had made, and burnt it in the fire, and ground it to powder, and strawed it upon the water, and made the children of Israel drink of it.[15]

As is well known, the book of Exodus proceeds to detail how Moses and the sons of Levi go on to slay all those who had partaken in the dance around the golden calf as punishment for their 'great sin'.[16] The law is rewritten in Moses's hand and God's authority is restored. Schoenberg, however, omits these occurrences, choosing instead to draw out the confrontation between the two brothers in order to illuminate the fundamental stakes of their conflict: 'God's eternity opposes idol's transience';[17] '[n]o folk can grasp more than just a partial image, the perceivable part of the whole idea.'[18] God *cannot* be pictured, God *must* be pictured. This designates the 'tragic' dimension of *Moses und Aron*: '[T]he insoluble conflict between the finite and the infinite inherent in the subject matter Schoenberg chose.'[19] Against this backdrop, the Viennese composer's 'biblical opera' invites two preliminary observations.[20]

(i) Insofar as the origin of the law cannot be dissociated from Moses's breaking of the tables, the source of its authority remains obscure. That is, the relation between law, authority and scripture remains somewhat under-determined, thus arguably posing a stumbling block for subsequent efforts to ground binding ethical guidelines on a biblical basis.[21] At the same time, though, inasmuch as Moses acts in response to the Israelites' effort to supplant God with an intermediary – an idol – the breaking of the tables is supposed to substantiate the very law whose physical trace it obliterates, namely the 'Jewish prohibition on making images'.[22] This peculiar incongruity extends into the manifest motivations that underlie the biblical injunction '[t]hou shalt not make unto thee any graven image'.[23] For one thing, we are told, the God of Israel is a 'jealous' God; He demands an exclusive commitment.[24] Yet Moses's destruction of the golden calf seems only to confirm 'the charismatic power of the idol'.[25] In other words, if the golden calf poses a threat to God's authority – if it rouses His jealousy – then, surely, the very primacy of the monotheistic world view is under threat. At the same time, we are assured, the ban on using earthly means for picturing the absolute is not simply a way to manage God's jealousy; rather, it is supposed to guard against the gravest of hubristic errors: the attempt to determine that which eludes all determination. Thus '[t]he central effort of philosophical religion', as Moshe Halbertal and Avishai

Margalit observe, 'is the attempt to attain a proper *metaphysical* conception of God.'[26] Not only is such a conception necessary for the purposes of proper worship – after all, the ban on idol worship is nothing if not a practical directive – it also constitutes the 'high point of religious life'.[27] This 'high point', however, is marked by a double bind. For if the outlawing of idolatry goes hand in hand with Moses's smashing of the law, if the pronouncement of this prohibition thus assumes an ill-founded legislative authority – 'to act as the mouthpiece of the Almighty is blasphemy for mortal man'[28] – might it not be objected that the 'Jewish prohibition on making images' is essentially self-transgressive; that the commandment against idol worship contains its own infraction as an ineluctable condition of its formulation?

(ii) Schoenberg's libretto stops short of covering the events outlined in Exodus 34 – the passage that describes how God summons Moses to Mount Sinai for a second time, in order to have him write a set of replacement tables. Schoenberg's omission is striking because the episode instantiates the very contradiction that he seeks to stage: the replacement tables are 'no longer identified as "God's handiwork"', as Rebecca Comay highlights; they are 'inexorably marked as substitute or simulacrum'.[29] But if we concede this point, might it not be objected that the redrawing of the tables relies on the very self-transgression of the law outlined earlier – an act of second-degree idolatry? In other words, does the fact that Moses rewrites a law that originally appeared as *God*'s 'handiwork' not mark out the replacement tables as idols in their own right?

To begin with, these two preliminary observations concerning Schoenberg's biblical subject matter serve to frame the subsequent discussion in a double sense. With regards to the former point – Exodus 32 – this means the following: if the image ban chiefly concerns an immeasurable excess of absolute ideas over their limited representations, then Judaism's '*metaphysical* conception of God' – invoked, earlier, by Halbertal and Margalit – points beyond the sphere of Exodus. In other words, if the outlawing of images principally follows from a desire to attain a 'metaphysical *conception*' of God – rather than, say, from a fear of His jealous retribution – then it follows that Judaism appears above all as a '*philosophical* religion'. In this regard, Moses's destruction of the golden calf is supposed to signal the triumph of a certain metaphysical–philosophical understanding of the absolute over the fateful–mythical model that undergirds iconophilic paganism. God is intellectualized. To be sure, such a portrayal of Judaism runs the danger of equating the history of biblical monotheism with that of reason *tout court*, a premise that resounds tacitly throughout the work of early twentieth-century thinkers from the orbit of the *Wissenschaft des Judentums* (*Science of Judaism*), not least amongst them the pre-eminent neo-Kantian philosopher Hermann Cohen.[30]

Even though Cohen is barely ever cited by Adorno, his mapping of Kant's moral philosophy – rooted, as it is, in the workings of reason – onto central tenets of Judaism is of interest, here, because a broadly similar view is taken up and critically recast in *Dialectic of Enlightenment* (1947), the conjectural prehistory of sovereign subjectivity co-authored by Adorno and Max Horkheimer during their American exile. 'The disenchanted world of Judaism', we are told, 'propitiates magic by negating it in the idea of God. (. . .) It places all hope in the prohibition on invoking falsity as God, the finite as the infinite, the lie as truth. The pledge of salvation lies in the rejection of any faith which claims to depict it, knowledge in the denunciation of illusion.'[31] Of course, Adorno and Horkheimer do not endorse this view as such. They quickly qualify their apparent equation of Judaism and enlightenment by arguing that '[m]yth' – coded here as the fateful realm of paganism – is already a form of 'enlightenment' and that, in turn, subsequent forms of 'enlightenment' – including biblical monotheism – revert to 'mythology'.[32] What is at stake here is an immanent un-working of a seamless history of reason in the singular. As in the case of Sigmund Freud's *Moses & Monotheism* (1939), the speculative prehistory of Judaism serves as a case in point. We will return to these matters in due course. For now it suffices to note the following: what interests us here is less to do with what Adorno and Horkheimer may have had to say about the crossroads of Judaism and Neo-Kantianism in early twentieth-century Germany (in any case, their knowledge of such matters was surely limited); rather, what concerns us in the present context is that, in both cases – for better or worse – the image ban appears as a kind of philosophical–historical trope: a figure of rationalization. Inasmuch as Adorno and Horkheimer insist that such rationalization perpetually risks reverting into its opposite, however, the following question arises: Is it possible to challenge the perceived ills of enlightenment reason through recourse to a religious injunction that, on Adorno and Horkheimer's account, stems squarely from within its bounds?

With regards to the latter point – Exodus 34 – Comay's allusion to a tension between 'original' and 'simulacrum' similarly points to a wider philosophical issue. In this regard it might be said that Moses's smashing and rewriting of the law is echoed in the fundamental bifurcations that span the *longue durée* of 'Western metaphysics':[33] essence versus appearance, form versus content, subject versus object. This is borne out etymologically. Plato famously distinguishes the world of eternal and unchanging Forms (*eidoi*, 'ideas') from that of mere representations (*eikones*, 'images').[34] Sensible objects are mere shadows of the truth, partial and inadequate copies. Accordingly, the task of philosophy is to seek truth beyond the world of appearances, to determine the relationship between true ideas and deceitful images. Notwithstanding Nietzsche's sharp rebuke of such *Hinterwelt* metaphysics,[35] well known to Adorno, commentators including the historian Alain Besançon and the art historian Horst Bredekamp, amongst others, argue that iconoclasm – at least as it has come to be associated with the various strands of Exodus-reception, from the Babylonian Talmud to the Byzantine *Eikonomachía*, and from the Council of Trent to Islamic aniconism – is an eminently philosophical undertaking: the clearing away of *eidola* (apparitions) that obscure the true relation between the finite and the infinite.[36] In this regard, the role of Neo-Platonism in shaping Jewish, Christian and Islamic thought can hardly be overstated.[37] As above, the iconoclastic impulse is effectively identified with the triumph of reason in the face of overwhelming forces: the aforementioned 'denunciation of illusion'. By that token it is perhaps unsurprising that the image ban should survive into the present as a discourse of sublimity (from Immanuel Kant's *Critique of the Power of Judgement*, 1790, to Jean-François Lyotard's *The Inhuman*, 1988) and, in turn, as an aniconic tendency in modern art (from Kasimir Malevich's *Black Square*, 1915, to Ad Reinhardt's *Abstract Painting No. 1*, 1963).

It is not my aim here to dissolve the far-flung history of the image ban into the annals of philosophy, art history or theology. Instead, I propose to ask in what sense the tension designated by the Old Testament ban on making images of God can help to short-circuit the historical dynamic outlined in *Dialectic of Enlightenment*. Is it possible, in other words, to invoke the image ban – in its capacity as a philosophical–historical marker, rather than a theological edict – to formulate a critical theory of the present?

* * *

The present study aims to explore the conspicuous recurrence of the Old Testament ban on making images of God, the *Bilderverbot*, throughout Adorno's writings: from his musical works on Beethoven, Mahler and Schoenberg to his literary analyses of Hölderlin, Kafka and Beckett; from his philosophical–political reflections on Marx, Engels and Lenin to his sporadic notes on painting (Corot). To be sure, Adorno's references to the image ban recall this figure's prominent place in the history of modern German thought – a lineage that extends from Mendelssohn to Kant, Hegel, Cohen and beyond. Adorno's intimate familiarity with this tradition, in addition to his well-documented ignorance of theological issues,[38] indicates that his outwardly biblical lexicon in fact owes more to a deep engagement with the history of philosophy than to the concerted study of scripture. In any case, Adorno openly heeds the verdicts of his intellectual forerunners Nietzsche, Freud and Marx, arguing that 'positive religion has lost its (. . .) validity';[39] that '[t]raditional theology is not restorable'.[40] Far from lamenting the ostensible displacement of traditional religion in the present, though, Adorno turns the waning of religious authority into an opportunity; precisely by dint of its perceived redundancy, the image ban is transformed into a potent philosophical device. It signifies a refusal of the sense that that 'which merely is',[41] is, in fact, everything. Despite his much-maligned verdict that the moment for a Marxian actualization of philosophy has been 'missed',[42] Adorno's abidance by the image ban is supposed to signal his commitment to a mode of philosophical critique which aims to hold open the possibility that things might yet be otherwise. A highly qualified discourse of Utopia displaces that of transcendence: 'Utopia as the harmony between humankind and nature',[43] Utopia as the longing for 'undeluded happiness, including bodily pleasure, the wish for an end to suffering'.[44] Nevertheless, Adorno is aware that 'one may not cast a picture of Utopia in a positive manner'; 'one can only talk about Utopia in a negative way'.[45] To form an image of Utopia is to render it in terms of the present situation and thus 'to garnish the status quo with its ultimate apologia'.[46] The stakes are high. In the 'administered world' even utopian longing constantly risks reverting into its opposite.[47] Accordingly, the central aim of the present study is to illuminate the sense in which the image ban informs Adorno's effort to safeguard the minimal space within which something like a radical societal transformation might yet be thought.

In aiming to respond to these issues, the book focuses on three aspects of Adorno's thinking: his 'imageless materialism' (Chapter 1), his 'inverse theology' (Chapter 2) and his 'aesthetic negativity' (Chapter 3). Broadly speaking, each of these chapters concerns a seemingly discrete field of inquiry: the immanent critique of materialism (Chapter 1), the paradoxical recovery of metaphysics (Chapter 2) and the bearing out of their tension in the field of aesthetics (Chapter 3). This tension, for its part, attests to the mutual implication of these seemingly divergent registers: a meta-critique of philosophy whose material correlate is supposed to lie in the history of humankind's (self-)domination; a declared solidarity with metaphysics in the face of its purported fall; and an aesthetics that is thought to bear the weight of a displaced hope for something beyond the spellbound sphere of existence – a trace of something that cannot, for its part, be pictured. In a letter to Gershom Scholem, dated 14 March 1967, Adorno schematizes these connections with reference to *Negative Dialectics*:

> It seems to me that what does justice to the concept of materialism – at least once one has escaped the spell of identity – is what I have, in the immanent, epistemo-critical discussion, called the preponderance of the object; and this is not crudely asserted but can only be presented very gently within the dialectic. I take it that the weighty arguments, which I believe I have advanced against idealism, are located beyond this spell – they are stringently materialist. This means, however, that such materialism is not conclusive; it's not a fixed worldview. To me, it is this path to materialism – a path that is totally different from any dogma – that warrants an affinity with metaphysics (I would have almost said theology), which you rightly recognized as the book's central concern.[48]

To the extent that Adorno's question about the possibility of a properly materialist metaphysics – 'I would have almost said theology' – is finally reformulated as a question concerning the possibility of modern art, however, the singular outline of his 'imageless image of Utopia' comes into focus.[49] All three chapters, then, are couched in the structure of the historical narrative outlined in *Dialectic of Enlightenment*, whose credo, it has already been noted, proclaims that 'myth is already enlightenment' and 'all enlightenment reverts to mythology'. With respect to this maxim, each chapter places Adorno into a dialogue with an array of authors, whose work orients his argument: Marx versus Engels and Lenin (Chapter 1), Kafka and Benjamin versus Schmitt (Chapter 2), Hegel versus Kant (Chapter 3). In each case, a recent voice is introduced to complement the historical exposition: Meillassoux on materialism (Chapter 1), Agamben and Taubes on theology (Chapter 2), Lyotard on the limits of figurative art (Chapter 3). These voices are intended to show that Adorno's concerns continue to polarize opinion even fifty years after his death, and, moreover, that the questions addressed in his works are far from being settled. By centring each chapter around a set of prominent references to the image ban, I propose to reorganize Adorno's uneasily systematic 'anti-system' around the notion of imagelessness:[50] a 'thinking beyond itself', a thinking 'into *openness*', into that which resists presentation.[51] I take it that this is a timely task for at least two reasons: first, if Adorno's bleak assessment of his own historical situation has only been confirmed by subsequent events, then his echo of the Marxian claim that only a 'ruthless criticism of all that exists' can hold open the possibility of historical change gains poignancy.[52] Second, and more modestly, if the reception of Adorno's work has long been dominated by a slightly singular interest in questions of normative legitimacy, then highlighting his project's paradoxically utopian thrust – in all its negativity – might serve to reframe Adorno's actuality beyond providing a prelude to the achievements of the Frankfurt School's so-called second generation. The dual motivation of this study is thus, at once, to foreground the iconoclastic tendencies of Adorno's thought and to distance him from the broadly liberal political orientation of much Adorno scholarship today, which, I argue, is in many ways at odds with his own thinking, if not always with his stated intentions. How and why exactly will become apparent over the course of the book. Certainly, this effort is not exhaustive. My aim here has been neither to comprehensively reconstruct nor to 'complete' Adorno's philosophical project against the backdrop of its reception. Rather, I have sought to single out the image ban as a kind of leitmotif in Adorno's thought, whose significance – both critical and heuristic – has been largely overlooked. Under this aspect it remains to ask: What is the significance of the image ban for Adorno's thinking?

1

Imageless materialism

Quelle que soit la valeur, la puissance de pénétration d'une explication, c'est encore et encore la chose à expliquer qui est la plus réelle – et parmi sa réalité figure précisément ce mystère que l'on a voulu dissiper.[1]

Paul Valéry

'What could be at work in the Marxist rendition of the theological prohibition of images?'[2] This question posed by Rebecca Comay at the beginning of her essay 'Materialist Mutations of the *Bilderverbot*' (1997) addresses itself to the unlikely pairing of an ostensibly biblical motif – the Old Testament ban on making images of God – with an emphatically worldly disposition: historical materialism. Comay alludes here to the conspicuous recurrence of the image ban in certain articulations of what has come to be known – for better or worse – as *Western* Marxism: a critical re-imagination of the materialist philosophy of history outlined in works such as Karl Korsch's *Marxism and Philosophy* (1923) and Georg Lukács's *History and Class-Consciousness* (1923).[3] As Comay notes, the improbable tension between 'materialism' and 'theology' that characterizes particular strands of this tradition – from Ernst Bloch to Walter Benjamin – is discernible, not least, in the work of Theodor W. Adorno.[4] In fact, Comay's question is occasioned by a striking passage from Adorno's magnum opus *Negative Dialectics* (1966), fittingly titled 'Materialism Imageless'. There Adorno writes the following:

> Representational thinking would be without reflection – an undialectical contradiction, for without reflection there is no theory. A consciousness interpolating images, a third element, between itself and that which it thinks would unwittingly reproduce idealism. A body of ideas would substitute for the object of cognition, and the subjective arbitrariness of such ideas

is that of the authorities. The materialist longing to grasp the thing aims at the opposite: it is only in the absence of images that the full object could be conceived. Such absence concurs with the theological ban on images. Materialism brought that ban into secular form by not permitting Utopia to be positively pictured; this is the substance of its negativity. At its most materialistic, materialism comes to agree with theology. Its great desire would be the resurrection of the flesh, a desire utterly foreign to idealism, the realm of the absolute spirit. The perspective vanishing point of historic materialism would be its self-sublation (*seine eigene Aufhebung*), the spirit's liberation from the primacy of material needs in their state of fulfilment. Only if the physical urge were quenched would the spirit be reconciled and would become that which it only promises while the spell of material conditions will not let it satisfy material needs.[5]

In the first instance, this passage seems to stake an epistemological claim: that a purportedly materialist form of cognition which interpolates *images* – 'a third element' – between consciousness and 'that which it thinks' in fact 'unwittingly reproduces idealism'. Adorno's phrasing thus recalls the traditional opposition of materialism and idealism – the realm of 'material needs' versus that of 'absolute spirit'. Adorno had already outlined this opposition some thirty-five years earlier, in his 1931 inaugural address as a *Privatdozent* at the University of Frankfurt, which begins with a rejection of idealism, broadly conceived of as the view that 'the power of thought is sufficient to grasp the totality of the real'.[6] In *Negative Dialectics*, Adorno returns to this thought to draw attention to a '*risk* that supposedly materialist thinking will involuntarily turn into its opposite',[7] namely into a form of subjective domination that – in keeping with the terms laid out in *Dialectic of Enlightenment* (1947) – is associated with certain unnamed 'authorities'. But which 'authorities' are envisaged here?

To be sure, Adorno's reference to 'representational thinking' (*abbildendes Denken*) calls to mind the various forms of 'reflection theory' (*Abbildtheorie*) that punctuate the history of philosophical materialisms from Democritus to Locke.[8] In this respect, the German term *Abbild* – 'image', 'depiction', 'representation' – takes centre stage. Indeed, the prefix *Ab* – roughly translatable as 'of' – already implies that an *Ab-bild* is an image of an image so to speak: an impermissible tautology, if nothing else.

Yet Adorno's formulation suggests that the locus of the problem lies elsewhere – in 'the Eastern countries', as he puts it.[9] Notwithstanding this rather indelicate jab at the so-called East, it is striking that Adorno speaks here of a 'materialism come to political power', of 'governmental terror machines' that 'entrench themselves as permanent institutions', thus 'mocking the theory they carry on their lips'.[10] Accordingly, his invective appears to be directed chiefly against the official materialist doctrines of the Soviet sphere, not least, it would appear, Vladimir Ilyich Lenin's meta-scientific opus *Materialism and Empirio-Criticism* (1908). This suspicion is confirmed by the fact that Adorno explicitly names Lenin in the paragraph preceding the one from which the above-mentioned citation is drawn. As Adorno writes, 'When Lenin, rather than go in for epistemology, opposed it in compulsively reiterated avowals of the noumenality of cognitive objects, he meant to demonstrate that subjective positivism is conspiring with the powers that be'.[11] This is further borne out in a lecture, dated 17 January 1963, where Adorno describes 'the big book by Lenin about "Empirio-Criticism", which, through a sort of dogmatic repetition, declares the objective reality of the world vis-à-vis its reduction to subjective givens'.[12] But if Adorno's objections are, in fact, directed against the official materialisms of the 'Eastern Countries', then Comay's question – 'what could be at work in the Marxist rendition of the theological prohibition of images' – bifurcates: What kind of 'Marxism' is at issue here? What kind of materialism does it draw on?

Certainly, any effort to answer these questions today cannot go unqualified. That is to say, inasmuch as the theoretical and political sway of the Soviet Union has been all but consigned to the history books, Adorno's objections to the functionaries of 'Diamat' may appear to have lost much of their currency. However, there is a sense, I think, in which 'Materialism Imageless' points beyond its immediate context, raising wider questions about a material 'state of fulfilment' whose 'promise' (frustrated in both 'East' and 'West' alike) continues to haunt a present whose definitive feature appears to be the relinquishment of any sense 'that things *should*', or – indeed – *could*, 'be different'.[13]

Revisiting Adorno's interrogation of 'representational thinking', then, is more than an exercise in the history of ideas; rather, it calls to mind what he describes, elsewhere, as a 'Utopia of cognition' (*Utopie der Erkenntnis*), which – for its part – is supposed to inform a specific kind of politics.[14] We will return to this point later. For now it suffices to note that, in Adorno's view, 'the materialist longing to grasp the thing' means nothing less than a radical reconfiguration of the relationship between the 'subject' and 'object' of thought with respect to their socio-historical analogue: the relationship between 'humankind' and 'nature' in capitalist modernity. (After all, and in a duly Marxian fashion, Adorno sees philosophical problems, of the sort noted earlier, as having real material correlates.) Accordingly, elaborating a concept of materialism means, not least, a reinterpretation of what thinking itself means, albeit not without certain caveats. For what can we really say about a 'cognition that neither merely depicts nor constitutes things – how is it to be thought?'[15] This query raised by Adorno's erstwhile student, Alfred Schmidt, concerns precisely the requisite conditions for articulating a mode of materialist cognition that staves off the sacrificial logic which Adorno associates with 'identity thinking': subsuming, and thus sacrificing, particulars under universals; identifying phenomena that are not, as it were, identical. The central formula for this effort, I contend, is the 'theological ban on images'; its locus is the moment when materialism and theology come to 'agree'. But what is the nature of this agreement, if it is not identity? A different kind of universality, which does not violate its constitutive parts, perhaps? In any event, it might be asked how such a 'materialist prohibition against images [can] be enunciated' without transgressing against itself.[16] After all, the 'Utopia' intended by Adorno's 'imageless' materialism – 'harmony between humankind and nature', as Schmidt puts it – is itself subject to the ban on images.[17] As has already been noted, 'one may not cast a picture of Utopia in a positive manner'; 'one can only talk about Utopia in a negative way.'[18]

The outlines of such an 'imageless' materialism, then, require some elucidation. Accordingly, Part I of this chapter considers (i) what Adorno means by the mode of 'representational thinking' that he attacks in *Negative Dialectics*, and (ii) the terms in which he criticizes this approach. The point, here, is to stage a central facet of Adorno's 'method', if one can call it that, namely the fact that Adorno's own positions – provisional as they are – tend to emerge from a confrontation with existing materials; materials which are, as it were, determinately negated (albeit, again, in a qualified sense). In turn, the chapter will go on to consider (iii) how Adorno's criticisms apply to recent currents in philosophical materialism, particularly those outlined in Quentin Meillassoux's influential essay *After Finitude* (2006), which have frequently been likened to 'the big book by Lenin about "Empirio-Criticism"'. This excursus intends to emphasize the actuality of Adorno's thought by demonstrating the tacit political implications of outwardly theoretical problems, and by foregrounding the urgency of recasting, for example, 'materialism' as the possible basis for an altogether different way of relating to the world.

Against this backdrop, Part II of this chapter considers (i) the peculiarly autodeconstructive relationship between the notions of 'image' and 'imagelessness' that is yielded by Adorno's critique of Lenin et al. (after all, an image *ban* presupposes a conception of the *image*). Scrutiny of this relationship, in turn, reveals (ii) how the somatic and affective facets of Adorno's 'imageless' materialism inform his wider project: a restless and incessant dismantling of established philosophical dogmas that throws into relief a mode of thinking, and – by extension – living, that escapes the violence and coercion of the present.

Part I: Materialism

(i) The theory of reflection

It was suggested, earlier, that in 'Materialism Imageless' Adorno's intimation of the 'theological ban on images' follows from a critique of what he describes laconically as 'representational thinking'. Adorno's references to Lenin in the paragraph preceding 'Materialism Imageless', and in the 1963 lecture that appears to underlie these passages, suggest that such a mode of thinking means – above all – certain theories that gained traction during the early part of the twentieth century as part of the official Soviet codification of Marx's critique of political economy. Although the origins of such theories (theories of reflection) can be traced back to pre-Socratic and Hellenic Atomism, their specifically Soviet variants are couched in a self-avowedly scientific materialist world view (complete with a fully fledged epistemology), which is derived largely from Friedrich Engels's particular portrayal of his and Marx's common efforts, laid out in works including *Anti-Dühring* (1878), *Dialectics of Nature* (1883) and *Ludwig Feuerbach and the End of Classical German Philosophy* (1886).[19] Without presuming to summarize the sense in which early Marx-reception depends on a number of ideas that are distinctly Engels's own – a task that is, in any case, tangential inasmuch as Adorno appears to have only a passing interest in the texts in question – any attempt to unpack the concept of an 'imageless' materialism must nonetheless take stock of at least *some* characteristic features of the 'traditional Marxism' that gives rise to the aforementioned theories of reflection, if only to establish them as a foil.[20] Adorno's conceit appears to be that his critique of such a Marxism brings into focus the proper object of historical materialism: a true state of fulfilment brought about by the alleviation of bodily suffering. In order to grasp this, though, we must begin by considering (a) the epistemological precepts of Engels's concept of materialism, and (b) the sense in which Lenin elaborates a theory of reflection on the basis of Engels's views.

(a) In the present context, the salient point regarding Engels's concept of materialism is twofold: first, the characterization of his and Marx's project – taken up in different ways by figureheads of the Second Socialist International (e.g. Karl Kautsky, Eduard Bernstein), on the one hand, and leading Bolsheviks (e.g. Vladimir Lenin, Joseph Stalin), on the other – yields a 'general law of development of nature, society, and thought' that is essentially ontological.[21] That is to say, in *Dialectics of Nature*, for instance, Engels postulates a general correspondence between sociopolitical, philosophical and natural processes whose significance for the development of 'traditional Marxism' can hardly be overstated: '[W]hat is valid for nature' – the material world as such – 'must also be valid for history'; '[p]olitical praxis is (...) the consummation of historical' and – by extension – natural 'laws'.[22] Broadly speaking, then, Engels's construct depends on a reversal of Hegel's philosophy of nature.[23] That is to say, Engels follows Hegel in portraying the dialectic as the fundamental 'law' of nature, while refusing this law's deduction from philosophical first principles, that is, its purportedly subjective anchoring. Whereas the dialectic is believed to be at work '*in* the external world', it is supposed to be merely '*mirrored* by human thought'.[24] As Ingo Elbe explains, for Engels the 'law' of the dialectic is thus 'split into "*two* sets of laws"': '[T]he dialectic of "the external world"', on the one hand, 'and the dialectic of "human thought"', on the other.[25] The latter is thus understood as providing 'merely a passive mental *image* of the former', rather than acting as its active arbitrator.[26]

Engels fleshes out this claim in a letter to his friend Conrad Schmidt, dated 1 November 1891:

> The inversion of the dialectic in Hegel rests on this, that it is supposed to be the 'self-development of thought', of which the dialectic of facts is (...) only a reflection, whereas the dialectic in our heads is in reality the reflection of the

actual development going on in the world of nature and of human history in obedience to dialectical forms.[27]

By dislodging the dialectic from 'human thought' and locating it in the 'external world', Engels purports to put its focus on matter itself. He thus '"applies" Hegelian categories to', for instance, 'the biological concept of the cell' in order to demonstrate their operation in nature – an operation for which empirical science is, in turn, supposed to offer tangible proofs.[28] Engels thus suggests that Hegel's dialectic is marked by a simple mind–matter dichotomy that is unduly weighted in favour of thought. Undoing this supposed confusion means chiefly a reversal of these terms – putting the dialectic back on its feet, as it were. Sidestepping for a moment the sense in which this reading underestimates the tensions between 'thought' and 'matter' – subject and object – in the Hegelian dialectic, Engels's contention appears to be two-pronged: on the one hand, he seems to want to demonstrate the interconnectedness of all fields of intellectual inquiry (philosophy, political economy and the natural sciences are all seen as evincing the same historical tendency whose law is supposed to be dialectical in the materialist sense described earlier); on the other hand, this unifying endeavour is thought to put his political project on a firm footing – the authoritative ground of empirical science.

However, the consequence of this move escapes Engels's intentions. His view that 'the dialectic in our heads' is merely a '*reflection* of the actual development going on in the world' tends to portray humankind as a mere 'product of evolution and a passive reflection of the process of nature, not however as a productive force', as Schmidt notes.[29] This occurs at the expense of Engels's foremost concern – the affirmation of *praxis* – a point that is at odds with the stated intentions of older works, such as Marx's 'Theses on Feuerbach' (1845). After all, the 'Theses' open with the estimation that '[t]he chief defect of all hitherto existing materialism (. . .) is' precisely that 'the thing, reality, sensuousness, is conceived only in the form of the *object or of contemplation*, but not as *sensuous human activity, practice*, not subjectively'.[30] It might be said, then, that Engels's later view that 'the dialectical laws are really laws of the development of nature' leaves little room for such 'activity'.[31] His argument seems to entail that the 'external world' appears as a mere fact, a rigid system wherein humankind is 'limited to a mere mirroring of the factual', that is, the 'uncritical reproduction of existing relationships in consciousness', in Schmidt's words.[32]

The second point worth noting, here, concerns Engels's assertion that history is coterminous with certain natural processes, and that humankind merely mirrors these parallels in consciousness. This view leads Engels to unwittingly endorse a kind of historical determinism. That is to say, if in Engels's view the natural sciences prove that the dialectic lies '*in* the external world' – for example, in the development of cells – and history, as such, is presented as the analogue of this process; and if humankind, in turn, merely 'mirrors' these developments in consciousness (at the expense of praxis), then it follows that history is imbued with an almost tragic sense of inevitability. A deterministic concept of development thus comes to occupy a central place in 'Marxist doctrine'.[33] On this reading, socialism is effectively hypostatized as the inevitable *telos* of history. On this point, Adorno sarcastically observes that 'in the mightiest, most differentiated didactic edifices of dialectical materialism, a conception of the world is developed in which hunger, fear and self-denial actually *cannot* exist'.[34]

On this view, the mode of 'representational thinking' derided by Adorno appears to mean precisely the epistemological precepts of Engels's materialist dialectic, which are – in turn – taken up and elaborated by Lenin. The question thus arises as to what the consequences are of arguing that dialectics lies in things and that humankind merely mirrors their seemingly inevitable developments in consciousness.

(b) Lenin's book, *Materialism and Empirio-Criticism* (1908), was written in the wake of the failed revolution of 1905. It is couched in a string of factional debates within the Bolshevik Party, which outwardly concern certain developments in the natural sciences. The backdrop to this intra-Bolshevik conflict is the prevalent sense that a 'crisis' has occurred in modern physics that threatens the primacy of 'matter', which – in Lenin's view – ensures the very grounding of materialism.[35] Above all, the discovery of radioactivity is supposed to have led to a widespread rejection, amongst both physicists and philosophers, 'of an objective reality existing outside the mind', a sentiment that – in turn – provokes 'the replacement of materialism' (at least as Lenin sees it) 'by idealism and agnosticism'.[36] Scientific Marxism thus ostensibly relapses into bourgeois subjectivism. Without wishing to reconstruct the intricacies of these debates, it suffices to note that Lenin's misgivings are directed chiefly at Alexander Bogdanov's major three-volume work *Empirio-Monism* (1904–6), which, for its part, draws extensively on theories developed by the Austrian physicist Ernst Mach.[37] In brief: if Mach argues that physics proceeds not from the study of 'matter' but rather from the study of sense experience – '[n]ot bodies produce sensations, but element-complexes (sensation-complexes) constitute the bodies'[38] – then Bogdanov's effort to ensure the scientific grounding of Marxism must be understood along similar lines. Like Mach, 'Bogdanov espoused a strict empiricism and denied the possibility of a priori knowledge of any sort at all.'[39] Instead, he 'defined reality in terms of experience: The real world is identical with human experience of it.'[40] Bogdanov's specifically Marxist manoeuvre, then, is to recast the individual experiences described by Mach into those of a collective subject, namely the proletarian class itself. As he contends, '[t]he basis of "objectivity" must lie' not in matter but 'in the sphere of *collective* experience'.[41] That is, '[t]he objective character of the physical world consists in the fact that it exists not for me individually but for everyone, and for everyone has a definite meaning, exactly (. . .) as it does for me.'[42] Accordingly, knowledge of the external world – and, moreover, the ability to change it – is not supposed to be based on the merely subjective whims of individuals. Rather, '"[r]eality" is said to be made up of the shared perceptions of the collective consciousness of a society.'[43]

Despite the prominent invocation of a proletarian consciousness, Lenin charges that Bogdanov's idiosyncratic adaptation of Mach cannot escape its rooting in a fundamentally subject-centred outlook. Accordingly, the prioritization of sense experience is said to displace the primacy of mind-independent matter. The political consequence of this displacement is taken to mean that the materialist imperative to political praxis is transformed into an academic exercise, which Lenin associates with bourgeois conformism. To bolster this claim, Lenin outlines a highly polemical account of the history of philosophy in terms of a dichotomy between 'idealism' and 'materialism'. In a sweeping gesture, he charges that 'the idealism and agnosticism which characterized not only the Russian Machists but also Berkeley and Kant was the result of an (. . .) erroneous philosophical decision by all of them to adopt an empiricist epistemology'.[44] That is to say, the purportedly bourgeois 'belief that our knowledge of the world is constructed out of a field of sense-data resulted in this sense-data becoming an insuperable barrier between human consciousness and the external world'.[45] This 'belief', in turn, gives rise to all manner of sceptical attitudes that forestall political action.

The dubiousness of Lenin's identification of Mach with Kant and Berkeley hardly needs pointing out. Suffice it to note that all the while his aim is to defend a broadly Engelsian concept of materialism in the face of the supposed threat posed to it by the 'crisis' in modern physics. It is the character rather than the context of this defence that is of interest here. If, as noted earlier, the 'insuperable barrier' between 'human consciousness' and 'the external world' is the consequence of a fallacious 'decision' to 'adopt' certain allegedly bourgeois forms of 'empiricism', then any effort to defend the concept of 'matter' requires – above all – an alternative epistemology. Significantly, Lenin provides this by way of a theory of reflection.

In Lenin's estimation, 'sensation', rather than 'constituting bodies', appears as 'the direct connection between consciousness and the external world'.[46] The world is, above all, material, and consciousness is determined by it, not vice versa. Sense data is said to mirror the world as it really is, existing independently of and external to consciousness. Accordingly, Lenin argues that 'sensation, perception, idea, and the mind of man generally' are to be regarded 'as an *image* of objective reality'.[47] As far as Lenin is concerned, this framework guarantees the simple primacy of matter over ideas: '[C]onsciousness is only *an image* of the external world, and it is obvious that an image cannot exist without the thing imaged, and that the latter exists independently of that which images it.'[48] The proof that these images are bearers of objective truth is supposed to be provided by scientific experimentation, the analogue of which is seen as political praxis – a claim that is left largely unsubstantiated. Accordingly, Lenin appears to contradict himself when he contends that '[i]t is absolutely unpardonable to confuse, as the Machists do, any particular theory of the structure of matter with the epistemological category' of matter itself.[49] After all, if no 'particular theory' can pose a challenge to 'matter' as an 'epistemological category', then 'matter' itself – along with the revolutionary politics that it supposedly ensures – is dogmatically elevated to an unhistorical invariant. As Lance Byron Richey observes,

> In effect, Lenin is responding to the revolution which occurred in modern physics around the turn of the last century and the challenge it posed to traditional materialism by separating out the scientific and theory-laden features of it (. . .) and retaining only the philosophical content of it. The result is a conception of matter stripped of any specific theoretical content

and instead assigned the philosophical task of guaranteeing the extra-mental reference of our mental concepts.[50]

It cannot presently be our task to trace the sense in which the traditional view of matter does, in fact, come to be challenged by modern physics, albeit not in the way that Lenin intends; nor can it be our task to determine in what ways this development may or may not complicate the scientific self-understanding of Marx's theories and their reception.[51] Let it be noted only that insofar as Lenin's view of matter is apparently immune to any scientific contestation, his effort to escape the trappings of idealism runs the danger of underwriting (rather than refuting) the positions he rallies against: '[S]o much the worse for the facts'.[52] The point that follows from all this in the present context is this: if Adorno suggests that these ostensibly theoretical problems have far-reaching political consequences – what kind of Marxism is conceivable on the basis of Lenin's materialism? – then the precise nature of his criticism warrants further investigation.

(ii) Adorno's critique of reflection theory

As has already been noted, in 'Materialism Imageless' Adorno criticizes the official materialist doctrines of the 'Eastern Countries' by charging that certain 'deficiencies' in their epistemological frameworks – for example, their elevation of matter to an ontological invariant – are used to justify a political configuration where, 'on the threadbare pretext of a dictatorship (. . .) of the proletariat (. . .), governmental terror machines entrench themselves as permanent institutions' thus 'mocking the theory they carry on their lips'.[53] Rather than 'going in for epistemology', we have seen how Adorno charges that Lenin's 'political requirements turned him against the goal of theoretical cognition' with the 'disastrous result' that 'the unpenetrated target of criticism remains undisturbed (. . .) and not being hit at all (. . .) can be resurrected at will in changed constellations of power'.[54] Adorno thus asserts that Lenin tends to unwittingly reproduce the imperialism of spirit that he seeks to refute in a view of reality as seamlessly and causally mechanical, and that this view has political consequences. However, as might be objected, it is not clear why bad politics should necessarily follow from bad philosophy. The connection between a mode of thinking about the world and a manner of inhabiting it is implied but not exactly fleshed out. Nevertheless, Adorno's critique of 'representational thinking' does throw into relief the contours of his own conception of materialism, which has its own political implications, and which requires some unpacking.

(a) To the extent that Adorno's polemic appears to be directed at the epistemological precepts of Lenin's *Materialism and Empirio-Criticism*, his play on the ambiguity of the term 'reflection' (*Reflexion*) takes on a particular significance. As was seen earlier, Adorno writes that 'representational thinking would be *without* reflection – an undialectical contradiction, for without reflection there is no theory'. The equivocality of this term is fortuitously captured by the translation of the German *Reflexionstheorie* (or, indeed, *Abbildtheorie*) as 'reflection theory'. After all, the term 'reflection' connotes both mirroring and thinking in English and German alike.

On the one hand, then, it has already been noted that, for Engels and Lenin, 'reflection' principally means the imagistic reproduction of reality in the mind, which is – in turn – said to affirm the unshakable primacy of the material world as existing independently of and externally to consciousness. Adorno thus associates Lenin's reflections with idols and fetishes. As he argues, '[w]hat clings to the image remains idolatry, mythic enthrallment'.[55] By extension, he identifies the image *ban* with the monotheistic injunction against idol worship: 'Demythologisation, the thought's enlightening intent, deletes the image character of consciousness'.[56] On the other hand, Adorno means a mode of theoretical 'reflection', which he associates with Hegel. The derivation of 'theory' from the Greek *theoros* (spectator) and of 'speculation' from the Latin *specere* (to look) is not lost on Adorno. Vis-à-vis the image-laden phrasing of Leninist reflection theory, our opening question might thus be reformulated as follows: What kind of 'vision' is at stake in the formulation of an 'imageless' materialism? What would it mean to look in a manner that does not do violence unto phenomena?

At any rate, Adorno writes, in a discussion of Hegel's *Phenomenology of Spirit* (1806), which follows on from the passages on Lenin in the aforementioned 1963 lecture-series, that '[d]ialectics is a moving-through-contradictions. Without the moment of reflection, i.e. without the moment when a thing appears in its otherness (. . .) dialectics is in fact unthinkable'.[57] Adorno's implicit attempt to marshal Hegel against Lenin thus locates the 'deficiency' of Soviet materialism in its fraught relation to German Idealism.

Without presuming to detail the enormous scope of Hegel's propaedeutic effort to outline a 'science of the experience of consciousness',[58] making sense of Adorno's manoeuvre requires that we note the following, at least: as is well known, Hegel's *Phenomenology* starts out by critically recasting the view of cognition laid out in Kant's *Critique of Pure Reason* (1781/1787). Hegel describes Kant's outlook as a kind of 'natural assumption':[59] before one can start to deal with philosophy's 'proper subject matter one must first of all come to an understanding about cognition (. . .) either as the instrument to get hold of the absolute, or as the medium through which one discovers it'.[60] Hegel rejects this view on two counts: first, he argues that Kant's effort to delimit the conditions of possibility and the limits of legitimacy of cognition before cognizing, so to speak, is akin to the absurd attempt to learn how to swim without getting into the water;[61] second, he argues that Kant's 'fear of falling into error' leads him to falsely distinguish 'between ourselves and (. . .) our cognition'.[62] Instead, Hegel suggests that consciousness is co-extensive with cognition and that its truth is arrived at processually. Significantly for our purposes, Adorno views reflection as the motor of this process, or at least one side of it. Accordingly, he portrays phenomenology as the de-familiarization of certain established modes of cognition through reflection, conceived of, here, as the speculative operation proper to philosophy. He acknowledges that sense-certainty, perception, understanding and so on are partial articulations of what is ultimately recouped as absolute knowing, absolute cognition; that the progression through these stages follows from consciousness discovering the immanent limitations of each of its shapes. Upon reflection – Adorno suggests – the simple 'here and now' of sense-certainty, for instance, is revealed to be an empty universal, which contradicts its claim to be cognizant of a given particular. In turn, this contradiction forces consciousness into motion so that this incongruity might be overcome. Consciousness thus encounters itself as though it were looking in a mirror. This dialectical drive, conceived of as the reflexive movement of consciousness through contradiction, produces a series of shapes of consciousness whose sum appears as the history of its education to the standpoint of science. Such a mode of reflection, though, is speculative, not empirical.

Despite Adorno's somewhat tendentious use of Hegel, his invocation of the *Phenomenology* helps to clarify his objections to the proponents of 'representational thinking'. Broadly speaking, his criticism hinges on the claim that Lenin's theory of reflection corresponds to Hegel's description of sense-certainty – a naive mirroring of purportedly objective reality in the senses: this, here, now. By disavowing Hegel's supposed emphasis on reflection, however, Adorno suggests that Lenin cannot move forward from this stage. Accordingly, 'reflection theory' is – in fact – 'without reflection' and, indeed, without dialectics. That is, Adorno's treatment of materialism somewhat ironically pits Hegel against Lenin by arguing that while '[d]ialectics lies in things' (he is a materialist and a Marxist after all) 'it could not exist without a consciousness that reflects it'.[63] Since contradiction – the negative moment in all dialectics – can only be reflected within consciousness, 'the moment of subjectivity or reflection cannot be taken out of the dialectic. Where this does nonetheless happen' – as in Lenin's re-imagination of Hegel via Engels – 'the philosophical grounds for a transition to a state-religion are laid, wherein we can observe with horror the deterioration of dialectical theory'.[64] That is to say, '[w]hat is not reflected in itself does not know contradiction' and insofar as it 'does not know contradiction', it is eminently un-dialectical.[65] Adorno continues: '[T]he perversion of dialectical materialism into the state religion of Russia is theoretically based on the defamation of that element as idealistic.'[66] The proliferation of religious metaphors is decisive here. The idolatrous 'images' of Lenin's reflection theory are worshipped at the altar of Russia's 'state religion' – a formulation that further recalls the personality cult surrounding Lenin. Adorno's critique of Lenin, then, seeks to highlight the inadequacy of 'reflection' *through* 'reflection', that is, meta-critically, from the inside out. In other words, on Adorno's reading, there is a materialist moment to Hegel's speculative idealism and hence to the 'bourgeois' subjectivity that Lenin seeks to disavow. It is only by venturing through the proverbial desert of abstraction that something like materialism becomes conceivable.

(b) Following Adorno's play on the ambiguity of the term 'reflection', it is worth calling to mind that – in a second step – he likens the epistemological precepts of Lenin's dialectical materialism to those of pre-Socratic and Hellenic Atomism, particularly as advanced by Democritus and Epicurus. Adorno argues as follows: '[R]eflection theory' is rooted in 'an Epicurean-style materialist mythology, which invents the emission by matter of little images'.[67] This is, of course, a very partial account of Adorno's relationship to Epicurus. While Adorno is certainly critical of some epistemological precepts associated with Epicurean Atomism, his own notion of happiness as bodily fulfilment is clearly indebted to Epicurus. Nevertheless, the 'naïve replica-realism' of Leninist epistemology is thus said to depend on a 'materialist metaphysics, such as that advanced by antique Epicureanism, with its thesis that we continually receive little images from matter'.[68] In turn, this 'thesis' raises questions about how 'matter, which was previously characterised as wholly without soul or spirit, i.e. causal-mechanical material in the sense of Democritus comes to emit such images in the first place'.[69]

To be sure, Adorno's analogy between Soviet materialism and pre-Socratic Atomism must be taken with a pinch of salt. Unlike Heidegger, for instance, Adorno's knowledge of Ancient Greek Philosophy is resolutely second hand. In his lectures on *Philosophical Terminology* (1963), Adorno cites Eduard Zeller's *A History of Greek Philosophy* (1865) and Friedrich Albert Lange's *History of Materialism* (1866/1875) as his main sources. In an aside, he also refers to the surviving fragments of Marx's doctoral dissertation on *The Difference between the Democritean and Epicurean Philosophy of Nature* (1841).[70] A more thorough investigation of the latter might have prompted him to develop the condensed statement of his 'imageless' materialism, for example, by redrawing the genealogy of Marx's concept of materialism in order to contrast it with its Engelsian re-imagination. This task is, in fact, laudably taken on in Alfred Schmidt's doctoral dissertation, which was written under Adorno and Horkheimer's supervision. In the absence of more substantial textual evidence, however, Adorno's effort to uncover a Marxian materialism beyond its Soviet codification remains tacit. Notwithstanding the fact that Adorno's analogy appears in a kind of philosophical shorthand, what is of interest here is how the alignment of Moscow and Athens allows him to expose certain unacknowledged metaphysical presuppositions that underlie Lenin's purportedly scientific mode of 'representational thinking'.

In the aforementioned 1963 lecture series, then, Adorno outlines a highly condensed history of materialism, which includes some notable passages on Atomism. (Lectures 34–43 sketch a history of materialism from Democritus to Marx. Since these lectures coincide with Adorno's work on *Negative Dialectics*, they contain numerous formulations that are later echoed in passages like 'Materialism Imageless'.) Herein, he traces a development leading from Democritus's pre-Socratic effort to 'fixate the essence of matter' to Epicurus's Hellenic 'attempt to establish a materialism solely on the basis of experience'.[71]

Adorno highlights two aspects of this progression: on the one hand, he follows Lange in arguing that 'we have every reason to suppose that many features of the Epikurean Atomism (. . .) are due to Demokritos'.[72] That is, insofar as Democritus's 'whole philosophy was finally absorbed by Epikuros',[73] the two are presented as being de facto interchangeable. On the other hand, he distinguishes between Epicurus's alleged 'anti-scientism'[74] – his eudemonic commitment to bodily pleasure – and Democritus's 'fully formed scientific system'.[75] The significance of this discontinuity will become apparent shortly.

To begin with, Adorno describes the sense in which Democritus divides the physical universe into two distinctive realms: 'Atoms' and 'void'. Atoms (from the Greek *atomos*: 'indivisible') are supposed to be the irreducible building blocks of all material entities, as expressed in the theses that '*nothing arises out of nothing*', that '*nothing that is can be destroyed*', and that '*[a]ll change is only combination and separation of atoms*'.[76] In turn, atoms are said to move through space, which is conceived of as an infinite void. (As Lange puts it, '*[n]othing exists but atoms and empty space: all else is only opinion.*')[77] Over the course of their movements, then, atoms either repel one another or combine into groups that ultimately constitute objects, which is to say that '*[n]othing happens by chance, but everything through a cause and of necessity*'.[78] Once constituted, the continual movements of atoms cause these objects to change, thus accounting for phenomena such as growth and decay. In other words, '*[t]he variety of all things is a consequence of the variety of their atoms in number, size, figure and arrangement; there is no qualitative difference of atoms*'.[79] Against this backdrop, the Epicurean theory of perception comes into focus. As Adorno reports, in Epicurus's view all matter continually emits 'fine particles', which are absorbed by our sense organs.[80] The origin of our sense impressions – 'mental images' – is thus due to a constant flow of such particles from the surface of material bodies.[81] As Lange expounds, it is thus that 'actual material copies of things' are said to 'enter into us'.[82] Accordingly, it is the impact of these particles on our sense organs that enables us to perceive the 'images' sent out by matter.

Adorno's attempt to relate this reading of Democritus and Epicurus to Lenin hinges on the difference he posits between these figures. As he argues, in Epicurus 'the moment of sensory perception is far more forcefully accentuated than in Democritus';[83] it alone is presented as the 'true source of cognition'; relative to it '[s]pirit is (. . .) something thoroughly derivative, dependent, secondary'.[84] That is to say, 'sensory perception and' – indeed – '*sensory pleasure* have a much greater status' in Epicureanism than in the 'objectively oriented' natural–scientific model that typifies 'Democritean materialism'.[85] However, insofar as Lange notes that Epicurus takes up his forerunner's atomism part and parcel, he is apparently caught in a kind of contradiction. Adorno tries to resolve this by asking how it is possible 'to simultaneously teach the being-in-itself of nature as something independent of us, whilst assuming that our sensory perception is the source of all cognition'.[86] In order to square this contradiction, we are told, 'Epicurus is forced to posit a metaphysical thesis, which is irreconcilable with materialism's *denial* of metaphysics',[87] namely that matter, 'which was previously characterised as wholly without soul or spirit, i.e. causal-mechanical material in the sense of Democritus', emits images, whose truth is verified by sensory experience. The supposed convergence with Leninist reflection theory is thus characterized as follows:

> This reflection theory, then, played a significant role in the history of Marxist materialism. To this day it lives on in the form of DIAMAT reflection theory, according to which theory is supposed to be an *image* of reality, regardless of the fact that whilst the spiritual and intentional may be directed at particular states of affairs – it may mean them, make judgements about them – it does not resemble them (. . .) imagistically.[88]

To be sure, Adorno's identification of Lenin's dialectical materialism with Epicurean Atomism is polemical, and (consequently) it is not as seamless as he might like. For instance, if he is suggesting that there is an absolute correspondence between Democritus's belief that *'nothing happens by chance'* and Lenin's alleged historical determinism, then this reading does not account for the Democritean doctrine of the atomic swerve – *clinamen* – which states that the movements of atoms are ultimately random. Nevertheless, the critique of 'representational thinking' elucidated until now is beginning to take shape. As Adorno argues, Lenin's theory of reflection reproduces precisely those *meta*physical presuppositions that it seeks to recant by assigning an *extra*-physical quality to ostensibly disenchanted matter. By positing the mysterious ability of mind-independent bodies to emit 'little images', whose truthfulness is confirmed through sensory reflection; by elevating this reality to the status of an inalterable philosophical principle; and by asserting this principle as the guarantor of revolutionary praxis, Lenin's concept of materialism is said to succumb to the very 'metaphysical subtleties and theological niceties' that it aims to overcome.⁸⁹ That is to say, Lenin is portrayed as fetishizing matter by imbuing it with lifelike qualities, while simultaneously reifying humankind by turning people into passive objects: reflecting mirrors. It follows, then, that if the official materialist doctrines of the so-called East aid the 'uncritical reproduction of existing relationships in consciousness', then the kind of Marxism that these doctrines serve to ground is seen as being deficient not only theoretically but also politically. Accordingly, Adorno contends that Lenin's metaphysics of matter embeds humankind in a system of seamlessly determined nature that belies 'the possibility of freedom, whilst' paradoxically 'speaking at the same time of spontaneous action, even revolution'.⁹⁰ Wherever materialism consigns itself to affirming such a total order of blind nature, it betrays its emancipatory intention – a failure that has everything to do with the image character of thought.

(iii) Speculative realism

Having thus sketched the outlines of Adorno's misgivings about Lenin's mode of 'representational thinking', it remains to explore how his opposition reverberates today, more than thirty years after the collapse of the Soviet Union. It is striking, then, that certain characteristics of Lenin's philosophy (rather than, say, his revolutionary activity) recur – conspicuously – in the context of a more recent intellectual current, namely the programme for a 'Speculative Realism'⁹¹ laid out in Quentin Meillassoux's essay, *After Finitude* (2006).⁹² It has repeatedly been pointed out that Meillassoux's book 'often sounds like a repetition of Lenin's ill-famed *Materialism and Empirio-Criticism*'; that '*After Finitude* can effectively be read as *Materialism and Empirio-Criticism* rewritten for the twenty-first century'.⁹³ Before proceeding to interrogate this claim, however, it bears emphasizing that Lenin's spectral presence at this juncture is revealing for at least two reasons: first, because it throws into relief the sense in which Meillassoux's attempt to think mind-independent matter tacitly draws on a highly charged model from the history of (political) philosophy to delineate how a 'transformative materialism' might be thought today;⁹⁴ second, because if it is true that *After Finitude* seeks to 'complete and correct the programme of Marxist philosophy undertaken by Lenin',⁹⁵ then it too falls prey to Adorno's critique of dialectical materialism.⁹⁶ What this goes to underline, then, is that imagining something like an emancipatory politics, in some sense, hinges on the epistemic precepts within which emancipation is thought.

Without wishing to speculate on Meillassoux's explicit political commitments (neither Marx nor Lenin is named in *After Finitude*),[97] the consequence of this peculiar convergence points back to the point, raised earlier, that purportedly materialist thought tends to relapse into its opposite; that its theoretical 'deficiencies' serve to ground a kind of bad 'political creed'.[98] Set against this backdrop, then, Adorno's critique of Lenin et al. yields its current resonance, allowing us to approach his concept of an 'imageless' materialism under a more contemporary aspect.

Meillassoux's claim, in *After Finitude*, is two-pronged: on the one hand, he argues that it is possible to gain determinate knowledge of absolute reality through philosophical speculation; and on the other hand, he argues that it is possible to demonstrate the sense in which reality is radically contingent. 'Nothing is necessary, apart from the necessity that nothing be necessary. Anything can happen, at any place and at any time, without reason or cause.'[99] But if Meillassoux's concern is with reality itself, this does not mean thinking about what *is* so much as it means thinking about what *can* be: not 'being' (*être*) but 'may-being' (*peut-être*).[100] In other words, '[i]f Meillassoux can be described as a "realist", then the reality that concerns him does not involve the way things are' – this is only a first step – 'so much as the possibility that they might always be otherwise'.[101] Broadly speaking, then, Meillassoux expounds these theses in two steps: (a) through a critique of what he calls 'correlationism' and (b) through a radicalization of what he describes as 'Hume's problem'.

(a) Meillassoux's effort to demonstrate that we can know mind-independent matter depends on his objections to a central tenet of Kantian and post-Kantian critical philosophy, whereby 'we only ever have access to the *correlation* between thinking and being' – subject and object – 'and never to either term considered apart from the other'.[102] In the main, Meillassoux argues that European philosophers since Kant mistakenly surmise that 'anything (. . .) totally a-subjective cannot be',[103] since objectivity can only be construed on 'the foundations of the cognition in which it is grounded'.[104] From Hegel to Heidegger, we are told, philosophy has univocally demanded various forms of mediation between thought and being. It is the defensibility of this relation – 'whether it be clarified through logical judgement, phenomenological reduction, historical reflection, linguistic articulation, pragmatic experimentation or inter-subjective communication' – which supposedly determines the legitimacy of any present claim about reality.[105] Meillassoux illustrates this predicament by citing the preface to the second edition of Kant's *Critique of Pure Reason* (1787). Herein Kant famously likens the endeavour of critical philosophy to 'the first thoughts of Copernicus'.[106] As is well known, whereas, in Kant's view, traditional metaphysics assumed that 'our cognition must conform to objects' (the metaphorical analogue of the sun's supposed revolution around the earth), we must now consider the reverse: that objects 'conform to our cognition',[107] that is, that the earth revolves around the sun. Without presuming to recount the intricacies of Kant's first *Critique* in an aside, the comparison with Copernicus is important because – as Meillassoux points out – it contains an awkward slippage.

> [I]t has become abundantly clear that a more fitting comparison for the Kantian revolution in thought would be to a 'Ptolemaic counter-revolution', given that what the former asserts is not that the observer whom we thought was motionless is in fact orbiting around the observed sun, but on the contrary, that the subject is central to the process of knowledge.[108]

The point is clear: if Copernican heliocentrism places *reality* at the centre of intellectual inquiry, then Kant's critical turn entails a geocentric 'counter-revolution', such that the human becomes the measure of matter. Notwithstanding a certain bias in Meillassoux's reading,[109] his objection serves to frame the very questions that he shares with Lenin: How can philosophy gain access to mind-independent matter beyond its correlation with a thinking subject, and how can the transformation of such matter be accounted for?

In order to answer these questions, Meillassoux proposes to complicate the Kantian picture by introducing the problem of 'ancestrality', that is, statements about events anterior to the emergence of any form of human consciousness. (It hardly seems coincidental that one of the chapters in *Materialism and Empirio-Criticism* bears the title 'Did Nature Exist Prior to Man?') Accordingly, he asks, 'How are we to grasp the meaning of scientific statements bearing explicitly upon a manifestation of the world that is posited as anterior to the emergence of thought and even of life – posited, that is, as anterior to every form of human relation to the world?'[110] Put in Kantian terms: '[H]ow is one to legitimate the assertion that something subsists beyond our representations when one has already insisted that this beyond is radically inaccessible to thought?'[111]

Certainly, Meillassoux is not advocating for a simple regression to pre-Kantian metaphysics. Rather, he seeks to 'overcome the correlational obstacle to his acausal ontology' by showing that Kant's 'correlationist critique of metaphysical necessity *itself* enables (. . .) the speculative affirmation of non-necessity'.[112] To this end Meillassoux enlists an unlikely ally – Hegel – whose critique of Kant he claims to turn against itself. As he argues, 'instead of concluding that the in-itself is unknowable', Hegel transforms the correlation between thought and being into 'the *only* veritable in-itself'.[113] If Kant's 'instrument of empirico-critical de-absolutisation' becomes the 'model for a new type of absolute',[114] then this has a double consequence. On the one hand, absolute knowledge is reintroduced (we *can* know absolute reality); on the other hand, a slippage in the first *Critique* is retroactively illuminated. In turn, the correlation of thought and being itself is supposed to be exposed as a mere contingency. As Hallward explains, 'the correlationist' – Kant – 'in order to guard against idealist claims to knowledge of absolute reality' – Hegel – 'accepts not only the reduction of knowledge to knowledge of facts' (i.e. to knowledge of appearances within certain irreducible intellectual strictures); he also accepts that this 'reduction' itself is nothing but a fact amongst other facts: '[A]nother non-necessary contingency'.[115] The point for Meillassoux is that if such correlation is not necessary, then it is possible to imagine its suspension. In other words, 'the only way the correlationists can defend themselves against idealist absolutisation requires them to admit "the impossibility of giving an ultimate ground to the existence of any being", including the impossibility of giving a ground for this impossibility'.[116] It is in this unspoken admission that Meillassoux locates the affirmation of non-necessity on which his project hinges. Far from experiencing things in themselves as limit cases of thought, he pronounces their facticity as knowledge *of* their absolute reality. However, this raises the question as to how Meillassoux proposes to *know* this sheer contingency.

(b) In order to grasp this issue, we must briefly consider the second aspect of the argument announced earlier, namely Meillassoux's radicalization of 'Hume's problem'. As he recounts, Hume – in those sections of the *Enquiry*

Concerning Human Understanding (1748) that contest the principle of sufficient reason – teaches that 'any cause may actually produce any effect whatsoever, provided the latter is not contradictory'.[117] In other words, 'we may well be able to uncover the basic laws that govern the universe – but the cause that underlies those laws themselves, and which endows them with necessity, will remain inaccessible to us.'[118] (This is another reason why the subject–object correlation in post-Kantian thought is presented as being ultimately arbitrary.) Meillassoux concedes Hume's basic point but objects that he shies away from the full consequence of his insight. Instead of abandoning the idea of causal necessity, Hume simply consigns it to a realm beyond demonstration. In the end, he is thus said to 'believe blindly in the world that metaphysicians thought they could prove'.[119] By contrast, Meillassoux contends that the impossibility of rationally grounding the principle of sufficient reason – of demonstrating that things are as they are of necessity – in fact proves that there is no such reason or necessity at all. 'Rather than try to salvage a dubious faith in the apparent stability of our experience' – Meillassoux speaks here of 'fideism', Lenin's term to describe the Machists' supposed attitude towards the existence of an external world – 'we should affirm the prospect that Hume refused to accept': that 'an infinite variety of "effects" might emerge on the basis of no cause at all, in a pure eruption of novelty *ex nihilo*'.[120]

Here a decisive difference between Meillassoux and Lenin comes into focus. Whereas Lenin holds that ordinary sense experience provides the ultimate proof of matter's primacy – a primacy that is, in turn, supposed to ensure the pre-eminence of political praxis – Meillassoux argues that it is precisely the 'stability' of ordinary sense experience that prevents us from surrendering to the full consequence of absolute contingency, to transformation 'ex nihilo'. Hallward describes this shift as follows: the '[c]onversion of Hume's problem into Meillassoux's opportunity' requires a 'deflation of experience and the senses'.[121] It requires, in other words, 'that thought must free itself from the fascination for the phenomenal fixity of laws, so as to accede to a purely intelligible Chaos capable of destroying and of producing, without reason, things and the laws which they obey'.[122] That is to say, 'intelligibility' takes the place of 'phenomenal fixity'; 'speculation' takes the place of 'reflection'.

Meillassoux proceeds to buttress this point by reviving the ostensibly pre-critical notion of a purely 'intelligible' form of intuition so as to overturn the supposed strictures of Kant's critical turn. He extrapolates from the Cartesian account of objective reality's 'primary qualities', that is, those aspects of matter – for example, weight – that can be determined independently of its phenomenal appearance. But if Descartes conceives of these qualities in geometric terms – in terms of an object's physical parameters – then Meillassoux goes one step further by isolating this mathematical aspect from extension altogether: '[W]hat is mathematically conceivable' – however hypothetical – 'is absolutely possible.'[123] In other words, the irrefutable reality of a mind-independent matter whose mode of being is utterly contingent is supposedly proven *ex hypothesi* through recourse to mathematics.[124]

There are at least two aspects of such a 'Speculative Realism' that resonate with the critique of 'Diamat' outlined earlier: one regarding the locus of transformative agency in Meillassoux's philosophy; the other regarding the tendency of *After Finitude* to lapse into a strange kind of idealism. The first point concerns Meillassoux's equivocation between metaphysical and physical necessity, that is, between epistemology and ontology. We have already seen a version of this equivocation in Engels and Lenin's view that the material world evinces a kind of dialectical-developmental logic – that cells as much as societies necessarily evolve according to a historical dynamic that proceeds through overcoming internal contradictions, sublating them and carrying them forward into ever-higher degrees of articulation which are in turn mirrored by consciousness. By contrast, Meillassoux seems to invert this tendency (to put it back on its head, to stick with the Marxian metaphor) by claiming to deduce the absolute contingency of being by transposing Hume's repudiation of the principle of sufficient reason onto physical and natural laws more generally. From this he infers that 'there is *no* cause or reason for anything to be the way it is', and that consequently the transformation of material conditions may be both absolute and instantaneous.[125] Although the consequence of the Engelsian–Leninist materialist dialectic is a strong form of historical *necessity*, whereas the outcome of Meillassoux's speculative-realist deduction is an absolute form of *contingency*, both positions converge in mistaking metaphysical claims for binding natural–scientific facts. But whereas the former over-determines the course of the historical dynamic that is supposed to follow from the identification of physics and metaphysics, the latter can provide no real account of what drives its process of transformation. Accordingly, Meillassoux – for his part – has no adequate substitute for what others have called 'substance, or spirit, or power, or labour.'[126] That is to say, '[h]is insistence that anything might happen' ex nihilo 'can only amount to an insistence on the bare possibility of radical change.'[127] If Meillassoux's model is thus supposed to 'correct and complete' the perceived shortcomings of Engels and Lenin's ontology, then it is unclear how the strictures which the latter unwittingly impose on revolutionary praxis are supposed to be lifted by displacing the affirmation of matter from the domain of the sensual to that of the mathematical. Despite this shift of emphasis, Meillassoux ultimately faces the same problem as Engels and Lenin: by hypostatizing a trans-historical metaphysics of matter – be it on the basis of sense-certainty or mathematics – all three unwittingly negate the possibility of freedom while paradoxically speaking at the same time of spontaneous and total transformation.

The second point worth noting here concerns the view that '[i]n trying to maintain the speculative sovereignty of philosophical reason',[128] Meillassoux in fact reintroduces idealism at the level of form. It is unclear why an account of material reality in terms of pure number should be any less anthropocentric than its verification through sense impressions. The claim that the meaning of 'ancestral statements' can be grasped apart from a thinking subject does not account for the fact that the very terms of their mathematical reformulation stem from the eminently human discourse of mathematics. As Hallward explains,

> As a matter of course, every unit of measurement, from the length of a meter to the time required for a planet to orbit around a star, exists at a fundamental distance from the domain of number as such. If Meillassoux was to carry through the argument of 'ancestrality' to its logical conclusion, he would have to acknowledge that it would eliminate not only all reference to secondary qualities like colour and texture but also all conventional primary qualities like length or mass or date as well. What might then be known of an 'arche-fossil' (. . .) would presumably have to be expressed in terms of pure numbers alone (. . .). Whatever else such (. . .) knowledge amounts to, it has no obvious relation with the sorts of realities that empirical science tries to describe.[129]

Meillassoux's misstep, then, lies in the suggestion 'that a speculative philosophy in conjunction with a mathematized science can struggle against abstractions that are perceived as mere errors of the intellect, and not as abstractions that have any basis in a social, material and extra-logical reality'.[130] That is to say, the mathematical form of Meillassoux's argument undermines its purportedly materialist content. His parochial defence of mind-independent matter tends to obfuscate the material grounds of techno-scientific and capitalist abstraction.

* * *

To recap: the preceding pages recounted Adorno's critique of 'representational thinking' with reference to the epistemological precepts of dialectical materialism. Building on this reconstruction, an attempt was made to weigh up the actuality of Adorno's objections by mapping them onto Meillassoux's programme for a 'Speculative Realism', not least because *After Finitude* has repeatedly been portrayed as a contemporary version of Lenin's *Materialism and Empirio-Criticism*. In both cases the point has been to demonstrate that Adorno allows us to uncover the common metaphysical presuppositions that underpin these outwardly materialist philosophies in a manner that at least implies a certain kind of politics. Nevertheless, it ought to be noted, the claim that the political deficiencies of dialectical materialism follow directly from its theoretical shortcomings presumes a somewhat *un*-dialectical relation between theory and praxis.

Adorno himself wrestles with this issue in a late text titled 'Marginalia on Theory and Praxis' (1969). Herein he identifies the division between thought and action with the separation of subject and object, a schism that – in turn – sits in a wider historical narrative outlined chiefly in *Dialectic of Enlightenment*. 'Just as the division of subject and object cannot be revoked immediately by a decree of thought' – a point to which we will return later – 'so too an immediate unity of theory and praxis is hardly possible: it would imitate the false identity of subject and object and would perpetuate the principle of domination that posits identity and that a true praxis must oppose.'[131] A 'true praxis', here, can, I think, finally be taken to mean something like 'politics'. Existing modes of 'thought' cannot present a true 'identity of subject and object' because they inevitably 'perpetuate' a 'principle of domination', which subordinates objects under the reign of sovereign subjectivity. What is at stake in Adorno's singular reorientation of materialism in terms of the Mosaic interdiction against idol worship, then, is a reorientation of 'thought' away from an epistemic violence, whose material correlate is supposed to be bodily suffering, the capitalist division of labour, state violence and societal injustice. The stated aim of Adorno's imageless materialism is thus to think the condition of possibility for a life free from privation.

Part II: Imagelessness

The preceding pages have paid close attention to the opening lines from the passage of 'Materialism Imageless', cited at the outset, where Adorno observes that 'a consciousness interpolating images, a third element, between itself and that which it thinks would unwittingly reproduce idealism'. As was seen, Adorno's critique targets the 'representational' character of dialectical materialism – an epistemic precept that he polemically likens to idol worship. It was noted, then, that this ironic interjection aligns Adorno's concept of an 'imageless' materialism with the monotheistic proscription of idol worship. ('What clings to the image remains idolatry, mythic enthrallment'; 'demythologisation, the thought's enlightening intent, deletes the image character of consciousness.')

The subsequent lines from this passage, in turn, contain further clues for how to understand Adorno's notion of an 'imageless' materialism. (i) First, this concerns the manner in which Adorno seeks to figure the relationship between image and imagelessness, as expressed in the verdict that 'the full object could be conceived' only 'in the absence of images'. 'The full object', in this context, should, I think, be taken to mean a phenomenon apprehended in a manner that does not 'perpetuate the principle of domination' – something other than the subject–object, theory–praxis, nature–culture split which, nonetheless, emerges from within these schisms. The object of Adorno's materialism, then, would be the critical delineation of the conditions under which such apprehension might become possible; and I take it that, moreover, this effort is, in fact, the final aim of Adorno's 'politics'. (ii) The second point concerns the somatic and affective features of such a materialism, as expressed in Adorno's reference to a 'resurrection of the flesh', that is, his estimation that 'the perspective vanishing point of historic materialism would be its self-sublation, the spirit's liberation from the primacy of material needs in their state of fulfilment'. If nothing else, the move from 'matter' to 'flesh' requires some degree of qualification.

(i) Image and imagelessness

In order to determine the relationship between 'image' and 'imagelessness' as a turning point of Adorno's politics, the following should briefly be considered: if the image ban designates a negation of the images associated with Leninist reflection theory, and hence a confrontation between 'representational' and 'non-representational' *thinking*, then the locus of what has been called Adorno's 'Utopia of cognition' – a mode of grasping and acting upon objectivity beyond instrumentality, intentionality and means-ends relations – lies precisely in the particular dynamic that is unfolded in the latter part of the passage cited at the outset: '[I]t is only in the absence of images that the full object could be conceived. Such absence concurs with the theological ban on images. Materialism brought that ban into secular form by not permitting Utopia to be positively pictured; this is the substance of its negativity.'[132] Put differently: if, as was suggested, 'the materialist longing to grasp the thing' means nothing less than a radical reconfiguration of thinking as such (the haptic connotation of the German term *begreifen* – to grasp – anticipates Adorno's effort to elaborate what might be called a mimetic kind of cognition); if, in turn, this intellectual modality is supposed to stave off the sacrificial logic that Adorno associates with all historical iterations of identity thinking (including Soviet materialism and cold war capitalism); and if, finally, formulating such a mode of materialist cognition hinges on the figure of the image ban, because positively formulating it in extant terms would simply reproduce the status quo, then it follows that Adorno's phrasing illuminates – however carefully – the vexed political stakes of his own idiosyncratic Marxism.[133]

The salient question, here, is how Adorno proposes to present his 'Utopia of cognition', with all of its far-reaching resonances, if it cannot be 'positively pictured'. Indeed, the question of presentation (*Darstellung*) is central here. Its significance for Adorno goes back to the 'Epistemo-Critical Foreword' to Walter Benjamin's ill-fated *Habilitationsschrift* on the *Origin of the German Trauerspiel* (1928), a text that Adorno knew well.[134] For its part, the text can be viewed as the summative statement of Benjamin's early philosophical project. Although *Darstellung* defies easy summary (for Benjamin it is to do with the presentation of what he calls 'ideas'),[135] one way of approaching this term in the present context is to note that Adorno inherits from this work the view that conventional ways of philosophizing effect a kind of epistemic violence perpetuated on what Benjamin calls 'phenomena'.[136] For Adorno, in turn, these 'phenomena' seem to designate something like the lived stuff of experience; and insofar as philosophy does not do justice to 'phenomena' through knowledge, that is, in the guise of conceptual thought (de facto, philosophy's *only* guise), it is taken to be incapable of entering into a relation with *truth*, which is, after all, its stated aim. Adorno's take on what Benjamin calls 'truth',[137] then, appears to mean something like a non-coercive mode of relating to phenomenal reality. Knowledge, on this account, is rejected for subsuming particulars under universals and, hence, obfuscating their inimitability. Truth, in the emphatic sense, would mean grasping the world of phenomena in its particularity, that is, non-violently, or at least by way of 'a different kind of violence'.[138] In this regard, philosophy must undergo an 'Epistemo-Critical' recalibration; its principal task becomes recasting its own time-honoured modes of apprehending and (re)presenting reality in a manner that opposes its seemingly in-built tendency to coercion. However, since philosophy *as such* is deemed to be complicit with the problem it is trying to overcome – the view that thought is sufficient for grasping the totality of the real – the whole enterprise of Adorno's negative dialectic is, at first glance, self-contradictory. Indeed, it is on this point that critics of Adorno, according to whom his whole project is insufficiently grounded, get going. For Axel Honneth, for instance, Critical Theory of the Adornian cast 'cannot really justify what makes the ideals from its own culture', for example, its appeal to truth, 'normatively defensible or desirable in the first place';[139] but while for Honneth and other thinkers from the Frankfurt school's so-called second and third generations, this normative deficit is to be remedied through a recourse to more traditional concepts, such as communication – the arena in which the promise of reason (and, with it, philosophy) is to be fulfilled – for Adorno, following Benjamin, the point is, rather, to immanently recast philosophy in such a way that an altogether different way of thinking might yet emerge. The 'truth' that philosophy is supposed to articulate, on this view, cannot be positively figured but only negatively intimated.

To this end, I take it, Adorno makes use of at least two strategies, which might provisionally be placed under the headings (a) inversion and (b) negation.

(a) The dynamic figure of 'inversion'[140] designates a characteristic movement of Adorno's dialectic: the paradoxical attempt to glean a kind of photographic negative of reconciliation between the subject and object of thought from within the 'bewitched, distorted and upside-down world' of capitalist modernity.[141] Adorno thus gestures *ex negativo* towards a third term (vulgarized in the sequence thesis-antithesis-synthesis) by dwelling in the moment of dialectical contradiction, that is, by refusing what he considers to be an extorted form of *rapprochement* between subject and object. This emphasis on non-identity, however, is not reducible to a merely methodological quirk. Rather, Adorno, in a duly Marxist fashion, views dialectical antitheses as philosophical sedimentations of socio-historical antagonisms. These demand that we highlight their incommensurability, push against their limits and strengthen our resolve that 'things *should* be different' – a resolve that, for its part, cannot be satisfied abstractly. In brief, by emphasizing what is false, Adorno seeks the inverted image of what is true.[142] To illustrate this point he upends a famous dictum from Spinoza's correspondence with Albert Burgh: 'Verum Index sui et falsi'[143] becomes 'Falsum (. . .) index sui et veri'.[144] In the present context, this strategy of syntactical inversion is remarkable to the extent that it reflects back on Adorno's iconoclastic critique of dialectical materialism: the images of Leninist reflection theory are revealed as unwittingly underwriting the very dogmatism they sought to displace in favour of transformative praxis; and, in turn, this revelation is supposed to yield a negative imprint of its opposite as a kind of 'mirror-writing'.[145] Put differently, the demonstration of the internal contradictions of – in this case – Leninist reflection theory is supposed to throw into relief the outline of what *ought* to be: not the blind insistence on a priority of matter, but a concern with the alleviation of suffering.

Adorno frequently intimates codes, puzzles and riddles that rely on inversions of different kinds, a tactic that recalls Leonardo Da Vinci's practice of encrypting sensitive texts by inverting their script using a mirror. Benjamin's presence is palpable when we learn that it is the task of philosophical 'interpretation' to discern the truth content of such puzzle images (*Vexierbilder*) by reading them as though they were sacred texts.[146] Hence, Adorno notes that '[d]ialectics discloses (. . .) every image as script. It teaches us to read from its features the admission of falseness which cancels its power and hands it over to truth.'[147] This tendency is borne out in Adorno's own *Habilitationsschrift* on Kierkegaard, *Construction of the Aesthetic* (1933), once memorably derided by Gershom Scholem as a 'sublime plagiarism' of Benjamin's study of the German *Trauerspiel*.¹⁴⁸ Adorno's book contains some notable passages on Søren Kierkegaard's description of a curious Biedermeier contraption,¹⁴⁹ the so-called window mirror (*Reflexionsspiegel*).¹⁵⁰ On Kirkegaard's account, window mirrors were attached to the outside of window frames in urban apartment buildings in a manner that made it possible for inhabitants to see a reflection of the streets outside without being visible to passers-by. Reflections of the outside world thus appeared as projections in the private interior – a metaphor for the relationship between individual consciousness and the objective, material world.

Broadly speaking, Adorno's study of Kierkegaard considers the Danish thinker's critique of Hegel as a bourgeois counterpart to Marx's concurrent confrontation with speculative idealism. Susan Buck-Morss notes that '[a]lthough both', Marx and Kierkegaard, 'rejected Hegel's identity theory because it lost sight of lived reality, Kierkegaard rested his case on the reality of individual existence' – a tendency that Adorno sees echoed in the work of Martin Heidegger – 'whereas for Marx existence is a social category',¹⁵¹ that is, *not* one that is exhausted in the appeal to subjectivity. Adorno's attempt to 'explode' Kierkegaard's philosophy of inwardness from the inside out thus shows itself as having two principle aims: first, 'to rob (. . .) existentialism', conceived of, here, as the retreat to bourgeois interiority, 'of its validity, and to justify simultaneously a (. . .) Marxist alternative'; and second, 'to argue against the view (. . .) that aesthetics', the lowest order of thought, according to Kierkegaard, 'was the realm of subjective immediacy and irrationalism, and to validate in its place the Hegelian conception of aesthetics as a medium for knowing objective truth'.¹⁵² In order to demonstrate the validity of these claims, Adorno seeks to expose what he perceives as the internal contradictions of Kierkegaard's thought so as to glean from them the unintended expression of historical truth: that 'the inner realm into which the logic of his theory led' – the subject's retreat from the object world – 'was itself a historical manifestation, marking the passing of the bourgeois era'.¹⁵³ This, according to Adorno, is the unintended – inverted – truth content of Kierkegaard's philosophy.

In particular, Adorno's reading proceeds by reversing the hierarchy of existential spheres – aesthetics, ethics, religion – outlined in Kierkegaard's pseudonymous opus *Either/Or* (1843). As is well known, Kierkegaard views the aesthetic sphere as the lowest stage of his peculiar dialectic. It is associated with the sensual, with worldly matter, rather than with the higher domains of ethics and religion. The figure of Johannes the Seducer, who inhabits the bourgeois interior, and in whose guise Kierkegaard narrates those sections of *Either/Or* that outline the aesthetic attitude, is emblematic of this outlook. Accordingly, Adorno homes in on the portrayal of Johannes's relation to his material surroundings, not in the form of the outside world but in the form his home furnishings. The 'window mirror' in Johannes's apartment becomes a case in point:

> Why can't you just be nice and quiet? What have you done all morning but shake my awnings, tug at my window mirror and the cord on it, play with the bellpull wire from the fourth floor, push against the windowpanes – in short, proclaim your existence in every way as if you wanted to beckon me out to you?[154]

Adorno comments on the inside–outside relation in this passage as follows: 'The window mirror is a characteristic furnishing of the spacious nineteenth-century apartment';[155] '[t]he function of the window mirror is to project the endless row of apartment buildings into the isolated bourgeois living room';[156] '[t]he window mirror testifies to objectlessness – it casts into the apartment only the semblance of things – and isolated privacy.'[157] Adorno views this seemingly innocuous feature of Johannes's lodgings as a material expression of Kierkegaard's inward turn. It inadvertently registers 'the alienation of subject and object'.[158] That is to say, the window mirror stands for the fact that '[i]n Kierkegaard there is so little of a subject/object in the Hegelian sense as there are given objects; there is only an isolated subjectivity' – the private resident of the 'spacious nineteenth-century apartment' – 'surrounded by a dark otherness'.[159] In other words, Johannes is connected to the world of objects only in semblance, by the reflections from the 'window mirror'. On this basis Adorno draws the following analogy:

> In his philosophy the knowing subject can no more reach its objective correlative than, in a society dominated by exchange-value, things are 'immediately' accessible to the person. Kierkegaard recognised the distress of incipient high-capitalism. He opposed its privations in the name of a lost immediacy that he sheltered in subjectivity. He analysed neither the necessity and legitimacy of reification nor the possibility of its correction. But he did nevertheless (. . .) note the relation of commodification and the commodity form in a metaphor that need only be taken literally to correspond with Marxist theories.[160]

This 'metaphor that need only be taken literally' is none other than that of the bourgeois *intérieur*: the smoke and mirrors of Johannes's reified consciousness amid the fetish world of commodities. To put it simply, Adorno's question is how to mobilize this figure, how to turn the impasse of Kierkegaard's objectless interiority against itself. In other words, he wonders how the reflections from the window mirror can be seen to contain a negative image of their opposite. Like Marx's account of the 'camera obscura',[161] the window mirror casts into the apartment an image of the topsy-turvy world of capitalist modernity. But as Adorno suggests, when critically interrogated, these projections do not re-double the world so much as they 'displace and estrange' it by literally putting it on its head, thus calling to mind the myriad modernist *Verfremdungs-stratagems* of the Weimar-era.[162]

Whatever one makes of this (what might it mean to put something on its head that is already upside down?), the metaphorical thrust of Adorno's phrasing appears to be that the window mirror divulges the perversion of the present as the code of its own undoing – 'the mirror writing of its opposite' – not as a 'blueprint for Utopia', but as an 'encrypted message' containing a '"prolegomenon" to a new reality', as Elizabeth Pritchard perceptively puts it.[163] This 'message' requires philosophical 'interpretation' – the labour of criticism – in order to uncover the history of domination that lies concealed in, say, Johannes's petrified interior. There may be 'no true life in the false',[164] as Adorno famously remarks; but the negative contours of a prospective reconciliation between subject and object are to be sought, amongst other places, in the reflections of the 'window mirror'.

(b) The inversions described earlier are essentially rhetorical modifications of the central moment in Adorno's thought, namely negation. In a pivotal passage from *Dialectic of Enlightenment*, for instance, Adorno notes, in terms that chime with the present effort to determine the relation between 'image' and 'imagelessness', that '[t]he right of the image' (the image of what is *true*, presumably) 'is rescued in the faithful observance of its prohibition': an 'observance' that is – in turn – associated with the Hegelian figure of 'determinate negation'.[165] What kind of a 'right' is envisaged here?

Again, the matter hinges on Adorno's singular remodelling of Hegel. The broad outlines of what Hegel means by determinate negation can be found already in central works, such as the introduction to the *Phenomenology of*

Spirit, though the movement designated by this term is decisive for virtually all of Hegel's mature thinking. As above, Hegel's exposition turns on his critique of Kant. Insofar as – for Kant – objects are only knowable as appearances, they are supposed to remain indeterminable as things in themselves. This is because the differentiation of one object from another (*this*-not-*that*) – a differentiation which proceeds through negation (this-*not*-that) – cannot, so long as it is governed by the sceptical consciousness that Hegel associates with Kant, truly determine an object. In Hegel's estimation, then, Kant stalls at the recognition that there is a difference between *this* and *that*, but he is unable to adequately express this difference. Hegel claims to overcome this impasse by absolutizing it: the Kantian thing-in-itself is knowable *as* unknowable. Hegel associates this gesture with a certain productivity of the negation contained in the judgement that x is not y. When the result of a dialectical reflection is 'conceived as it is in truth, namely, as a determinate negation, a new form has thereby immediately arisen'.[166] In other words, if the appearance of an object is followed by reflection on whether it is adequate to the conception of knowledge held by the subject at a given stage of consciousness; and if, in turn, the object is found lacking so that a new one is posited, which includes the unity of the process that produced it, then negation does not just produce nothing: it produces a 'determinate nothingness' which follows the arithmetic principle that the negation of a negation yields a positive term.[167] (Hegel, of course, describes this cumulative movement of supersession as 'sublation', *Aufhebung*, from the German verb *aufheben*, meaning literally 'to pick up' or 'to preserve', but also 'to lift', as in the lifting of sanctions.)

As has already been noted, in the case of the *Phenomenology*, this insight – first articulated vis-à-vis Kant – inaugurates a movement through all conceivable stages of consciousness (at least as Hegel sees it). Its sum, finally, appears as the standpoint of absolute knowing from whence the true work of philosophy – outlined in Hegel's *Science of Logic* (1816) – can finally begin. It is well known, too, that Adorno explicitly conceives of his own philosophical enterprise along Hegelian lines. However, to the extent that Hegel's philosophy is supposed, by some commentators, to chart a purposeful forward movement of the development of consciousness, history and so on, Adorno charges that what 'wins out' in such a *positive* dialectic is in fact an 'anti-dialectical principle: that traditional logic which, *more arithmetico*, takes minus times minus for a plus'.[168] The point is not so much that Adorno in any sense *opposes*

Hegel; rather, he aims to be more Hegelian than Hegel himself: the moment of negation, central to all dialectics, is assigned absolute primacy. Accordingly, Adorno contends that '[t]o negate a negation does *not* bring about its reversal'; *negative* dialectics 'proves, rather, that the negation was not negative enough'.[169] That is, insofar as, in conventionally Marxian terms, Adorno views philosophical contradictions as expressions of societal antagonisms, dialectics must not prematurely smooth over a given set of antitheses. Accordingly, Adorno argues that Hegel shies away from the full consequence of the negativity that drives his dialectic. He 'could not resolve the contradiction between his dialectic and his experience: it was this alone that forced Hegel the critic to maintain the affirmative'.[170] To affirm the moment of synthesis, of a unity – however provisional – between subject and object, means to sanction the status quo. A genuine resolution of contradiction would mean nothing less than the reconciliation between humankind and nature, and – hence – Utopia.

To be sure, if the image of a false reconciliation between subject and object were simply sublated in the act of banning it, that is, if Adorno's argument followed the positively dialectical schema of determinate negation that he presents, then (eventually) an image of the true life would irresistibly emerge. In the terms presented here, this would mean that Adorno's critique of Leninist reflection theory would necessarily resolve into a higher form of cognition (a truer form of materialism), just as the monotheistic injunction against idol worship ineluctably supersedes polytheistic paganism in Hegel's philosophy of religion.[171] But given that Adorno apparently identifies the synthetic moment of Hegelian dialectics with the actualization of philosophical universality – a clear echo of Marx's final thesis on Feuerbach – this will not do. That is to say, if, in Adorno's view, the historical moment for such synthesis in the guise of, say, a proletarian revolution has been 'missed',[172] as the famous opening line from *Negative Dialectics* proclaims; if philosophy is thus suspended in the moment of contradiction, and its principal task is marked out as perpetual critique, then the *ban* on images means – above all – holding open the possibility that what is represented in 'representational thinking' is not, in fact, everything. This sentiment is forcefully expressed in a passage from 'Marginalia on Theory and Praxis', where Adorno writes: 'The hostility to theory in the spirit of the times, the by no means coincidental withering away of theory, its banishment by an impatience that wants to change the world' (belabour it as an image) 'without having to interpret it while so far it has been chapter and verse that philosophers have *merely* interpreted – such hostility becomes praxis's weakness.'[173] Put differently, if – as Adorno suggests – the images of dialectical materialism are in fact static reflections of immutable matter, then surely their elevation to a philosophical principle grants the status quo absolute authority. If, by contrast, the image ban forbids the 'uncritical reproduction of existing relationships in consciousness', then Adorno's iconoclasm designates a clearing away: forging a space in which the subject–object relation can be recast, albeit negatively. To borrow a famous formulation of Benjamin's, Adorno 'sees no image hovering before him'; he 'knows only one watchword: make room', not 'for the sake of the rubble but for that of the way leading through it'.[174] On Adorno's model, to determinately negate the images of self-identical reality produced, in this case, by Leninist reflection theory means to underscore their inadequacy to the lived experience of un-freedom. The 'right' of the *true* image – the rightfulness of the promise it holds – is thus 'rescued' through the unswerving criticism of the present, a criticism that is carried out for the sake of the possibility that things might yet be otherwise. It is against this backdrop that Adorno's reference to the Old Testament ban on making images of God serves to frame his meta-critique of materialism – a materialism whose central concern is not the prioritization of matter but the abolition of suffering.

(ii) Adorno's concept of materialism

As we have seen, an 'imageless' mode of materialist cognition is initially occasioned by the sense in which Adorno seeks to subvert the images of Leninist reflection theory. In this respect, Adorno's polemical invocation of the 'theological ban on images' is supposed to bolster his alternative conception of a Marxian materialism, which departs from Soviet orthodoxy by foregrounding neither 'matter' nor 'praxis' but rather the elimination of suffering and privation. We will return to the question as to what kind of 'theology' informs Adorno's phrasing in Chapter 2; in the meantime, it will be recalled, 'Materialism Imageless' concludes with the estimation that materialism's 'great desire would be the resurrection of the flesh, a desire utterly foreign to idealism, the realm of the absolute spirit'. In this regard Adorno contends that 'the perspective vanishing point of historic materialism would be its self-sublation, the spirit's liberation from the primacy of material needs in their state of fulfilment. Only if the physical urge were quenched', we are told, 'would the spirit be reconciled and would become that which it only promises while the spell of material conditions will not let it satisfy material needs.' For Adorno, then, materialism is neither a method nor a goal but rather 'an impulse', a drive, as Simon Jarvis observes: 'the utopian wish for undeluded happiness, including bodily pleasure, the wish for an end to suffering.'[175] Nonetheless, this passage marks a crossroads at which various strands of Adorno's thinking coincide. That is, on the one hand, 'materialism' emerges from the immanent critique of idealism, the dictate of 'identity thinking' (as Adorno notes, 'the concept does not exhaust the thing conceived');[176] on the other hand, this ostensibly epistemological concern is supposed to have a material correlate in the history of domination outlined in *Dialectic of Enlightenment* where whatever falls outside given societal parameters is brutally expunged. With regards to the former, this means that thinking objectivity, in the emphatic sense, is, in fact, a contradiction in terms: 'To think is to identify.'[177] Accordingly, Adorno's 'Utopia of cognition' means paradoxically thinking thought against itself so as to throw into relief a materiality beyond thought's bounds, albeit not for the purposes of attaining any ontological mastery, but rather to recast the way in which subject and object *relate* to each other: '[T]o use concepts to unseal the nonconceptual with concepts without making it their equal.'[178] With regards to the latter, this means that the putative polarity between idealism and materialism is dissolved. Adorno, in a sense, deconstructs the binary.[179] Idealism entails a corporeal subject just as much as materialism entails a reflecting consciousness. However, the terms are not just dialectically mediated; they short-circuit each other's stable position in the very structure of thought. This is the sense in which Adorno argues that while 'the spell of material conditions' obstructs the transformation of society, the burden of critical theory lies in the much-maligned 'interpretation' of the world: critique (after all, he chides, the premature Marxist pronouncement of having dispensed with theory in favour of praxis 'miscarried').[180]

To the extent that Adorno accepts that social and historical injustices are inscribed in the workings of philosophy, his ethical, political concern with overcoming socio-historical antagonisms is occasionally expressed in oddly stiff philosophical terms. At least on one level, then, the tension in Adorno's thought is between (a) his insistence on a formal preponderance of objectivity and (b) his emphasis on what he calls the somatic moment of thought.

(a) In his late essay 'On Subject and Object' (1969), Adorno seeks to challenge the predominance of an always–already ill-constituted subjectivity – a point that harks back to his writings from the 1940s. In quasi-epistemological terms, Adorno highlights an asymmetry in the relationship between the subject and object of cognition by citing certain markers from the history of philosophy.[181] Contrary to certain unspecified epistemological models – perhaps Husserl, whose phenomenology Adorno had worked on in some detail – Adorno argues that the relation of objects to subjects is qualitatively different from that of subjects to objects. This signals not only the reciprocal dependence and mutual production of subjects by objects and objects by subjects but also the fact that '[a]n object can be conceived only by a subject but always remains something other than the subject, whereas a subject by its very nature is from the outset an object as well'.[182] Subjects, in short, are special kinds of objects. However, their objective character has become obscured and distorted over the course of history (one can imagine a psychoanalytic analogue to this point). This affects both the subject's self-relation in its capacity as a special kind of object and its relation to the material world.

As Adorno argues, the terms 'subject' and 'object' are exceedingly equivocal. '"[S]ubject" can refer to the particular individual as well as to universal attributes of "consciousness in general", in the language of Kant's *Prolegomena*.'[183] While the element of 'individual humanity' cannot be subtracted from the concept of the subject, the very conceptual articulation of subjectivity transforms it into a 'universal'.[184] By the same token, 'object' does not merely mean mind-independent matter: the 'object cannot be known except through consciousness'.[185] In other words, '[o]bjectivity can be made out solely by reflecting, at every historical and cognitive stage, both upon what at that time is presented as subject and object as well as upon their mediations.'[186] The mutual constitution of these terms, however, is historically produced. This point is borne out in *Dialectic of Enlightenment*,[187] where Adorno and Horkheimer argue that the emergence of individuated consciousness from the enchanted union with 'nature' marks the process of enlightenment as a splitting asunder of 'subject' (mind) and 'object' (matter), thus at least implying a kind of immemorial oneness beyond this split.

Such an implied oneness, though, is deceptive. Adorno relies here on Lukács's concept of 'second nature', which designates a world of capitalistic convention that masquerades as God-given and law-like. For Adorno, as for

Lukács, the notion of an authentic 'first nature' is an ideological projection made from the standpoint of 'second nature'. As Lukács puts it,

> [t]his second nature is not dumb, sensuous and yet senseless like the first: it is a complex of senses – meanings – which has become rigid and strange, and which no longer awakens interiority; it is a charnel-house of long-dead interiorities; this second nature could only be brought to life – if this were possible – by the metaphysical act of reawakening the souls which, in an early or ideal existence, created or preserved it; it can never be animated by another interiority.[188]

Accordingly, enlightenment must be seen, on the one hand, as the dual process of rationalizing deadly 'natural' forces from without (both physically and intellectually) and, on the other, as the self-imposed bondage necessary to persist under such conditions – a point memorably illustrated by Adorno and Horkheimer with reference to Homer's *Odyssey*. This immemorial rift, which – for its part – is read as a prehistoric division between mental and manual labour, inaugurates a historical dynamic that is characterized from the outset by the subjective domination of objects, including the subject's unwitting (and hence all the more calamitous) *self*-domination.[189] We will return to this point in subsequent chapters; for now it suffices to note that what Adorno and Horkheimer identify as the predominance of the subject in the philosophies of, for example, Bacon, Descartes or Kant is the expression of a historically fraught relation between humankind and the world of matter – nature. Humankind has had to renounce aspects of its bodily being in order to dominate the external world. Humanity thus becomes estranged from its own objectivity, which – in turn – leads to a disastrous form of blind self-instrumentalization. The epistemological categories 'subject' and 'object' thus lend 'expression to the real separation, the rivenness of the human condition', which is – in fact – 'the result of a coercive historical process' of which the mind-body dualism is only one prominent instantiation.[190] The subject's relationship to objectivity is thus portrayed as the undergirding of an instrumental rationality, whose path, Adorno wagers, leads directly into the great cataclysms of the twentieth century.

Nonetheless, such a relation between subject and object is not set in stone. In 'On Subject and Object' Adorno seeks to criticize this intellectual configuration by intimating a 'second reflection' of Kant's Copernican turn, that is, an immanent destabilization of, in this case, critical (as opposed to speculative) idealism.[191] If, as has already been seen, the Kantian revolution is supposed to demonstrate the (inter)subjective constitution of objectivity, then the 'second reflection' of this turn should – by extension – put this picture on its head. As Adorno argues, such an inversion exposes the Kantian view of 'consciousness in general' as a reification of the subject.[192] The alleged self-sufficiency of constitutive consciousness relies on an objectification of the subject that is not transparent to it. The autonomous subject is, in fact, not self-identical: '[M]ind's claim to independence announces its claim to domination. Once radically separated from the object, subject reduces the object to itself; subject swallows object, forgetting how much it is object itself.'[193] Yet, in a characteristic move, Adorno seeks to redeem this purported failure of Kant's thought by crediting him with inadvertently registering a historical truth: that the idealist conception of subjectivity is a real, albeit ill-begotten, abstraction.

Following the cue of Alfred Sohn-Rethel, Adorno thus reads Kant through a Marxian prism. The intellectual abstraction of the transcendental subject is an expression of the real abstraction of capitalist exchange relations. As Sohn-Rethel writes to Adorno in a long letter dated 4 November 1936, 'the formation of subjectivity is the inextricable correlate of the establishment of the money form of value.'[194] In the present context, this means that Adorno's effort to elaborate a materialist mode of cognition aims, not least, to break the spell of capitalist exchange relations that prevents the subject from recognizing its objective entanglements. He does so by dialectically exposing an asymmetry in the configuration of subject and object. That is to say, Adorno attempts to throw into relief the possibility of a non-coercive 'communication' between subject and object as truly differentiated entities.[195] His aim is not so much to reunite subject and object in the sense of forging a positive, self-identical figure of thought – this would be 'romantic', he objects – but rather to expound the reasons for the subject's constitutive inability to recognize its own objective ties.[196] As he argues, '[i]n its proper place, even epistemologically, the relationship of subject and object would lie in a peace achieved between human beings as well as between them and their Other. Peace' – the ethical–political maxim of Adorno's 'Utopia of cognition' – 'is the state of differentiation without domination, with the differentiated participating in each other.'[197] This view marks the beating heart of Adorno's politics, not in a narrowly administrative sense but in immanently reconfigured philosophical terms. Significantly, for our purposes, and as has already been pointed out, this Utopia cannot be positively pictured lest it be entered into the very economy it seeks to overcome. However, to the extent that this theoretical reconfiguration of the subject–object relation is supposed to correlate with the material transformation of society, the stakes of these considerations are extremely high.

(b) As Adorno argues, '[t]he object, the positive expression of non-identity, is a terminological mask.'[198] It covers over an elusive excess of matter that cannot be captured by thought. 'Once the object becomes an object of cognition', as it does for idealist and materialist epistemologies alike, 'its physical side' – its irreducibly material moment – 'is spiritualised'.[199] It is 'called "object" only from the viewpoint of a subjectively aimed analysis in which the subject's primacy seems', once again, 'beyond question'.[200] As Adorno contends, leaving this primacy uncontested reduces sensation – 'the crux of all epistemology' – to a mere 'fact of consciousness'.[201] There can be no sensation without a somatic moment. In this sense, conventional epistemologies run the danger of misconstruing the thing that is registered in sensation as simply another link in the chain of cognitive functions. By contrast, Adorno argues, sensation is not spent in consciousness. 'Every sensation is a physical feeling also.'[202] The echoes of Adorno's critical engagement with Husserlian phenomenology and its afterlife are unmistakable here. It is this 'feeling', which is associated with the aforementioned 'resurrection of the flesh'.[203] As will become clear in the final chapter, this is to do with what Adorno describes as a 'feeling of resistance'.[204]

As indicated previously, however, this 'resurrection' is negatively coded. That is to say, in the first instance 'physical feeling' means suffering. Suffering is marked out as the somatic index of the non-identity between subject and object, humankind and the world of matter, nature and culture. Adorno suggestively illustrates this point in a passage from *Negative Dialectics* titled 'Suffering Physical': 'All pain and all negativity, the motor of dialectical thought, is the variously mediated, sometimes unrecognisable form of physical things.'[205] In a typical gesture, Adorno identifies the antithetical moment of dialectical thought – 'negativity' – with the experience of 'pain', which, for its part, is an enduring feature of his philosophy of history.[206] Adorno's 'Utopia of cognition' is intended as the mirror image of this negativity. It is supposed to signal, inversely, a state of hedonic fulfilment. In the present, however, the perceived disparity between mind and matter causes one to experience the full weight of the dialectic of reason as somatic torment.

For Adorno, this experience is imbued with an ethical imperative.[207] As Adorno writes, the 'physical moment tells our knowledge that suffering ought not to be, that things should be different "Woe speaks: Go". Hence the convergence of the specifically materialist with the critical, with socially transformative praxis.'[208] Once again, Adorno's multifarious concerns converge. As he argues, '[t]he *telos* of such an organisation of society' as would allow for the satisfaction of want 'would be to negate the physical suffering of even the least of its members'.[209] The insistence on a *negation* of 'physical suffering' in such a society in turn recalls a formulation from an earlier, but thematically related text by Adorno – his 'Theses on Need' (1942). 'The question of the immediate satisfaction of needs should not be posed under the aspects "social" and "natural", "primary" and "secondary", "true" and "false". Rather it falls into the same category as the question of the suffering of the vast majority of all the people on earth.'[210] In a 'classless society', we are told, the relation between 'need and satisfaction *will* be transformed' – an unusually confident pronouncement for Adorno.[211] This transformation, then, is coextensive with that of the relation between the subject and object of thought; its locus is the tortured body; and, accordingly, epistemology, ethics and politics converge. Notwithstanding the question as to what kind of anthropology informs Adorno's slippery conceptions of humankind's 'need' and 'satisfaction', this passage – for its part – points forward to the central motivation of Adorno's final unfinished work, *Aesthetic Theory* (1969), treated at length in Chapter 3. The alleviation of bodily suffering, the reconciliation of subject and object, the overcoming of societal antagonisms – in short, Utopia – can only be intimidated *via negativa* in rendering conscious the 'spell' that obstructs these transformations: through the self-consciousness of semblance achieved in autonomous works of art. For the present discussion this means the following: while the possibility of societal transformation is mandated by an individual experience of bodily suffering, the 'satisfaction of material needs' hinges on the continued criticism of a philosophical tradition that had been prematurely left for dead, but whose real exercise of epistemic violence continues to determine the shape of politics. In this context, '[t]he power of determinate negation', outlined earlier, 'is the *only* permissible figure' of fulfilment.[212] If Adorno argues, then, that 'the spirit' would 'be reconciled and would become that which it only promises while the spell of material conditions will not let it satisfy material needs', then this means – in René Buchholz's words – that 'such spirit may only emerge undiminished when the conditions of lack (*Mangel*) and privation (*Not*), which it repressed, will come to an end'.[213] This 'end', however, is not a positive *telos*.

Nevertheless, the image ban that undergirds Adorno's 'imageless' materialism stands in for the refusal to foreclose on the possibility that such an 'end' may, prospectively, be realized. Moreover, Adorno is careful to qualify that the strategic efficacy of the image ban must not be overstated, lest the image ban itself degenerates into a mere image. In a passage from *Minima Moralia*, titled 'Picture Book Without Pictures', for instance, he notes:

> The objective tendency of the Enlightenment, to wipe out the power of images over man, is not matched by any subjective progress on the part of enlightened thinking towards freedom from images. While the assault on images irresistibly demolishes, after metaphysical ideas, those concepts once understood as rational and genuinely attained by thought, the thinking unleashed by the Enlightenment and immunized against thinking is now becoming a second figurativeness, though without images or spontaneity.[214]

The image ban itself is thus only a strategic, provisional figure for the kind of thinking that Adorno has in mind.

* * *

In a lecture on the concept of materialism, dated 17 January 1963, Adorno argues that '[o]ne of the substantive misinterpretations of materialism believes that, since it teaches the preponderance of matter or, indeed, of material conditions, this preponderance itself is desired and wanted, that it is itself positive'.[215] Rather, Adorno argues that '[t]he telos (...) of Marxist materialism is the abolition of materialism, i.e. the introduction of a state in which the blind coercion of people by material conditions would be broken and in which the question of freedom would become truly meaningful'.[216] On Adorno's reading, then, a truly Marxian concept of materialism is ultimately self-sublating. This is the sense in which he argues that 'the perspective vanishing point of historic materialism would be its self-sublation, the spirit's liberation from the primacy of material needs in their state of fulfilment'. That is to say, properly speaking, materialism would mean its own undoing, erasing even the trace of itself in the satisfaction of need. Adorno's self-sublating – *imageless* – mode of materialist cognition, then, points beyond the critique of 'representational thinking' to a 'Utopia of cognition' whose 'weak messianic'[217] promise motivates the unlikely deployment of an ostensibly biblical motif in the critical re-imagination of a Marxian materialism.

2

Inverse theology

Ihr sollt euch kein Bild –[1]

Franz Kafka

The previous chapter explored a reference to the Old Testament ban on making images of God in a passage from Adorno's magnum opus *Negative Dialectics* (1966). It will be recalled that particular attention was paid to Adorno's concept of an 'imageless' materialism. However, the biblical provenance of Adorno's terminology also raises questions concerning the theological weighting of his enigmatic formulation.[2] Such an inquiry demands considerable qualification for at least two reasons. First, Adorno does not engage at any point in a sustained scholarly inquiry into the nature of God that might be called properly theological in an academic sense (certainly, he never received any formal training in such matters). Second, as noted at the outset, Adorno explicitly echoes the verdicts of his intellectual progenitors Friedrich Nietzsche, Sigmund Freud and Karl Marx, by arguing that 'positive religion has lost its (. . .) validity'[3] and '[t]raditional theology is not restorable'.[4] Accordingly, his invocation of a biblical motif is indeed rather surprising.

Once again, the problem can be framed with a view to Adorno's reflections on Arnold Schoenberg's unfinished opera *Moses und Aron* (1932). In his essay 'Sacred Fragment' (1963) Adorno describes Schoenberg's Exodus adaptation as a work of 'sacred music'.[5] As he argues, '[s]acred works of art – and the fact that *Moses und Aron* was written as an opera does not disqualify it from being one – claim that their substance is valid.'[6] That is to say, Schoenberg's opera insists on the continuing actuality and the binding validity of its biblical 'substance' or subject matter. But, Adorno argues, 'a secular world can scarcely tolerate (. . .) sacred art.'[7] This estimation designates a two-pronged difficulty for Schoenberg's piece. On the one hand, this impasse is conditioned by historical factors, '[t]he impossibility (...) of sacred art *today*';[8] on the other hand, there is a contradiction 'intrinsic to the work':[9] 'God, the absolute, eludes finite beings. Where they desire to name him, because they must, they betray him. But if they keep silent about him, they acquiesce in their own impotence and sin against the other, no less binding, commandment *to* name him.'[10] Finite beings 'lose heart', Adorno continues, 'because they are not up to the task' of naming the infinite.[11] (They are not up to this task because after the expulsion from paradise the Adamitic language of names becomes mere chatter, *Geschwätz*). As Adorno argues, Schoenberg is aware of these difficulties. He has 'an intuition of the link between the possibility of sacred works and the actual historical situation', which is 'uncongenial' to religious sentiments.[12] His opera thus stages a kind of necessary failure: on the one hand, the piece 'must extend a hand to the sacred if it is not entirely to fail its own intention';[13] on the other hand, this extending-of-a-hand must overreach.

In light of this short gloss, Adorno's challenge to the Viennese composer comes into focus. Adorno asks: '[H]ow is cultic music possible in the absence of cult?'[14] In other words, how does Schoenberg's opera resist lapsing into wanton anachronism? Leaving in suspense Adorno's solution to this quandary (he describes Schoenberg's opera in terms of 'negative theology', which, it will become apparent, is not quite how Adorno views his own recourse to theology),[15] I propose to reformulate his question and direct it back at its author. How is it possible for Adorno to invoke the language of theology given that he explicitly rejects its legitimacy? My claim is that Adorno turns to theology in spite of itself, thus assigning figures such as the image ban a curious afterlife. As we will find, the modern dislocation of traditional theology thus serves as the condition of possibility for the deployment of its terms in the immanent critique of reality under the rule of what might be called a capitalist cult religion.[16]

The opening half of the present chapter will consider, first, the peculiar role of religion and theology in Adorno's thinking, which might be characterized as firmly second-hand. Adorno eccentrically repurposes those religious and theological terms that do find their way into his thinking, mostly – I argue – via his friendship with Walter Benjamin, although Paul Tillich also warrants mentioning at this juncture. Second, the chapter will consider the manner in which Adorno distinguishes between theology, religion and a more general view of metaphysics as aspects of a dialectic of enlightenment. Ultimately, it will be shown, this is to do with a logic of supersession that marks Adorno's philosophy of history, where what is superseded is ascribed a kind of posthumous existence. Such posthumous terms, I argue, can – in certain circumstances – resurface to assume a renewed actuality. Third, the chapter will look at how this afterlife of theology maps onto a historical moment in interwar Europe that Benjamin perceptively frames in terms of the aforementioned capitalist cult religion. In short, theological terms return – transfigured – in the midst of a purportedly secular modernity as the improbable register most appropriate to a critique of this situation. Finally, though, this chapter will aim to show why such a return is not, in any straightforward sense, a secularization of theological terms. Adorno is not attempting to uncover God as the repressed legitimating agent of modernity, as in the case of, say, Carl Schmitt's political theology; rather, he is aiming to address a historical circumstance where the terrible logic of fungibility addressed in the previous chapter appears in an essentially religious guise as a logic of sacrifice.

The second part of the present chapter, then, seeks to develop Adorno's concept of an '"inverse" theology'.[17] This formulation occurs in a letter from Adorno to Walter Benjamin, dated 17 December 1934, wherein he responds to his friend's essay, 'Franz Kafka: On the Tenth Anniversary of His Death'.[18] Adorno writes:

> Do not take it for immodesty if I begin by confessing that our agreement in philosophical fundamentals has never impressed itself upon my mind more perfectly than it does here. Let me only mention my own earliest attempt to interpret Kafka, nine years ago – I claimed he is a photograph of earthly life taken from the perspective of the redeemed, of which nothing appears but the edge of a black cloth, whereas the terrifyingly displaced optic of the photographic image is none other than that of the obliquely angled camera itself – no further words seem necessary to demonstrate our agreement, however much your analyses also point beyond this conception. And this also, and indeed in quite a principled sense, concerns the position of 'theology'. Since I always insisted on such a position, before entering your Arcades, it seems to me doubly important that the image of theology, into which I would gladly see our thoughts dissolve, is none other than the very one which sustains your thoughts here – it could indeed be called 'inverse' theology.[19]

The first part of this passage contains an early articulation of a notable figure from Adorno's writings. The reference to a 'photograph of earthly life taken from the perspective of the redeemed' occurs at least three times in Adorno's published writings: in his early review of Bertolt Brecht and Kurt Weill's *Mahagonny* (1930);[20] in 'Finale', the closing aphorism from *Minima Moralia* (1951);[21] and in 'Notes on Kafka' (1953).[22] This formulation is treated later, with a view to exploring what it might mean to speak of such a 'perspective' (or – indeed – *from* it). After all, Adorno's self-professed abidance by the image ban prohibits him from furnishing the 'standpoint of redemption' with any positive determinations.[23] This question is explored with an eye to some of the criticisms that this phrasing has provoked in recent years, specifically from Jacob Taubes and Giorgio Agamben, who charge that the ostensibly 'messianic', 'theological' current in Adorno's work amounts to little more than empty aestheticism written in the mode of the 'as if'. As will become clear, the effort to respond to this charge resonates with ongoing debates concerning the remarkable intersection of a newly fangled view of Jewish Messianism with revolutionary politics, which was characteristic for certain German-Jewish thinkers in the early part of the twentieth century. As Michael Löwy observes, during this period a particular constellation of social and historical factors inspired a generation of largely assimilated German Jews to turn to their ancestral religion as it appeared to them through the prism of Romanticism, and in an often volatile political climate. Accordingly, authors like Gustav Landauer, Georg Lukács, Ernst Bloch, Walter Benjamin and Franz Kafka are all said to have oriented their work, in various ways, around the kabbalistic idea of *Tikkun*. According to Löwy, *Tikkun* – Hebrew for 'restoration' – refers to two tendencies 'that are at once intimately linked and contradictory: a *restorative* current focusing on the re-establishment of a (...) shattered Edenic harmony; and a *utopian* current which aspired to a radically new future, to a state of things that has never existed before'.[24] Certainly, Adorno's proximity to the romantic and anarchistic tendencies ascribed to these authors by Löwy must not be overstated. However, insofar as his main interlocutors in the formulation of an 'inverse' theology are Benjamin and Kafka, I take it that a certain affinity with this tradition should not be wholly discounted.

The second part of this passage concerns Adorno's self-avowed agreement with an 'image of theology' that he attributes to Benjamin. To be sure, this enthusiastic declaration of allegiance, too, must be taken with a pinch of salt. Adorno's assertion is complicated by at least two factors: first, the role of theology in Benjamin's writings is notoriously unstable, displaying a great range of facets between early works, such as 'Dialogue on the Religiosity of the Present' (1912) and later texts such as the piece on Kafka or the theses 'On the Concept of History' (1940). In this regard, speaking of Benjamin's 'image of theology' in the singular is in fact untenably reductive. In any case, it will not be our aim to survey the many guises of theology in Benjamin's thought (from the blotting pad to the wizened dwarf) as if to suggest that they form some self-sufficient framework in which Adorno figures as a mere afterthought. Rather, inasmuch as Adorno's reading of Benjamin contains an element of projection – the as-yet nascent 'image' of a 'theology' into which he '*would gladly*' see their 'thoughts dissolve' – I take it that his views possess a degree of independence that is easily understated.

Second, it is worth noting that little over a year after writing the letter cited earlier, Adorno sharply criticizes one of Benjamin's *Arcades* exposés, demanding a radicalization of his friend's dialectic 'right into the theological glowing core'.[25] However, instead of recounting the catalogue of familiar grievances concerning the rift between Adorno and Benjamin, contained in their 1935 exchange,[26] the present chapter aims to trace a different thread leading from Adorno's singular over-identification with Benjamin's 'image of theology' to his use of theological terms in a secular critique of capitalist modernity. As I will argue, Adorno views the 'image' of an 'inverse' theology as suggesting a shift in the topography on which traditional theological inquiry rests: the supposedly stable, antithetical orders of the 'sacred' and the 'profane'. On the one hand, this means a standard enlightenment narrative, which teaches that the authority of a religious world view is displaced by the advancement of the natural sciences; on the other hand, it means that the seemingly secular-scientific phenomenon of capitalism is itself imbued with religious characteristics.

Part I: Theology

(i) Life and work

The fact that Adorno is neither a religious nor a theological thinker in any straightforward sense is reflected, in part, by his biography. Adorno's father – the German wine merchant Oskar Wiesengrund – converted from Judaism to Protestantism before his son's birth, whereas Adorno's mother – the Corsican singer Maria Calvelli-Adorno – was Catholic.[27] Adorno was nominally raised as a Lutheran, but organized religion appears to have played no particular role in his upbringing.[28] Nevertheless, it is worth noting a few points about Adorno's relation to his Jewish and Christian heritage, if only to give an indication of his sources and coordinates.

As Detlev Claussen argues, Adorno was strongly influenced by his upbringing amongst the luminaries of Frankfurt's Jewish *Bildungsbürgertum*, the assimilated, Jewish bourgeoisie to which his father belonged.[29] This is clear, not least, from his relationship with the close family friend Siegfried Kracauer, whose interest in Judaism is well documented, despite being less famous than his cultural criticism.[30] Kracauer, for his part, introduced the young Adorno to many major philosophical works. For instance, in addition to studying key philosophical texts by Kant and Hegel, Kracauer and the Adorno read seminal works of interwar Jewish thought, such as Franz Rosenzweig's *The Star of Redemption* (1921). However, Adorno is said to have been quite unmoved by Rosenzweig's book, referring to it in a letter to Leo Löwenthal as 'linguistic philosophemes, which I wouldn't understand even if I understood them'.[31] This dismissive attitude is echoed decades later in *The Jargon of Authenticity* (1964), which contains a biting critique of Rosenzweig's colleague, the celebrated Jewish philosopher of religion, Martin Buber. There, Adorno rather uncharitably argues that Buber's account of the 'I-Thou' relation removes the 'thorn' from 'theology, without which redemption is unthinkable'.[32] Though it is not the aim of this chapter to explore Adorno's objections to Buber in any depth, at the very least this grievance indicates that his view of Judaism, in general, and the circle around the *Freies Jüdisches Lehrhaus*,[33] in particular, appears to have been broadly unsympathetic.

Adorno's engagement with Christianity, by contrast, appears to have been more substantial. This is discernible from his *Habilitationsschrift* on Kierkegaard (1933), which was written under the supervision of the Protestant theologian Paul Tillich, with whom Adorno stayed in contact throughout his later life. This work contains Adorno's most sustained engagement with the work of any single 'theologian'. However, as Hermann Deuser points out, Adorno sides with a resolutely *philosophical* Kierkegaard. That is to say, his reading contrasts 'a critical and aesthetic Kierkegaard, on the one hand' with 'a theologian of sacrifice, suspected of existential ontology, on the other'.[34]

Without wishing to focus on Adorno's reading of Kierkegaard as such, it suffices to note the following: in light of the above, any claim to a theological current in Adorno's thinking must take into account not only that he was generally suspicious of religion and theology but – more importantly – that his sources were resolutely second-hand.

It seems clear, therefore, as has often been noted, that Adorno's understanding of Judaism owes more to the acquaintance with Benjamin than it owes to the Talmud; and that his knowledge of Christianity, in turn, owes more to Kierkegaard (and Tillich) than it does to any catechism. In both cases, though, the point is that Adorno is not concerned with a return to God, despite his explicit declaration of 'theological intentions'[35] vis-à-vis Max Horkheimer. These 'intentions', it will become apparent, hold only in a very qualified sense. Accordingly, it is better to ask not how accurately Adorno's particular reception of theology maps onto its traditional variants, but rather how he critically repurposes theological terms, however limited his awareness of their original context might be.

(ii) Negative universal history: Religion – theology – metaphysics

Adorno conceives of religion, theology and metaphysics as particular formations within a larger philosophical–historical edifice. As such, they lie embedded in a highly speculative civilizational metanarrative, characterized by an 'unmissable logic and rhetoric of exaggeration, hyperbole, and excess,'[36] as Hent de Vries notes, which traces the vacillations of rational thought from prehistory to the present. Adorno first outlines the broad contours of this narrative in his early lectures, 'The Actuality of Philosophy' (1931) and 'The Idea of Natural History' (1932). It is then elaborated in his *Habilitationsschrift* on Kierkegaard from whence it is taken up into *Dialectic of Enlightenment* (1947). The piecemeal theses contained in these texts finally receive their full philosophical articulation in a section of *Negative Dialectics* titled 'World Spirit and Natural History: An Excursion on Hegel'. There, Adorno proposes two divergent approaches: on the one hand, he outlines an idea of 'natural history', which is largely derived from a cross-reading of Benjamin and Lukács; on the other hand, he presents a concept of 'negative universal history'.[37] On closer inspection, it becomes clear that these ideas – (a) the negatively universal character of history and (b) the dialectical structure of reason – sit uneasily beside each other.

(a) Adorno views the negatively universal character of history in terms of an immanent recasting of Hegel's concept of (positive) universal history. In order for there to be history at all, Adorno suggests, universal history has to be at once 'constructed and denied'.[38] That is, in Adorno's view, the basic movement of Hegel's concept of universal history charts a series of dialectical stages through which history itself moves purposefully forward towards freedom. Universal history, at least as Adorno sees it, means the totality of this movement conceived of as 'the continuous history of mankind' as a whole.[39]

Inasmuch as Adorno is concerned with constructing a *concept* of history, then, he must affirm the totality of this movement. After all, concepts always aim at universality, and, since – for Adorno – philosophy necessarily deals in concepts, it follows that the concept of history must be *a priori* universal. However, although Adorno deems the structure of Hegel's reflections to be necessary for constructing a concept of history, he is nonetheless careful to emphasize its perceived Achilles heel: that universal history is apparently unable to account for contingency.[40] Characteristically, Adorno rather immodestly suggests that it is *his* approach that brings into focus a position that was only implicit in Hegel. Without presuming to settle this issue here, it suffices to note that Adorno turns to an unlikely ally in his re-reading of Hegel: the positivist critique of universal history. As he argues, the minutiae of contingent historical events cause inconsistencies to emerge in the supposedly seamless narrative of historical progress with which certain vulgarized strands of Hegelianism are sometimes associated. 'As long as you do not have too great a knowledge of historical detail', he claims, 'you not only have the benefit of (. . .) distance which enables you to gain a better overview, but, by the same token, you are blinder to facts that make things awkward for philosophical theory.'[41] That is to say, universal history falsifies those events that do not conform to its narrative thrust. To this extent, universal history has to be negated, 'denied'.

Negative universal history, then, is a kind of counter-narrative that seeks to tell the history of domination and defeat rather than progress. Adorno approvingly cites Benjamin on this point, arguing that universal history is always written from the standpoint of the victor of historical struggle.[42]

> [B]y pointing out that the element of consent, of apologia, that is to say the element that justifies history from the standpoint of the victor and defends everything that has happened on the grounds of its necessity – this element

of consent is connected with the construction of a theory of universal history because the assumption of such a continuous *unity* in history seems to point to the idea that history has meaning.⁴³

We will return to the point about the breakdown of meaning in history in the context of Adorno's 'Meditations on Metaphysics'. For now, let it be noted that if universal history is supposed – by Adorno – to tell the story of an inevitable unfolding of consciousness towards freedom, then *negative* universal history must mean the story of humankind's (self-)domination and the ensuing state of *un*-freedom. This, of course, is the theme of *Dialectic of Enlightenment*, to which we will turn momentarily. First, however, it remains to account for a criticism that Adorno opens himself up to on this point.

One might object that if Adorno aims to expose the logic underpinning a providential history that leads 'from savagery to humanitarianism' by reversing its course to go 'from the slingshot to the megaton bomb',⁴⁴ as the famous formulation from *Negative Dialectics* goes, then he is in fact simply reproducing it as a kind of 'bad' universality. Adorno seeks to pre-empt this charge by unfolding a dialectic of continuity and discontinuity. As he argues, 'discontinuity and universal history must be conceived together.'⁴⁵ That is to say, on the one hand, history is '*discontinuous* in the sense that it represents life perennially disrupted', and, on the other hand, it is *continuous* in the sense that this 'disruption' is itself deemed to be permanent.⁴⁶ Accordingly, Adorno's materialist rebuttal of Hegel (at least as Adorno portrays him) is that historical events do not take place *in* a predetermined flow of history, but rather that the events themselves contain a historical 'nucleus' – a *Zeitkern* – 'that can be decoded by interpretation'.⁴⁷

Adorno's explanation speaks to a larger issue with his philosophy of history, which is expressed in the fact that his main statement on this topic – the excursus on 'World Spirit and Natural History' in *Negative Dialectics* – contains two divergent models, which, as already noted, are not necessarily compatible with one another. On the one hand, the text describes an idea of natural history which is fragmented, melancholic and committed to the particularity of historical suffering; on the other hand, it proffers an account of negative universal history which is linear, albeit not progressive, and – at least in principle – all-encompassing. But if Adorno insists that the incongruity between these models can be surmounted dialectically, then it is not clear how he envisages their mutual mediation. As with his discussion of materialism, his conceit appears to be that 'the trace of possible developments, of something hopeful',[48] can be thrown into relief by interpreting the fragments of 'bad' universality as containing the 'mirror writing' of their opposite;[49] but the particulars of this appeal to particularity remain conspicuously absent.

(b) Having thus sketched the broad contours of Adorno's negative universal history, it is possible to take another step towards determining how his concepts of religion, theology and metaphysics sit therein. For this purpose, we turn to *Dialectic of Enlightenment*. Adorno and Horkheimer's central thesis – '[m]yth is already enlightenment, and all enlightenment reverts to mythology'[50] – already contains the metanarrative outlined earlier. The markers of this arc are different historical guises of 'enlightenment', conceived of not as a chronological marker (e.g. the eighteenth-century European enlightenment) but rather as human intellectual endeavour as such. This development, in turn, is supposed to stretch from a kind of imaginary prehistory to the present in a manner that encompasses (amongst many other moments) religion, theology and metaphysics. By paying attention to the ways in which Adorno distinguishes between these three exemplary markers, one can gain a clearer sense of how an ostensibly outmoded moment in the dialectic of enlightenment – theology – can gain the kind of untimely actuality intimated at the start of this chapter.

This point is refracted through the more general historical dynamic outlined in *Dialectic of Enlightenment*. Myth, here, designates two divergent tendencies that Adorno and Horkheimer extract – above all – from their reading of Homer's *Odyssey* (only to then show how it plays out elsewhere). As they argue,

> the *Odyssey* as a whole bears witness to the dialectic of enlightenment. In its oldest stratum, especially, the epic shows clear links to myth: the adventures are drawn from popular tradition. But as the Homeric spirit takes over and 'organises' the myths, it comes into contradictions with them. The familiar equation of epic and myth, which in any case has been undermined by recent classical philology, proves wholly misleading when subjected to philosophical critique. The two concepts diverge. They mark two phases of an historical process, which are still visible at the joints where editors have stitched the epic together.[51]

On the one hand, the authors loosely characterize myth as a particular narrative form, which is 'derived from popular tradition'.[52] With explicit reference to Ulrich von Wilamowitz-Moellendorff and Jacob Burckhardt (and an implicit nod to Lukács's *Theory of the Novel*, 1916), they argue that the overarching characteristic of myth is that humankind is ruled over by perennial forces of murky provenance, which they describe as 'fate' or 'destiny' (*Schicksal*). Accordingly, Adorno and Horkheimer present the world of myth as emphatically prehistoric inasmuch as past, present and future appear undifferentiated therein. In myth, they argue, 'nothing can be defined as lasting, and yet everything remains one and the same'.[53] In this regard, they assert that myth operates according to the timeless law of cyclical recurrence (as in the myth of Sisyphus, for instance).

On the other hand, however, the authors characterize myth as an early product of emphatically rational thought. That is to say, in Adorno and Horkheimer's view, 'myth is already enlightenment' to the extent that it serves as an explanatory device designed to dispel humankind's ostensibly elementary terror before the death-bringing forces of nature – a form of rationalization. Hence the famous estimation that '[e]nlightement, understood in the widest sense as the advance of thought, has always aimed at liberating human beings from fear and installing them as masters',[54] both physically and intellectually. In turn, the concept of 'enlightenment' extends far beyond any particular school of thought. Rather, it is taken to mean a much more general comportment by which human beings assert their place in the world through the mastery of nature. Without rehearsing the specifics of this point, it is significant that Adorno and Horkheimer's account is tied to a wider, quasi-ontogenetic reflection on the emergence of subjectivity, conceived of – in particular – as a prehistory of bourgeois individuality. As they argue, humankind's individual consciousness emerges at the moment when it is wrested from the realm of brute physicality. At the same time, there remains an irreducibly 'natural' dimension to human bodily being (although, as already noted, 'nature', here, always means *second* nature). Accordingly, the struggle against nature must also be seen as a struggle against oneself. That is to say, for humankind to safeguard itself against the fearful world from which it emerges, but which it fears may at any point reclaim it, it must deny its own ties to nature. Through various twists and turns, Adorno and Horkheimer argue, this internalized sense of domination returns as the calamitous revenge of repressed nature: the domination of human beings over each other. In this sense the book tells a story about the fateful cycle of self-preservation and its grave cost. The 'mythical sacrifice of reason' is endlessly replayed in ever more terrible scenarios that extend right into the present age.[55]

Adorno and Horkheimer illustrate this point with reference to Odysseus's cunning efforts to outsmart the powers of mythical nature (Circe, the Cyclops, the Lotus-Eaters, etc.). As they argue, Odysseus becomes a slave to his self-preservational drive and thus relapses to a fateful state of un-freedom that is akin to mythical nature. In Adorno and Horkheimer's view, this is particularly evident in book XII of the *Odyssey*, the tale of Odysseus and the Sirens.[56] Herein, it will be recalled, Odysseus orders his oarsmen to stuff their ears with wax and tie him to the mast of their ship as they pass by the Sirens' island. This way the crew remain impervious to the Sirens' irresistible call while Odysseus may experience it from a position of relative safety. In the present context, this episode is significant because it serves as an analogy for the self-abnegation of reason that Adorno and Horkheimer claim to diagnose. As they argue, Odysseus – the prototype of the bourgeois subject – resists the Sirens' mythical call only by having himself restrained. The cost of his self-preservation, however, is nothing less than his precarious autonomy. Adorno and Horkheimer derive a general historical paradigm from this image. As they suggest, a 'history of civilisation' conceived along the lines of the *Odyssey* (being bound in order to persist) appears as a 'history of the introversion of sacrifice':[57] a sacrifice of the self to itself, so to speak. This dialectical view of history, construed as a wilful re-imagination of civilization as such, is illustrated – without any claim to systematicity or completeness – with reference to an assortment of examples that are as wide-reaching as they are eccentric: from accounts of animistic rituals to the emergence of modern science; and from the rise of biblical monotheism to that of fascism.

Notwithstanding the book's problematic blind spots (the negative universality it presents surely proceeds from a resolutely Western standpoint), *Dialectic of Enlightenment* nonetheless contains some important insights in the present context, especially concerning the possibility of theology's critical afterlife. This possibility, however, hinges on a series of distinctions that Adorno makes between theology, religion and metaphysics.

Religion

Although Adorno makes free use of religious motifs throughout his writings, his explicit references to religion *as* religion are scant. They typically occur indirectly in works like *The Jargon of Authenticity*, where he argues that certain unacknowledged religious sentiments live on in the ostensibly secular thought patterns of thinkers such as Jaspers and Heidegger. Where Adorno does speak of religion as such, however, he is generally concerned with various forms of Judaism and Christianity. He appears to rely on the etymological derivation of 'religion' from the Latin *religare* (to bind), for instance, when he speaks of the 'renaissance of revealed religion' in terms of 'bonds' (*Bindungen*).[58] It might be inferred, then, that for Adorno religion means being bound *to* and, indeed, *by* a tradition that claims to derive its authority directly from divine revelation, for example, Moses's reception of the Ten Commandments at Mount Sinai. The operative terms here are 'revelation', meaning God's direct communication with humankind (God *reveals* certain injunctions to the prophet Moses), and 'tradition' (the term 'comes from *tradere*, to hand down'),[59] which designates the mode of transmission by which God's injunctions arrive in the present. That is to say, Adorno seems to perceive the defining trait of religion as a submission to the traditional authority of revelation.

The problem with positive religion in the present, then, is that – for Adorno – modernity marks precisely a *crisis* of tradition, following a broadly Marxian account of the capitalist dissolution of bonds paired with a more thoroughgoing Nietzscheanism. Leaving in suspense the resonance of this point with Benjamin's writings on Kafka, which treat the concept of tradition at some length, we note the following: on the one hand, religion has a socially normative function inasmuch as it binds individuals to each other through a shared observance of divine injunctions received from tradition (e.g. the ban on images), and as such it is the model for a certain kind of sociality; on the other hand, it has an explanatory function inasmuch as it designates what Freud has called a 'system of thought',[60] which – like myth – provides an account of the origins of the universe, the meaning of life and so on. In its capacity as a 'system of thought', to borrow Freud's expression from *Totem & Taboo* (an explicit point of reference for Adorno), religion must thus be grasped as a form of rational thought that is proper to one, or more, specific historical moments. As noted in the Prelude to the present book, Adorno and Horkheimer cite Judaism as the paradigmatic example hereof.

As *the* monotheistic religion par excellence, Judaism is presented as a rationalization of polytheistic paganism: a more 'advanced stage' in the dialectic of enlightenment (though, of course, such a view is purely illustrative, insofar as Adorno would surely deny that the dialectic has discrete 'stages' which are more or less 'advanced' in quite this way). Nevertheless, Judaism's central feature, we are told, is that it 'outlaw[s] the principle of magic'.[61] Accordingly, Adorno and Horkheimer assure us that, in Judaism, spells give way to concepts, and taboos give way to laws – above all, the law against idol worship (since there is only one God who demands a specific form of worship). In this regard, it follows that Judaism is repeatedly equated with reason itself in a curious, albeit presumably unintentional, echo of Hermann Cohen's famous characterization of Judaism as the religion of reason, and, hence, of law.[62] This is why, unlike Christianity, Judaism has no particular need for faith.

In any case, Adorno and Horkheimer present the Jewish idea of God as annihilating the spirited cosmos of animism: '[A]s its creator and ruler', they claim, the Jewish God '*subjugates* nature'.[63] This interpretation, tendentious though it may be, allows the authors to discern the dialectic of reason in Judaism, inasmuch as the effort to vanquish myth through a seamless domination of nature only ensnares it deeper in its fateful cycle. As Adorno and Horkheimer argue,

> God as spirit is the principle *opposed* to nature; it not only stands for nature's blind cycle as do all the mythical gods, but offers liberation from it. But in its remotest abstractness, the incommensurable has at the same time become more terrible, and the pitiless statement: 'I am who I am', which tolerates nothing beside itself, surpasses in its inescapable power the blinder and therefore more ambiguous judgement of anonymous fate.[64]

The passage clearly illustrates the historical dynamic outlined earlier with reference to Odysseus. While 'God as spirit' is said to 'offer liberation' from the 'blind cycle' of 'nature', His 'remote abstractness' ultimately turns out to be even more 'terrible' than what preceded it. It remains, then, to take this partial and peculiar definition of 'religion' (as applied to Judaism), and to ask how Adorno envisages its difference from 'theology'.

Theology

As will be recalled, it was asserted at the outset that Adorno views theology as something like the intellectual superstructure of religion: a reasoned discourse *about* God as opposed to a binding faith *in* God. However, the historical dynamic, outlined previously with reference to religion, is, in fact, operational in this context too. This is important, in the present context, because it gives some indication as to the manner in which, for Adorno, all theological content will, ultimately, 'have to put itself to the test of migrating into the realm of the secular, the profane'.[65] Accordingly, I propose to approach this matter with a view to Adorno's essay 'Reason and Revelation' (1958)[66] in order (a) to account for the direction of this 'migration' and (b) to distinguish this position from more full-blooded forms of 'negative theology', which have, on occasion, been invoked polemically by some of Adorno's critics to characterize his views (not least amongst them, Jürgen Habermas).

(a) In 'Reason and Revelation' Adorno reflects on a series of interrelated questions. First, he is concerned with a tension between two ostensibly divergent tendencies that span the history of Christian thought from Augustine to Karl Barth. On the one hand, this means 'faith in revelation' (*Offenbarungsglaube*); on the other hand, it means 'autonomous reason' (*autonome Vernunft*). To begin with, the investigation is prompted by what Adorno perceives as a disconcerting 'turn toward positive religion' in post-war West Germany.[67] Although Adorno cites only anecdotal evidence for this alleged development, he insists that this 'turn' expresses an altogether spurious sense – pervasive in the German Federal Republic – that one could simply 'breathe back that meaning into the disenchanted world under whose absence we have been suffering for so long'.[68] As he suggests, the danger of this tendency is that it legitimates a wanton obscurantism: '[T]oday', he claims, 'the turn toward faith in revelation' is a 'desperate reaction' to the perceived failings of '*ratio*', an estimation that recalls the argumentative pattern familiar from *Dialectic of Enlightenment*.[69] Adorno's general point appears to be that, at best, the 'new religious attitude'[70] – whatever it may mean – offers a false sense of consolation about the ills of capitalist modernity; and, at worst, its irrationalism serves to reinforce existing injustices by wishing away socio-historically conditioned problems rather than facing them.

Second, as in *The Jargon of Authenticity*, Adorno's exposition is underpinned by an indictment of certain strands of contemporary philosophy that he perceives as forms of crypto-religious irrationalism, by which he appears to mean chiefly Heidegger.[71] Accordingly, Adorno writes that 'the endeavours of ontology today' are little more than a desperate attempt to 'leap without mediation' from an 'ongoing nominalistic situation' into 'realism, the world of ideas in themselves' – a tendency that is, in turn, supposed to be 'closely related' to the 'renaissance of revealed religion'.[72] Although Adorno's own insistence on particularity also brings him into the orbit of a certain nominalism,[73] his reference to a 'nominalistic situation', here, is surely meant polemically. It implies that Heidegger and his followers try to get immediately at what they deem to be essential – the ontological, in Heidegger's terms, coded here counter-intuitively as a 'world of ideas in themselves' – instead of paying due attention to the ontic, conceived of as the disenchanted world of capitalist modernity. The claim, in short, appears to be that 'ontology today' positively appeals to something *beyond* the present situation (namely to noumenal ideas), which Adorno, following Kant, deems to be impermissible.

Without wishing to judge the feasibility of these charges (to be sure, Adorno has far more in common with Heidegger than he lets on), it will prove telling that the *topos* of a Kierkegaardian 'leap' from one 'situation' to another recurs throughout Adorno's text. It marks an illegitimate movement, a corrupt form of 'migration' from the sphere of the profane to that of the sacred. Nevertheless, the text should not be read simply as an atheistic diatribe against religious sentiments or theologically inclined modes of philosophizing per se. After all, Adorno notes that, 'vis-à-vis the hardening of the world in late Antiquity', for instance, 'Christianity had an infinitely liberating and humane effect'.[74] To say that Christianity 'has never been anything more than ideology would really be the most narrow-minded sociologism'.[75] Instead, Adorno's claim is that 'today' – that is, in the aftermath of the Second World War – Christianity runs the 'infinite danger' of becoming a surrogate for certain nebulous 'authoritarian' tendencies, although these remain unspecified.[76] Presumably, given Adorno's swipe at Heidegger, he means a mode of thought that – in his estimation – enables and sustains a kind of intellectual fascism by dressing it up in a spiritual garb.

However, in the present context, 'Reason and Revelation' is of interest less because of its concern with contemporary religious trends, or because of its objections to 'ontology today', including its putative connection to authoritarianism, but rather because, between the lines, it contains a schematic account of how Christian *thought* sits in the larger philosophical metanarrative that we have been tracing. That is to say, in the present context, 'Reason and Revelation' clearly indicates two things: first, Adorno's account of the historical tensions between 'reason' and 'revelation' (cited to illustrate his plaint against the alleged 'renaissance of revealed religion') constitutes – however scantly – a history of Christian *theology* in the sense of a reasoned discourse about God (after all, Adorno surveys a number of divergent efforts to treat God intellectually and discursively). Second, as noted previously, Adorno frames the history of these efforts in terms of the dialectic of enlightenment itself, thus giving some important insight into how he imagines the peculiar afterlife that he ascribes to theology.

Having begun with the premise that the supposed 'turn to positive religion' in 1950s West Germany is a reaction to the mounting dissatisfaction with reason as such, Adorno suggests that in eighteenth-century Europe the situation was the other way around. Here, he assures us, the Scholastic concept of faith, 'which was inherited from (. . .) tradition', began to come under attack from 'an autonomous *ratio* that refuses to accept anything other than what stands up to examination in its own terms'.[77] Without specifying who launched these attacks (the *Philosophes* perhaps?), Adorno asserts that any 'defence' of theology 'against *ratio* had to be carried out with rational means'.[78] That is to say, the 'defence already assumed the principle that belonged to its adversary'.[79] In this regard, the effort of rationalist theology, in particular, to ground faith in reason turned out to be self-undermining. The question thus becomes by what other means theology might negotiate the tension between faith in revelation and the modern demands of reason if older thinkers failed to provide satisfactory answers.

Certainly, one possible response is to resolve the tension between 'reason' and 'revelation' by leaping into the ostensible irrationality of the latter, as Kierkegaard somewhat unfairly is sometimes supposed to have done (Adorno briefly discusses this possibility). Nevertheless, Adorno is careful to set apart Kierkegaard (and, indeed, Pascal) from the facile anti-intellectualism that he associates with the German return to religion in the 1950s. As he argues,

> [t]he sacrifice of the intellect that once, in Pascal or Kierkegaard, was made by the most progressive consciousness and at no less a cost than one's entire life has since become socialised, and whoever makes this sacrifice no longer feels any burden of fear and trembling; no one would have reacted to it with more indignation than Kierkegaard himself. Because too much thinking, an unwavering autonomy, hinders the conformity to the administered world and causes suffering, countless people project this suffering imposed on

them by society onto reason as such. According to them it is reason that has brought suffering and disaster into the world.[80]

Alternatively, one might want to overcome the polarity between these terms in a more dialectical fashion. For example, Adorno suggests, '[h]igh Scholasticism, and especially the *Summa* of St. Thomas, have their force and dignity in the fact that, without absolutising the concept of reason, they never condemned it: theology went so far only in the age of nominalism, particularly with Luther.'[81] This suggestion is startling for two reasons.

First, it is true that in his *Summa Theologica* (c. 1274), Thomas Aquinas teaches that if there were no mediation between faith and reason, then faith would be empty and reason would be blind, to put it in Kantian terms. That is to say, within certain bounds, the philosophical tools that Scholasticism derives principally from Aristotle can be used to verify the contents of revealed religion. At the same time, however, such a theological effort can never directly grasp that with which it is chiefly concerned, namely God. In short, although theology can provide *some* reasoned insights into matters concerning the Divine, in metaphysical terms, God remains beyond the grasp of reason. In Adorno's view, then, Aquinas maintains a 'productive tension'[82] between faith and rationality, inasmuch as he posits a transcendent realm that cannot be reduced to either the terms of reason or those of faith alone. (It is curious, in this respect, that, throughout the text, Adorno remains conspicuously silent about Kant's reflections on *Religion Within the Limits of Reason Alone*, 1793.)

By contrast, second, Adorno charges that 'in the age of nominalism, particularly with Luther', theology renders reason absolute and thus 'condemns' it. He does not elaborate on the historical connection between Luther and nominalism,[83] nor does he indicate why this association should be seen as either 'absolutising' or 'condemning' reason (presumably fleshing out this claim in due detail would require a comprehensive inquiry into the intellectual prehistory of the Reformation, which Adorno is not quite able to provide). Nonetheless, a number of points can be inferred from this passage. For one thing, Adorno implies that nominalism – the view that universals do not possess any objective reality, adopted by certain late medieval theologians to distance themselves from Aristotelian realism – breaks with the Thomist conception of God as an incomprehensible *esse*. It implies that God has to denote a discrete entity (an *ens*), however much this entity may differ from all other things. Accordingly, Adorno claims that in order to avoid sacrificing God's transcendence, Luther has to qualify his apparent nominalism by distinguishing between 'two types of truth':[84] one (inferior) expressed in terms of logic, confirming certain things about the natural world *hic e nunc*; the other (superior) attainable by means of faith alone – *sola fide*. That is, for Luther, only faith can reconcile the paradoxes of revealed religion: Christ as man *and* God, historical *and* eternal and so on. Reason is thus 'absolutised' to the extent that it is pronounced sufficient for the attainment of *worldly* knowledge, which is – in turn – associated with 'progress' and hence 'the increasing domination of nature', in Adorno's terms.[85] At the same time, though, reason is 'condemned' to the extent that it is subordinated to the primacy of faith. Put differently, Luther's 'age' – that is, early modernity – is nominalistic in the sense that it proclaims the absolute reign of reason over a world whose higher spiritual significance (*qua* 'Realism') has been forfeited. Nominalism, for better or worse, seems to be intended here as a byword for disenchantment, or at least its foreshadowing in Luther. In duly Weberian fashion, then, Adorno suggests that by proposing that there are 'two types of truth', Luther inadvertently made the world into a kind of spiritless, fungible material – a view that, for its part, is often seen as undoing, in the long run, the religious rooting from which it sprang. This, too, is, in a sense, a 'migration' from the sacred to the profane, albeit an unintended one.

To be sure, Adorno's speculations hinge on a conflation of numerous historically disparate phenomena. For instance, it is not clear how the 'current religious mood', which is supposed to respond to 'the prevailing positivism' of capitalist modernity, is supposed to be mirrored by 'the endeavours of ontology today'. Nor, for that matter, is it explained how this form of 'positivism' is supposed to be rooted in Luther's particular take on 'nominalism'.[86] That is to say, Adorno's diagnosis of the present as a 'nominalistic' or 'positivistic' *situation*, from which the likes of Heidegger and Barth are said to 'leap' (however unsuccessfully) into the world of 'realism', is framed rather too generally to be persuasive. In this regard, it is surprising that Adorno does not, in fact, cite Weber's account of how capitalist modernity might be seen as homologous with the Reformation, and how – in turn – it undermines its religious roots; after all, Adorno knew Weber's work well, and the introduction of his theses may have allowed him to avoid the slightly clumsy foray into medieval theological debates in which he was hardly well versed.

Whatever may have inspired Adorno's claims, for the purposes of the present chapter 'Reason and Revelation' is of interest less for its rather imperfect historical exposition, but because it contains a timely demand. Set against the backdrop of debates in Christian theology, Adorno argues that 'reason' (like revelation) must itself be immanently criticized, 'not as an absolute, regardless of whether it is then posited or negated, but rather as a moment within the totality'.[87] It is 'precisely this theme' – apparently 'familiar to the great religions' – that 'requires "secularisation" today' if the dialectic of reason is 'not to further the very darkening of the world'.[88] The critique of secular modernity, in other words, must take its cue from the manner in which 'the great religions' negotiated the tension between reason and revelation. This is the point at which Adorno writes that 'nothing' of the 'theological content' skimmed in 'Reason and Revelation' will survive this process of critique (which he demands but does not carry out) 'without being transformed; every content will have to put itself to the test of migrating into the realm of the secular, the profane'.[89]

(b) It has been suggested by various critics, and occasionally by Adorno himself, that his negatively dialectical mode of philosophizing is akin to forms of 'negative theology'. In its simplest form, negative theology, or – more properly – *apophatic* theology (from the Greek *apophasis*, to deny or negate), means that God is utterly transcendent, wholly ineffable and does not admit of any positive description.[90] In this regard, negative theology designates a philosophical device that addresses itself to problems arising from the convergence of broadly Old Testament views regarding the transcendence of God and ontological questions about His *being* – an effort to gain knowledge of God through negation. Put simply, on this model, since one cannot say that 'God *is* great', the statement 'God is not *not* great' is taken to provide more adequate knowledge of God's greatness according to the arithmetic principle that two negatives make a positive. In its more mystical guise, this *via negativa* is said to produce an extra-rational, spiritual encounter between humans and God: 'The Divine', as Christopher Craig Brittain notes in his study on Adorno and theology, 'experienced as *mysterium tremendum*, shatters the presuppositions of mere human beings and reveals the incomplete, if not erroneous, nature of existing beliefs or actions. Divine transcendence interrupts as "wholly other", completely beyond the range of human experience.'[91]

The most enduring identification of Adorno with negative theology occurs in an influential essay by Jürgen Habermas, titled 'The Primal History of Subjectivity' (1981). There, Habermas characterizes Adorno's thought as a negative theology in the sense that his 'critique of totality and "identity thinking"' appears to him as 'sharing in negative theology's aversion to asserting positive claims about the absolute, while continuing to posit the usefulness of the category of ultimate truth' as a kind of regulative ideal.[92] Habermas thus characterizes Adorno in the following terms: 'Despairing of the barbaric course of human history, and refusing to identify any solid foundation for hope or consolation', as per the image ban, 'Adorno is (...) left with nothing but a vague longing' for an amorphous 'wholly other'.[93] Accordingly, Habermas claims that Adorno's abidance by the image ban is akin to a negative theology inasmuch as this 'wholly other may only be indicated by indeterminate negation, not known'.[94]

Given the wording, it is possible that Habermas's objections are directed at a passage from *Dialectic of Enlightenment*, which declares the following: '[T]he right of the image' – the 'image of theology' referred to in Adorno's 1934 letter to Benjamin, perhaps – 'is rescued in the faithful observance of its prohibition': an 'observance' that is in turn equated with "determinate', as opposed to *in*determinate or abstract, 'negation".[95] As seen in the previous chapter, the 'images' to which Adorno and Horkheimer allude are not pictures so much as they are figures of thought. They insist on their 'right' only in the refusal of the 'false', never directly (bearing in mind the recalibration of the Hegelian movement of determinate negation outlined previously). Accordingly, since for Adorno and Horkheimer there can be no positive expression of 'the absolutely good', these 'images' are subject to a ban.

Against this backdrop, Habermas's critique of Adorno *qua* negative theology comes into focus. James Gordon Finlayson summarizes this in four steps. First, we are told, Habermas argues that Adorno's position is *irrational*. He 'accuses Adorno of abandoning reason in favour of some other mode of apprehension of Utopia', or, for that matter 'God'.[96] Second, he charges Adorno with *mysticism* since he 'posits a divine, wholly transcendent being that is consequently ineffable and unknowable', and because he 'holds out the prospect of an extra-conceptual experience of the divine presence, won through the dialectical self-subversion of discursive reason'.[97] Third, he maintains that Adorno's position is *incoherent*, that is, that it is in the thrall of a 'performative contradiction' (i.e. that his critique of reason must take recourse to the very reason it professes to criticize).[98] And, finally, he contends that 'negative dialectics, like negative theology, is theoretically *empty*', that is, that it is 'unproductive or pointless' inasmuch as it lacks any 'viable political dimension'.[99]

Taken together, Habermas's objections effectively show up the differences between the so-called first and second generations of the Frankfurt School. As noted in the previous chapter, this difference hinges on the degree to which the legitimacy of Critical Theory is supposed to depend on its normative thrust. The argument goes something like this: if the state of un-freedom diagnosed in a work like *Dialectic of Enlightenment* is, in fact, as emphatically universal as Adorno and Horkheimer suggest, then it follows that the first generation's proposed modes of addressing this condition – say, the movements of 'determinate negation' – can have no real determinacy since they too are embroiled in the all-encompassing nexus of delusion. Put in terms of the passages cited above, any attempt to refuse an 'image' of, for example, worldly injustice, in the manner proposed by Adorno et al., cannot logically yield the sorts of 'mirror writing' that could tell us what would be just in a normatively binding way. The characterization of Adorno's position as a negative theology is intended to indicate, polemically, that without some positive content, the negative dialectic must, as it were, fall short of its stated intentions: 'God', the 'wholly other', is only ever what is not *not*.

Instead of the infinite labour of negation, then, Habermas proposes a different foundation for Critical Theory, which is supposed to assure a kind of endogenous normativity: a framework for reaching a reasoned consensus on matters of politics and civil society, which is seen – above all – as legitimate and legitimating (in the absence of a divine legislator). This framework is most fully articulated in Habermas's opus, *The Theory of Communicative Action* (1981). There, a particular conception of communication is said to remedy Critical Theory's supposed normative deficit. On this view, communication, properly speaking, does not mean, in the first instance, the empirical phenomenon of inter-subjective exchange (through language) between different actors; rather, it is taken to mean the historically invariant structures governing the conditions under which any such exchange could occur. In this respect, Habermas's view of communication, in the emphatic sense, recalls Kant's critical safeguarding of reason, and hence his concern with questions of philosophical legitimacy.

As Raymond Geuss notes in a recent piece, 'the mere existence' of 'the kinds of transcendental 'communicative structures' that Habermas posits 'is taken (. . .) to imply that the agents communicating stand in what he calls a *Verständigungsverhältnis*', a relation of, both, understanding and (at least by implication) agreement.[100] In other words, Habermas holds that 'to speak', in the full sense of the word, is inevitably 'to be committed to coming to (ideal) moral agreement with the person to whom one is speaking', notwithstanding, of course, the 'potential (. . .) ideological distortions' that arise when the rules of speech are not observed. This ideal, moral agreement is supposed to be inscribed into the very structures of communication itself. Accordingly, Habermas argues that so-called ideal speech situation is the arena, and, moreover, the legitimating ground – the analogue of Kant's court of reason – for the establishment of valid norms for determining the outlines of life in a democratic society.[101] Put differently, discussion, carried out according to the inherently reasonable workings of speech itself, lends the requisite positivity to a Critical Theory that is otherwise deemed lacking in normative power.[102]

The divergence between Adorno and Habermas, then, stems in no small measure from their opposing attitudes towards language, and, hence, communication. (As Geuss points out, Adorno speaks mockingly, in *Minima Moralia*, of the 'the liberal fiction of the universal communicability of each and every thought'.)[103] Habermas deems that the insistence on a 'wholly other' is 'irrational', 'mystical', 'incoherent' and 'empty' because it lacks positive content according to the established parameters of a broadly Kantian liberalism, which, as Geuss suggests, was characteristic of post-war, reconstruction-era West Germany – the context in which he locates Habermas's thought. Not only does Habermas not share Adorno's conviction that *all* intellectual, linguistic and communicative regimes – including Kant's – are, in some sense, implicated in a universal state of un-freedom; rather, he appeals, from within these parameters, to a positive image of redeemed life in his own right: a Utopia of communication. In this regard, the estimation that Adorno 'stubbornly refuses' to positively delineate 'the structure of a life together in communication (. . .) free from coercion', for example, through a well-functioning parliamentarianism, is telling:[104] it indicates that Habermas views this 'life' as being available in a fraught, but ultimately uncomplicated sense, for example, by invoking reasoned debate as the means for hashing out, agreeing and – in turn – implementing political reforms. But, it might be objected, it is not clear that such an 'ideal speech situation' is any more 'determinate', according to the terms laid out by Habermas himself, than Adorno and Horkheimer's appeal to a 'wholly other'. In Geuss's words,

> No amount of human exertion will permit us to establish within the domain of the natural phenomenon 'communication' a safe-zone that is actually completely protected on all sides from the possible use of force, nor can we even realistically anticipate in some utopian sense a form of communication where relations of domination were completely suspended or cancelled out. Even if (...) there is something in the 'inherent logic' of speech that 'implies' freedom from domination, any particular theory that tries to claim that it is insulated against history and the real existing forms of communication will eventually turn out to do nothing more than absolutize some contingent features of our present situation.[105]

According to Geuss, then, the ideal of communication itself is prey to Habermas's criticism of Adorno and Horkheimer; it is, in the pejorative sense, 'utopian', the hallmark of a 'liberal fiction'. However, the decisive issue here is less to do with whether the particulars of Habermas's appeal to communication can serve as the legitimating ground for Critical Theory within certain established parameters; rather, it is to do with how one might interrupt these parameters completely, 'wholly'. However, in order to grasp more fully why Habermas's analogy between Adorno and negative theology cannot quite hold (other than as a polemical quip), it is necessary to turn to a third guise of rational thought, which – like religion and theology – is concerned with 'the wholly other', 'the constitutive structures of being',[106] namely what Adorno calls metaphysics.

Metaphysics

We have seen, then, where religion and theology, conceived of as guises of rational thought, sit in Adorno's historical metanarrative; but before concluding this section, it remains to consider a final example, which is revealing of the overall historical condition that Adorno's recourse to an 'inverse' theology, years earlier, sought to address, namely his treatment of metaphysics. In the final part of *Negative Dialectics*, the twelve 'Meditations on Metaphysics', and in line with his views that 'positive religion has lost its validity' and 'traditional theology is not restorable', Adorno suggests that 'the whole' has indeed become 'the untrue' and an affirmative concept of metaphysics is thus no longer sustainable.[107] What is of interest, here, is (a) what, exactly, prompts Adorno's diagnosis, since it is elaborated more fully here than in occasional essays like 'Reason and Revelation', and (b) what – if anything – he proposes to remedy this condition, since the ostensible lack of positivity is at the heart of the objections raised by Habermas.

To begin with, then, Adorno distinguishes, in a 1965 lecture series that underlies his 'Meditations', between theology and metaphysics in the following terms:

> It is quite certain that metaphysics and theology cannot simply be distinguished from each other as historical stages (. . .) since they have constantly crossed over historically: one appeared at the same time as the other; one was forgotten only to re-emerge in the foreground. They form an extraordinarily complex structure which cannot be reduced to a simple conceptual formula. Nevertheless, there is an element of truth in the theory of stages (. . .) in that metaphysics in the traditional sense (. . .) is an attempt to determine the absolute, or the constitutive structures of being, on the basis of thought alone. That is, it does not derive the absolute dogmatically from revelation, or as something positive which is simply given to me, as something directly existing, through revelation or recorded revelation, but (. . .) it determines the absolute through concepts.[108]

In Adorno's view, then, the difference between theology and metaphysics is as follows: theology means the attempt 'to determine the absolute, or the constitutive structures of being' dogmatically, that is, through reliance on the truth of revelation over and above what can be verified conceptually or rationally. That is to say, theology relies on (and constantly reasserts) the validity of an external *given* – God – knowledge of whom is passed down through tradition. By contrast, metaphysics means the attempt to determine these constitutive structures out of thought alone. This distinction is repeated in *Negative Dialectics*, where Adorno writes: 'Vis-à-vis theology, metaphysics is not just a historically later stage, as it is according to positivistic doctrine. It is not only theology secularised into a concept. It preserves theology in its critique, by uncovering the possibility of what theology may force upon men and thus desecrate.'[109] That is to say, for Aristotle – Adorno's main point of reference – metaphysics means 'the form of philosophy which takes concepts as its objects'.[110]

All the same (and despite his slightly wilful chronology), Adorno continues, 'it is certainly true that metaphysics has something in common with theology in its manner of seeking to elevate itself above immanence, above the empirical world.'[111] In other words, metaphysics, theology and – we might add – religion share a concern with transcendence, a realm beyond mere positivity, which, according to Adorno, may have, at one time or another, existed, but which has since become unavailable. The deliberately paradoxical gesture of Adorno's philosophy, then, lies in his declaration of solidarity with this impulse 'at the time of its fall',[112] as the famous final line of *Negative Dialectics* solemnly declares. After all, the utopian dimension of Adorno's thought aims precisely at breaking out of the closed system of immanence that he associates with the positivistic 'cult (. . .) of facts'[113] that characterizes the disenchanted world of capitalist modernity. We have already noted some of the reasons as to why this 'beyond' cannot be positively pictured (notably because it does not, in fact, simply pre-exist its actualization); however, it remains to be seen how Adorno accounts for this historical unavailability in the first place.

(a) In a postscript to the second edition of his study on Kierkegaard (1966), which is not included in the standard English translation, Adorno describes his opposition to metaphysics as a 'doctrine of the unhistorical, unchangeable':[114] a true and immutable world behind the world of mere appearances, a *Hinterwelt*, to borrow Nietzsche's term.[115] Indeed, he seems to associate this view of metaphysics with philosophy more generally. After all, Adorno argues that the traditional aim of philosophy *qua* idealism is precisely to grasp the totality of the real – the constitutive structures of being – bindingly and lastingly out of thought alone. Accordingly, it will be recalled that Adorno's philosophical project begins and ends with a resolute disavowal of this undertaking, conceived of as an immanent critique of idealism: the supposed self-sufficiency of thought.[116] The historical impasse of philosophy is thus deemed to be co-extensive with that of metaphysics. It is against this backdrop that one must view Adorno's reformulation of Kant's epistemological question – 'how is metaphysics possible?' – into a historical one: 'Is it *still* possible to have a metaphysical experience?', or rather: Can it be possible again?[117]

Starting with his earliest works, Adorno's reasoning echoes a wider sense that traditional structures of meaning have deteriorated – a view of modernity as loss once memorably captured by Georg Lukács in terms of 'transcendental homelessness'.[118] After the Second World War, however, his emphasis shifts markedly; the issue is no longer the unfulfilled promise of modernity (e.g. the occurrence of a proletarian revolution in Germany), but rather the question as to how something like fascism could arise and flourish in Europe. For Adorno, the irrevocable dissolution of a purposeful view of history, religion, theology and metaphysics is thus expressed in a proper name: *Auschwitz*.[119] On this point, Adorno notes:

> In face of the experiences we have had, not only through Auschwitz but through the introduction of torture as a permanent institution and through the atomic bomb – all these things form a kind of coherence, a hellish unity – in face of these experiences the assertion that what *is* has meaning, and the affirmative character which has been attributed to metaphysics almost without exception, becomes a mockery (*Hohn*).[120]

For Adorno, then, Auschwitz (though 'not only' Auschwitz but rather the institutionalization of 'torture' for which it stands) becomes the marker of a radical meaninglessness in history. It is supposed to belie not only the fact of purposive historical forward movement, and hence the positive claim to grasping a 'wholly other' through religion, theology or metaphysics, but also its possibility within the established parameters of identity thinking (the difficulty, of course, continues to be that no other mode is positively available). Certainly, similar claims have been made long before Adorno; one need only think of reflections on the 1755 Lisbon earthquake by eighteenth-century critics of rationalism. The *differentia specifica* is that Adorno views Auschwitz as the outcome of an intra-historical process, which proceeds through the technological domination of nature, and is expressed – at the level of philosophy – in the always–already coercive configuration of subject and object (including the subject in its own objective self-relation). Auschwitz, on this view, marks the apotheosis of the dialectic of enlightenment, the historical expression of a problem that is – elsewhere – treated in a range of different registers. The particular significance of 'Auschwitz', though, lies in the fact that it focuses Adorno's previous insights into a more thoroughgoing expression of historically occasioned nihilism.[121] Hence, for Adorno, the fact of Auschwitz quite literally changes everything.

(b) As has already been noted, Adorno is keen to salvage the transcendent orientation of metaphysics 'at the moment of its fall'. As he argues, 'thinking beyond itself, into *openness* – that, precisely, is metaphysics', or at least what metaphysics ought to be.¹²² As was argued previously, though, Adorno deems that the metaphysical orientation towards transcendence is only sustainable negatively as an experience of unavailability. Pain – visceral, somatic suffering – throws into relief the contours of something beyond the spellbound sphere of existence.¹²³ Such experiences inscribe an opening into the historical process in the form of the ethical imperative that '[w]oe' must 'go'.¹²⁴ In this respect, Adorno ultimately affirms the possibility of metaphysical experience, however qualified or paradoxical the character of this affirmation may be. As Peter Osborne argues, pace Habermas, this 'affirmation' is best understood as a '*materialist metaphysics of modernity*, rather than (. . .) a negative theology', because Adorno does not readmit God through the backdoor, so to speak.¹²⁵ Rather, Adorno's reflections concerning metaphysics operate on at least three overlapping registers: the first is *epistemological*, which concerns the idea that 'the absolute, as it hovers before metaphysics, would be the nonidentical';¹²⁶ the second is *ethical*, which concerns the pervasive sense of 'guilt' implied in the question 'whether after Auschwitz you can go on living'¹²⁷ (we will return to this point in due course); and the third is *aesthetic*, which concerns the displacement of metaphysics into the realm of aesthetics (this will be the focus of Chapter 3).

Adorno situates these three guises of rational thought, treated previously, within the bounds of his negative universal history. The red thread connecting religion with theology and metaphysics is a shared concern with transcendence. In Adorno's view, however, the object of this concern has become historically insubstantial. The cause of this impasse lies in the dialectic of reason itself, not least in its catastrophic culmination at Auschwitz. Accordingly, as has already been noted, Adorno attempts to salvage the orientation towards a realm beyond the spellbound sphere of existence by negatively intimating a sense of metaphysical experience in terms of unavailability. What is experienced as unavailable, lacking, in other words, is supposed to intimate what ought to be: a world free from domination, coercion and suffering; but since the full articulation of this *ought* absolutely exceeds what *is*, it cannot (and yet must) be fully figured in the available terms. Presenting what *is* in such a way that it yields what *ought* to be (at least in outline) is the basic movement of Adorno's thinking, although with the additional difficulty that this *ought* does not, for its part, pre-exist the possibility of its presentation. Accordingly, Adorno's negative reformulation of metaphysics is supposed to cast into relief a historical opening: an indeterminate realm of possibility, albeit not a 'negative theology' – or, in Hent de Vries's formulation – a theology of the 'trace',[128] insofar as the residual positivity of these approaches implies a more emphatic form of theology than Adorno can allow.

Before concluding this section, however, it is worth emphasizing one last point: Adorno's historical verdict concerning the impossibility of positively grasping the absolute in the present can be complemented with a view to a text cited at the outset, namely Walter Benjamin's fragment 'Capitalism as Religion'. To be sure, there is an asymmetry here in cross-reading large parts of Adorno's mature philosophy with a minor fragment of Benjamin's, which was – by all accounts – neither finished nor intended for publication. This is all the more troubling since it is not even clear whether Adorno was familiar with this sketch (although, given that Adorno co-edited the first collection of Benjamin's works in 1955, this is perhaps not improbable). In any case, there is a striking correspondence between certain precepts of Benjamin's text and the reconstruction of Adorno's position proffered here. Exploring this admittedly speculative correlation will allow us to substantiate the opening assertion that Adorno's heretical repurposing of theological motifs, 'far beyond' what they 'once originally meant',[129] serves the criticism of a reality disfigured by what might be called a capitalist cult religion. After all, as we have seen in 'Reason and Revelation', Adorno argues that in the present, 'nothing of theological content will persist without being transformed'; 'every content will have to put itself to the test of migrating into the realm of the secular, the profane'. With this in mind, we turn to Benjamin's text.

(iii) Capitalism as religion

Walter Benjamin's unfinished sketch, 'Capitalism as Religion' (1921), barely fills three pages. Nevertheless, its characteristic density has given rise to much debate since it was first published posthumously in 1985. Indeed, the diagnostic force of this short fragment is arresting. Over its course, Benjamin radicalizes Max Weber's analysis of capitalism's religious conditioning, famously elaborated in *The Protestant Ethic and the Spirit of Capitalism* (1904). As Benjamin argues, religion is not just the causal precondition of capitalism, its historical antecedent, as (on Benjamin's reading) Weber claims; capitalism is itself an '*essentially* religious phenomenon', designed to 'allay the same anxieties, torments, and disturbances' as other 'so-called religions'.[130] However, before attempting to weigh up the continuity of this text with our discussion of Adorno, it is worth (a) briefly situating the piece in the wider context of Benjamin's work and (b) summarizing the main thrust of its argument.

(a) 'Capitalism as Religion' takes its title – and in some ways its cue – from a section of Ernst Bloch's book *Thomas Münzer als Theologe der Revolution* (*Thomas Münzer as Theologian of the Revolution*) (1921). Bloch and Benjamin had become acquainted around 1918, when they both lived in Switzerland, and Benjamin had reportedly read a typescript of Bloch's book as early as 1920.[131] Indeed, Bloch writes that the Reformation 'inaugurates (. . .) not merely the misuse of Christianity', particularly in Calvinism, 'but rather its complete desertion and even elements of a new religion: of capitalism as religion and the true church of Mammon'.[132] Despite the explicit echo of Bloch's formulation in Benjamin's text, however, their approaches differ markedly: 'Though Bloch identifies capitalism as a religion (. . .), his judgement is nevertheless a moderate one: for the capitalism in question does not represent for Bloch, as it does for Benjamin, the metamorphosis of Christianity into its true form, but rather the "complete desertion" from it.'[133] Benjamin fleshes out this view over the course of three interlocking sections: a relatively polished opening passage followed by some shorthand notes and – finally – a literature review.

As Uwe Steiner demonstrates with a view to the texts cited in the latter part (including works by Erich Unger, Georges Sorel and Gustav Landauer), 'Capitalism as Religion' belongs to a largely unrealized cycle on politics that Benjamin was planning around 1921, a period before his self-professed conversion to Marxism in 1924 during which he displayed decidedly anarchistic leanings.[134] Indeed, Benjamin's letters suggest that the series was supposed to comprise at least three parts: first, an essay entitled 'Der Wahre Politiker' ('The True Politician'); second, a piece titled 'Die Wahre Politik' ('The True Politics'), which – in turn – was to consist of two sections, respectively called 'Abbau der Gewalt' ('Dismantling of Violence')[135] and 'Teleologie ohne Endzweck' ('Teleology Without Ends'); and third, a political reading of Paul Scheerbart's asteroid novel *Lesabéndio* (1913). Curiously, the editors of Benjamin's *Gesammelte Schriften* (*Collected Writings*) omitted a section from their transcript of the fragment, titled 'Geld und Wetter (Zur Lesabéndio-Kritik)'.[136] It is reproduced elsewhere as part of the supplementary materials for *One-Way Street* (1928). Presumably this is because certain formulations in Benjamin's note are, indeed, reworked and included in this later text. However, the particular point of interest here is Benjamin's mention of Scheerbart, whose novel he had reviewed some years earlier. As the correspondence with Scholem indicates, Benjamin planned to revisit *Lesabéndio* in a long-form piece set against his reflections on 'Capitalism as Religion'. Steiner suggests that this unwritten piece on Scheerbart along with a lost review of Ernst Bloch's *Spirit of Utopia* (1918) were intended to delineate the contours of Benjamin's concept of politics.[137] However, without presently wishing to attempt a reconstruction of this extremely dense and much-contested effort, we turn to a reading of Benjamin's fragment.

(b) 'Capitalism as Religion' contains four main hypotheses, which Samuel Weber helpfully summarizes as follows:

1. Capitalism is a cult-religion, and indeed, perhaps 'the most extreme that ever existed'.
2. The cult of capitalism is extreme because it never pauses. It is characterized by 'permanent duration'.
3. The incessant cult of capitalism is *verschuldend*, which, according to the dual meaning of *Schuld* itself, must be translated both as 'guilt-producing' or 'culpabilizing' and as 'debt-producing' or 'indebting'.
4. The God of this religion, far from redeeming from guilt, is drawn into it. As a result this God 'must be kept secret and addressed only at the zenith of its (his) culpability-indebtedness'.[138]

Indeed, with regard to the first point, Benjamin writes that '[i]n capitalism, things have a meaning only in their immediate relationship to the cult; capitalism has no specific body of dogma, no theology'.[139] As such, it is not concerned with 'higher' or 'moral' matters.[140] Accordingly, Benjamin describes the cult as 'pagan', in contrast to the ethical standpoint of biblical monotheism.[141] The cultic rites of the former are performed blindly and endlessly in the accruing of profits (tellingly, Benjamin characterizes 'banknotes' as the idols of the capitalist cult);[142] but the tenor of this first hypothesis also points in another direction. In Benjamin's view, namely, capitalism does not require any outside impetus. As Weber notes, 'this radically transforms its relation to the divine.'[143] Instead of deriving meaning from theology, or – for that matter – from economics, 'the capitalist cult is itself the locus and source of all meaning'.[144]

Moreover, Benjamin argues, the duration of the cult is permanent. 'Since the cult no longer draws its meaning from something radically separate from it, but only from itself, that self consequently becomes its own measure.'¹⁴⁵ It becomes, in other words, autonomous, self-sufficient in the sense that '[t]he measure of a self is its ability to (...) withstand the transformative effects of time'.¹⁴⁶ That is to say, the capitalist cult withstands the weathering of time because it is figured as time*less*, mythical. At this point, Benjamin's cryptic notion that '[c]apitalism is the celebration of a cult *sans trêve et sans merci*' (*without truce or mercy*) comes into focus.¹⁴⁷ In capitalism, he writes, 'there are no "weekdays". There is no day that is not a feast day, in the terrible sense that all its sacred pomp is unfolded before us.'¹⁴⁸ The 'sacred pomp' is 'terrible' because it appears as 'a *war* without pause or end' – without truce or mercy – 'a life-consuming exertion', perpetrated on the living.¹⁴⁹

Without expanding on this notion, Benjamin turns to his third point. As he claims, 'the cult makes guilt pervasive. Capitalism is probably the first instance of a cult that creates guilt (*Schuld*) not atonement.'¹⁵⁰ That is to say, a kind of mythical, primordial guilt – not unlike that later diagnosed in *Dialectic of Enlightenment* – is universalized to the extent that even God himself becomes embroiled in it. As Benjamin writes, 'God's transcendence is at an end. But he is not dead; he has become involved in human fate.'¹⁵¹ Bracketing the fourth point – that an 'unmatured', hidden God, a *deus absconditus*, can only be addressed 'when his guilt is at its zenith'¹⁵² – we note the appearance of two central terms: on the one hand, this concerns Benjamin's use of the term 'fate' (*Schicksal*), which recalls the passages on myth discussed earlier; on the other hand, it concerns his play on the 'demonic ambiguity'¹⁵³ of the term *Schuld*, which, as we have already seen, means both 'guilt/culpability' and 'debt'. As Hamacher explains, 'it is the ambiguity (...) by which' in capitalism 'financial debts (*Schulden*) always serve as an index of legal, moral and affective guilt (*Schuld*) – and by which every guilt manifests itself in debts, and every debt in guilt.'¹⁵⁴ In order to tie Benjamin's text to our discussion of Adorno, however, the complex network of ideas designated by the terms 'guilt' and 'fate' requires some elucidation.

According to Hamacher, the alleged pervasiveness of guilt associated with the capitalist cult religion is linked precisely to the assertion of its permanent duration. It stems from a particular conception of history as 'guilt history' (*Schuldgeschichte*). As Hamacher argues, for Benjamin guilt is inscribed into the very structure of time, at least as it is figured in its dominant historical iterations. (Indeed, many years after writing 'Capitalism as Religion' Benjamin will describe the Social Democratic vision of historical progress in terms of a 'homogeneous' and 'empty' time.)[155] Hamacher expands on this point with a view to the pre-Socratics, particularly Anaximander, for whom, we are told, 'the sequence of time orders the rise and fall of all things (. . .) in accordance with the law of guilt and punishment so that becoming (*génesis*) is a guilt (*adikía*) that must be expiated in perishing.'[156] Time, in other words, appears as 'an order of guilt and retribution, debt and payback',[157] a dual movement of coming-into-being and passing away. 'It is a time of economy,' indeed, a 'time of law': the lawful movement of quid pro quo, which is binding for every being 'as a decree, an ordinance'.[158]

Benjamin notes a number of other sources, which speak to a similar problem. For one thing, he alludes to the Christian doctrine of original sin. Though he does not unfold his criticism of this teaching here, the general point seems clear: 'Christianity (. . .) raised the doctrine of original sin' – in our sense: original guilt/debt – 'to the status of a dogma and extended this logic into the furthest reaches of its systems of faith, thought and behaviour.'[159] More pointedly, Benjamin invokes 'the Freudian theorem of originary repression (. . .), the ethno-psychological myth of the murder of the primal father', which locates the source of universal guilt in a speculative prehistory of civilization.[160] Indeed, Freud features prominently in Benjamin's fragment, albeit not without a hint of scathing (Benjamin names Freud alongside Nietzsche and Marx as one of the 'priests' of the capitalist cult religion).[161] It is telling, too, that Benjamin alludes to Nietzsche's *On the Genealogy of Morals* (1887), particularly the section on '"Guilt", "Bad Conscience" and related Matters'. After all, Nietzsche speaks there of a 'stroke of genius on the part of Christianity', which stems from the fact that 'God himself sacrifices himself for the guilt of mankind'.[162] That is, 'God himself makes payment to himself (. . .) as the only being who can redeem man from what has become unredeemable for man himself – the creditor sacrifices himself for his debtor, out of *love* (can one credit that?), out of love for his debtor!'[163] Finally, Benjamin points to Max Weber, who argues that guilt is universalized in the Calvinist doctrine of predestination, wherein every means of atonement – 'whether by the devout, through sacraments, through the church' or 'by God himself'[164] – is withdrawn.

Focusing on universal guilt as the red thread connecting Benjamin's sources, it is worth briefly turning to an untitled fragment from the orbit of 'Capitalism as Religion', where it is argued that 'guilt is the highest category of world history'.[165] For all the other meanings of this central term (and surely there are many), Benjamin observes here that the sheer fact of guilt puts every present in a deficient relation to both past and future. 'History, in short, is the process by which guilt is incurred – since in its every production the no-longer-being of something else is effected.'[166] In yet another crucial fragment from this period, 'Fate and Character' (1920), Benjamin equates this notion of a 'world history', whose 'highest category' is 'guilt', with a particular conception of fate, which he describes in an enigmatic turn of phrase as the 'guilt-nexus of the living'.[167] Fate is thus, in some sense, opposed to freedom; within its bounds humankind is at the mercy of mythical Gods. In the present context this means that fate returns in the guise of capitalist social relations, which present themselves as divinely decreed, law-like and eternally binding. Benjamin associates this seemingly fateful immersion in second nature with the ruling system of law and order in the administered world. That is to say, the order of fate is sustained by a violent 'mythical-legal system', which 'imposes identity upon difference, commensurability upon alterity, and universality upon singularity'.[168] Before the law, he argues, humankind is reduced to its 'purely (. . .) natural dimension',[169] to 'bare life',[170] or mere nature, as Adorno might call it. As such, humankind appears bereft of the capacity for ethical action – a facet of the young Benjamin's anarchism – because humanity is figured as constitutively un-free. In his essay 'Critique of Violence' (1921), the fullest surviving articulation of his early political project, Benjamin thus contrasts a certain conception of law (*Recht*) with a 'truly ethico-political standpoint of justice'[171] (*Gerechtigkeit*), which is on the side of 'singular, living beings'.[172] That is to say, if for Benjamin fate is the operational law in the time of guilt, then justice belongs to a qualitatively distinct order of freedom that would require the complete cessation of the status quo: the depositing (*Ent-setzung*), through 'pure means', of the mythical law (*Gesetz*) that, in effect, sustains the capitalist cult religion.[173]

Setting aside this partial and, admittedly, schematic reconstruction of Benjamin's fragment, we provisionally conclude by noting the following: the dominant regime of time (understood as a linear succession of cause and effect, means and ends) is structurally guilt producing. The pervasiveness of guilt reaches its 'terrible' climax in the capitalist cult religion, where it is finally universalized to the extent that even God is rendered culpable. In turn, Benjamin identifies the time of guilt with mythic fate, the law of the present. Before this law, human beings – and, indeed, the Man-God of Christendom – cannot settle their debts and can effect no atonement because they are structurally and constitutively un-free.

The question of how Benjamin proposes to bring about a breaking-open of this 'guilt history' is truly the theme for a separate book. Nevertheless, his fragment has significant implications for the reading of Adorno proposed here. After all, the verdict that 'God's transcendence is at an end' because He has become 'involved in human fate' resonates strongly with Adorno's argument that – in the present – any claim to transcendence made by 'positive religion', 'traditional theology' and 'affirmative metaphysics' becomes untenable, precisely because (in their capacity as historical iterations of a dialectic of enlightenment) all three are fatefully ensnared in myth. In this respect, Benjamin's view that capitalism is the 'most extreme' expression of a 'guilt-nexus of the living' finds a curious echo in *Dialectic of Enlightenment*, where Adorno and Horkheimer argue that '[t]he God of Judaism demands what he is owed and settles accounts with the defaulter'; He 'enmeshes his creatures in a tissue of debt and credit, guilt and merit'.[174] To be sure, Benjamin's claim is more far-reaching than Adorno and Horkheimer's. The point is not just that God 'enmeshes his creatures' in an economy of guilt and retribution; rather, God himself numbers amongst the guilty. That is why in capitalism all that remains is pure cult without 'dogma' or 'theology'. Moreover, the young Benjamin (under the sway of Cohen) would have presumably rejected Adorno and Horkheimer's characterization of Judaism – his target is very explicitly Christianity. Nevertheless, the reasoning that nourishes these verdicts is, in some sense, analogous. In the dialectic of enlightenment, the oldest returns in the guise of the new: myth as capitalism, capitalism as myth. The point is that if the earliest cultic practices are already a form of enlightenment – an exercise in the mastery of nature – and if, conversely, the most sophisticated modern phenomena bear the mark of these ancient rites, then it follows that the boundaries between our historical bookends are blurred. As such, the rationalization of cultic practices in capitalism speaks of an irrationality that is older than the cult itself.

(iv) Secularization

The following section returns us to an issue raised at the outset of the present chapter, namely whether Adorno's use of theological motifs, 'far beyond' what they 'once originally meant', can be grasped *sensu stricto* as a form of secularization. After all, as we have seen, Adorno argues that materialism brings the Old Testament ban on making images of God 'into *secular* form by not permitting Utopia to be positively pictured'.[175] Accordingly, it has been claimed by some commentators that Adorno's approach ought to be characterized as a paradoxical form of 'secular theology'.[176] However, I argue, Adorno's intentions are far from self-evident, and – upon closer inspection – complications arise from such readings. Accordingly, I propose to explore this matter with a view to three authors whose findings are instructive in this context, even though they do not, in fact, concern Adorno directly: first, this means Hans Blumenberg's critical reflections on the concept of 'secularization', laid out in his momentous study on *The Legitimacy of the Modern Age* (1966);[177] second, it means Giorgio Agamben's subsequent deliberations on the concept of 'profanation', laid out in his essay 'In Praise of Profanation' (2005); and, third, it means Sami Khatib's re-imagination of Freud's concept of 'dislocation', laid out in his book *Teleologie ohne Endzweck* (*Teleology Without Ends*) (2013). Although none of these texts address Adorno's work as such, all three offer helpful models for understanding the complex interplay between religious motifs and non-religious sentiments that is the subject of this section.

In *The Legitimacy of the Modern Age*, Hans Blumenberg highlights that the word 'secular' derives from the Latin *saeculum* (age). In its common usage, it can be taken to mean '"the present age", "this world" (as opposed to the next), and ultimately "the world" as opposed to the transcendent'.[178] As such, 'secularization' generally designates a long-term historical process 'by which a disappearance of religious ties, attitudes to transcendence, expectations of an afterlife, ritual performances, and firmly established turns of speech is driven onward in both private and daily public life.'[179] As Blumenberg reminds his readers, the term was first used in the seventeenth century to denote the expropriation of ecclesiastic goods by state authorities, for instance in the period leading up to the Peace of Westphalia, which ended the Thirty Years War in 1648. Broadly speaking, we are told, this process has a correlate in the history of ideas: like the signatories of the aforementioned treaty, figureheads of the European Enlightenment (e.g. Voltaire) are commonly seen as having 'secularise[d] knowledge in order to free man from the (. . .) illegitimate control of the Church'.[180] However, as Blumenberg emphasizes, this view is prey to a number of criticisms. For instance, one might object that if purportedly 'modern' ideas are, in fact, 'secularized' religious teachings, then their emphatic claim to modernity, to being new, unprecedented and inherently self-legitimating is undermined. As Blumenberg points out, this un-interrogated assumption more or less explicitly underlies the work of many eminent thinkers from the first half of the twentieth century, including (but not limited to) Max Weber, Carl Schmitt and Karl Löwith.

In the case of Weber this concerns the view that the modern work ethic is supposed to be a secularization of Christian asceticism.[181] In the case of Schmitt, this concerns the controversial estimation that '[a]ll significant concepts of the modern theory of the state are' at root 'secularised theological concepts'.[182] Finally, in the case of Löwith, this concerns the premise of his work *Meaning in History* (1949),[183] where it is argued that 'the modern idea of progress is a transformation into worldly form of Christian eschatology', that is, 'of the Christian preoccupation with the future as the dimension of the "last things", the end of the world, the Last Judgement, salvation, damnation, etc.'[184] Despite the far-reaching differences between these thinkers, Blumenberg's objection in each case is the same. In his view, the idea that modern phenomena should appear primarily as secularized versions of religious teachings obfuscates their claim to autonomy. In other words, 'the secularisation theorem obstructs the view of the *de facto* structure of an epochal threshold' – an epochal break between the modern and the pre-modern world – 'because the idea of a "historical constant" lies, unquestioned, at its basis'.[185] Blumenberg rejects this notion of historical constancy in the opening chapter of his book, 'Secularisation: Critique of a Category of Historical Wrong'. As he argues, such an 'unhistorical interpretation displaces the authenticity of the modern age, making it a remainder, a pagan substratum'.[186] In short: Blumenberg objects to the implication that the modern age is an illegitimate and unacknowledged derivate of religion, because such a view presumes a trans-historical religious original at its basis. However, instead of exploring how Blumenberg attempts to salvage the legitimacy of the modern age through charting its history in terms of a supposed self-assertion of reason, it remains to see how his insights pertain to our reading of Adorno.

To be sure, Adorno's notion of a negative universal history – 'from the slingshot to the megaton bomb' – presumes precisely the kind of constancy to which Blumenberg objects. As has already been seen, the entire metahistorical narrative outlined in *Dialectic of Enlightenment* might be read in this way (myth as the *incognito* of reason; reason as the *incognito* of myth). Nevertheless, it might be asked: What if the historical 'constants' assumed by secularization theory were themselves displaced in the historical process? In other words, what if the very grounds on which we map the putative polarity (and constancy) of the 'religious' and the 'secular', the 'sacred' and the 'profane', were to shift? Certainly, this would alter the stakes of the question as to whether Adorno's use of theological terms 'far beyond' what they 'once originally meant' can be adequately grasped as a form of secularization – as Blumenberg would have it, the illegitimate carrying-over of a religious original into a modern arena. After all, these terms would be uprooted from their traditional terrain.

An illuminating account of this dynamic is offered by Giorgio Agamben in his essay 'In Praise of Profanation' (2005). According to Agamben, the concept of secularization designates a particular relationship between the religious and the non-religious spheres – a passage from the former to the latter. He distinguishes between the 'sacred' and the 'profane' in the following terms: on the one hand, he cites the Roman jurist Trebatius, arguing that the term 'sacred' means belonging 'to the gods'.[187] Such things are 'removed from the free use and commerce of men'; they can be 'neither sold nor held in lien, neither given for usufruct nor burdened by servitude'.[188] On the other hand, 'if "to consecrate" (*sacrare*) was the term that indicated the removal of things from the sphere of human law, "to profane" (*profanare*) meant, conversely, to return them to the free use of men'.[189] In Agamben's view, religion can thus be defined as the operation that 'removes things, places, animals, or people from common use and transfers them to a separate sphere'.[190] Religious rituals sanction 'the passage of something from the profane to the sacred, from the human sphere to the divine'.[191] By contrast, we are told, 'profanation' – *sacrilege* – designates a movement in the opposite direction: the passage of a given thing from the sacred to the profane, from the ownership of the gods to the 'free use of men'.

Profanation, then, is *like* secularization insofar as it is supposed to designate the same direction of travel; however, it is *unlike* secularization insofar as it is not supposed to leave 'intact the forces it deals with'.[192] Unlike secularization, then, Agamben argues that profanation effects the passage of 'the forces it deals with' from one sphere to the other 'by means of (. . .) *play*', which – in this context – is taken to mean a particular 'use (or, rather, reuse) of the sacred'[193] because 'play frees and distracts humanity from the sphere of the sacred, without simply abolishing it.'[194] Accordingly, he sees great promise in the profanation of a '*religio* that is played with but no longer observed'.[195] Against this backdrop, Agamben distinguishes between 'secularisation' and 'profanation' in the following terms:

> Secularisation is a form of repression. It leaves intact the forces it deals with by simply moving them from one place to another. Thus the political secularisation of theological concepts (the transcendence of God as a paradigm of sovereign power) does nothing but displace the heavenly monarchy onto an earthly monarchy, leaving its power intact. Profanation, however, neutralises what it profanes. Once profaned, that which was unavailable and separate loses its aura and is returned to use. Both are political operations: The first guarantees the exercise of power by carrying it back to a sacred model; the second deactivates the apparatus of power and returns to common use the spaces that power had seized.[196]

Agamben does not develop this point here;[197] but whatever his stated intentions, it might be objected that his account of 'profanation' tends to reproduce the problems discussed earlier under a different name. After all, it seems as though Agamben too assumes the 'constancy' of a religious 'original' that can be playfully reclaimed, rather than illegitimately transposed from one sphere to another. As Alberto Toscano observes, '[t]hough Agamben does not straightforwardly embody the apologetic Christian purposes that Hans Blumenberg identifies in the discourse on secularisation', for example in Schmitt, 'he does manifest one key aspect of that discourse', namely 'the idea of a substantial continuity'.[198] Read in this way, it is unclear why profanation should be any more legitimate than secularization in designating the passage from the sacred to the profane. Both ultimately share the same 'belief in (. . .) continuity and concealment'.[199] Agamben's identification of 'secularisation' with 'repression', in fact, proceeds in much the same vein. It implies that religion continues to determine the character of the present in more or less unconscious ways. Agamben is playing on the fact that a well-known tenet of Freudian psychoanalysis teaches that repression leads to a return of the repressed in a distorted form. But if we follow Agamben in arguing that secularization is akin to a repression of religion, then it follows that the modern age appears principally as a series of psycho-pathological symptoms; and, indeed, on this reading the specifically religious character of these symptoms is only obliquely manifest. It requires an archaeological inquiry to unearth the biblical substrate of modernity.

Without wishing to situate this claim in the wider context of Agamben's project, I take it that there is another way to read this passage. After all, Freud describes repression as a dual operation of defacement and displacement. Freud's *terminus technicus* for this process is 'dislocation', *Entstellung*, which – in German – connotes both disfigurement or distortion and spatial dislodging, since the root *Stellung* denotes something like 'position', whereas the prefix *ent-*, roughly translatable as *de-*, designates a kind of de-positioning.[200] Accordingly, Freud specifies that dislocation means not only 'to change the appearance' of something – to deface, distort or disfigure it, in the manner that Agamben suggests – 'but also "to wrench [it] apart", "to put [it] in another place"'.[201] According to this double meaning of the term, the putative 'repression' of religion, described by Agamben in his account of secularization, cannot simply mean its unconscious persistence beneath the surface of capitalist modernity. If this were the case, then the modern age would, indeed, have to appear as the mere *incognito* of a religious original. However, if 'repression' does not just mean the distortion of religion, but also the uprooting from its traditional locale – dis*place*ment in the sense of its topographic *Stellung* – then it follows that religion cannot simply persist as a defaced substratum of the present, an original that has only been covered over, but never substantially altered. Rather, the stakes of the secularization theorem shift as its historical topography is destabilized.

On such a reading, it is hard to imagine how religion might be seen as a firmly rooted historical invariable, even in the context of a civilizational metanarrative like *Dialectic of Enlightenment*. This verdict is shared by Jean-Luc Nancy, who observes that 'the modern world does not transpose, in a secularized fashion, a theological structure' in the way that, for instance, Schmitt intends; rather, 'the supposed transposition displaces all the terms of the problem, as well as the structure itself'.[202] Against this backdrop our opening question is refocused: Where is religion displaced *to* if it is, indeed, removed from its traditional locality and thus from the undergrowth of the modern age?

Using this diagnosis as a point of departure, the Benjamin-scholar Sami Khatib argues that the wider precepts of Freud's reasoning can be productively applied to explain the critical function of theological terms in the context of Benjamin's 'secular' critique of capitalist modernity. Insofar as we have sought to establish a link between Benjamin and Adorno on this point, the brief discussions of Blumenberg, Agamben and Freud come to bear on the figure of an 'inverse' theology. As Khatib emphasizes, the concept of dislocation, which, as we have seen, is 'linked to questions of repressed conflict in Freud's writing',[203] designates a far-reaching topographic shift that lastingly displaces theology from its ancestral site. That is to say, the shift that we have described transposes the entire ground on which the putative polarity of the religious and the secular has historically been charted.

Siding with Blumenberg's critique of Schmitt et al., Khatib argues that for Benjamin, too, the present cannot appear as the simple covering-over of a religious foundation because this foundation has itself been lastingly undermined. In the present context, the point is that the radical epochal break invoked in *The Legitimacy of the Modern Age* (and figured by Khatib as a seismic shift) effects both a prospective and a retrospective change in the meaning ascribed to the historical markers of 'religion' and 'secular modernity'. To this end, Khatib cites Benjamin's fragment, 'Capitalism as Religion', arguing that 'with the emergence of capitalism as a new religious edifice (. . .) the positions of the old (. . .) world-religions shift'.[204] That is to say, the 'old world-religions' are no longer anchored to a stable, unchanging location, *Stellung*, from whence they cannot be dislodged, even if they are distorted beyond recognition. As Khatib continues, in its capacity as a 'remainder-less cult-context' capitalism advances both the absolute 'sacralisation' of 'profane life'[205] (i.e. the rendering-religious of ostensibly non-religious terrain) *and* the 'totalising secularisation of a realm that was hitherto sacred'.[206] In other words, Benjamin's fragment captures the Freudian double movement in the following terms: on the one hand, it describes the 'dislocation of the field of religion through the emergence of capitalism' as a new religion; and, on the other hand, it designates 'a shift of (monotheistic) theology' – the intellectual superstructure of religion – 'whose traditional place within the neo-pagan religious system of capitalism has become superfluous'.[207] However, far from consigning theology to the scrap heap of history, Khatib wagers that the becoming-superfluous of religion assigns theological terms a particular role in the immanent critique of the capitalist cult religion: a kind of critical afterlife. The significance of this shift has far-reaching consequences for our reading of Adorno.

Adorno's use of terms ostensibly derived from traditional theology, too, cannot be grasped as a form of secularization in any uncomplicated sense, despite his own occasional use of the term. If, as has been argued, capitalist modernity short-circuits the traditional polarity of 'sacred' and 'profane', then it follows that the concept of 'secularization' (and, indeed, the concept of theology) takes on a different meaning 'far beyond' what it 'originally meant', as Adorno puts it in 'Reason and Revelation'. This verdict brings us to the central question raised at the beginning of this chapter: In what sense can displaced theological terms, such as the image ban, be put to work by a Critical Theory like Adorno's without nostalgically reasserting an irretrievably lost authority? In other words, what perspectives are offered by Adorno's enigmatic notion of an 'inverse' theology?

Part II: Inversion

Having thus clarified some of the wider issues raised by Adorno's use of theological terms, it is now possible to turn to the letter cited at the start of this chapter where the notion of an 'inverse' theology is first articulated (as will be recalled, Adorno writes to Benjamin on 17 December 1934 to express his whole-hearted 'agreement' with an 'image of theology' that he locates in his friend's essay, 'Franz Kafka: On the Tenth Anniversary of His Death').[208] Let us recall, then, that Adorno describes the inverted 'image of theology' which he ascribes to Benjamin by use of a quasi-topographic term; as he argues, this image concerns, 'in quite a principled sense', theology's *position*. This peculiar description resonates with Adorno's own 'earliest attempt to interpret Kafka' in 1925,[209] which he paraphrases in the previous line: 'I claimed he' – that is, Kafka – 'is a photograph of earthly life taken from the perspective of the redeemed, of which nothing appears but the edge of a black cloth, whereas the terrifyingly displaced optic of the photographic image is none other than that of the obliquely angled camera itself.' Bracketing for a moment Adorno's prominent use of optical and photographic imagery with reference to Kafka,[210] as well as his striking use of personification – '*he*', Kafka, 'is a photograph' – it is worth highlighting that, as with the 'position' of theology, the 'perspective' of the redeemed ostensibly marks a determinate location, a viewpoint. This calls to mind the three critical junctures in Adorno's writing, noted previously, at which the topographic language of his letter appears: first, his review of Brecht and Weill's *Mahagonny* (1930); second, 'Finale', the closing aphorism from *Minima Moralia* (1951); and, third, his essay 'Notes on Kafka' (1953).[211] 'Finale', in particular, is worth citing in full, as it gives the strongest sense of what is at stake, for Adorno, in these formulations. Adorno writes:

> The only philosophy which can be responsibly practiced in the face of despair is the attempt to contemplate all things as they would present themselves *from the standpoint of redemption*. Knowledge has no light but that shed on the world by redemption: all else exhausts itself in reconstruction and remains mere technique. Perspectives would have to be fashioned that displace and estrange the world, reveal it to be, with its rifts and crevices, as indigent and dislocated [*entstellt*] as it will appear one day in the messianic light. To gain such perspectives without capriciousness or violence, entirely from felt contact with its objects – this alone is the task of thought. It is the simplest of all things, because the situation calls imperatively for such knowledge, indeed because consummate negativity, once squarely faced, shoots together into the mirror writing of its opposite. But it is also the utterly impossible thing, because it presupposes a standpoint removed, even though by a hair's breadth, from the scope of existence, whereas we well know that any possible knowledge must not only first be wrested from what is, if it shall hold good, but is also marked, for this very reason, by the same dislocated-ness [*Entstelltheit*] and indigence which it seeks to escape. The more passionately thought denies its conditionality for the sake of the unconditional, the more unconsciously, and so calamitously, it is delivered up to the world. Even its own impossibility it must at last comprehend for the sake of the possible. Vis-à-vis the demand thus placed on thought, the question of the reality or unreality of redemption itself hardly matters.[212]

The echo of Adorno's 1934 letter is unmistakable in this passage: a philosophy that contemplates 'all things as they would present themselves from the standpoint of redemption' recalls almost verbatim Adorno's own 'earliest attempt to interpret Kafka'. As we are told, such a philosophy aims to fashion – in an active sense – 'perspectives' from whence the world would appear 'dislocated' (*entstellt*), as though it were illuminated by a 'messianic light'. The figure of a 'messianic light' is in all likelihood an allusion to the Lurrianic Kabbalah, a source with which Adorno had a passing familiarity by the time he wrote 'Finale', not least through his reading of Scholem's influential book *Major Trends in Jewish Mysticism* (1941).[213] In this regard, the title of

Adorno's piece may be seen as deliberately evoking an eschatological 'end' to the existing order.

We might infer, then, that the 'perspectives' in question coincide with the vantage point from which 'the land-surveyor' Kafka 'photographs the earth's surface', as Adorno puts it in the aforementioned 1953 essay.[214] Here, too, the origin of the light-source in question is presented as determinate. It appears to shine from a distinct outside source, indeed, an 'optimal' place or locality. Its direction of travel is, moreover, captured by the preposition *zum* – a contraction of *zu* and the masculine, dative article *dem* – in the title of 'Zum Ende', which might thus be more adequately rendered as 'to' or 'towards' the end than as 'Finale'.[215]

Interestingly, then, Adorno goes on to state that this light reveals the world 'as it *would* be', hypothetically, 'for the *intellectus archetypus*',[216] thus calling to mind a prominent figure from Kant's writings, not least of all from the *Critique of Pure Reason*,[217] and – in turn – the *Critique of the Power of Judgement*.[218] In the first instance, the *intellectus archetypus* denotes a quasi-divine form of cognition: a positive grasp of noumena – God, the soul, things in themselves – as opposed to limited, phenomenal representations in space and time, which, alone, are the possible objects of human experience.

Kant contrasts the *intellectus archetypus* with an '*intellectus ectypus*',[219] which he describes as 'our' – that is, humankind's – 'discursive, image-dependent understanding', whose legitimate sphere of application is limited to the realm of appearances.[220] Having demonstrated, in the first *Critique*, that God, the soul and things in themselves cannot be adequately grasped through limited human modes of judgement, Kant, as it were, readmits these limit cases of experience as regulative principles, that is, as hypothetical postulates that orient our thoughts and actions. Thus, in theology, for instance, we cannot know whether God is, in fact, the ultimate cause of all things; but we can view all objects 'as if the objects themselves had arisen from that original image', that *archetype* 'of all reason', which is itself beyond representation by human means.[221] Accordingly, in the third *Critique* – in his discussion of teleological forms of judgement – Kant goes on to speak of an 'understanding through whose self-consciousness the manifold of intuition would at the same time be given', that is, 'an understanding through whose representation the objects of this representation would at the same time exist'.[222] Such understanding, he continues, 'would not require a (. . .) synthesis of the manifold for the unity of consciousness'; in other words, it would not require modes of judgement that imperfectly piece together the fragmented phenomenal multiplicity given in sensible intuition so characteristic of the 'human understanding'.[223] The human understanding, Kant concludes, 'merely thinks, but does not intuit', in the emphatic sense.[224] Instead, the mode of intellectual (as opposed to sensible) intuition, which is proper to the *intellectus archetypus*, is taken to be holistic in the sense that it makes no distinction between an object's existence, its representation in perception and its determination through the understanding because it is not limited by the constraints of the human mind. The 'standpoint' of the *intellectus archetypus*, however, is not accessible in a positive sense (either for Kant or for Adorno); it is implied by contrast with the 'special character of the human understanding', as the title of §77 in the *Critique of the Power of Judgement* puts it.[225]

The metaphorical topography of Adorno's phrasing, with its apparent invitation to contemplate the world as it would present itself to the *intellectus archetypus* from the 'standpoint of redemption', thus gives rise to a problem that has not eluded some commentators: '[H]ow can Kafka', or, for that matter, Adorno, 'look down on earthly life from a transcendent position if he is human', we might ask; 'if man is placed on earth and God cannot (. . .) be known'?[226] In other words, what might it mean to speak of such localities, or – indeed – *from* them, given (as we have noted) that Adorno's self-avowed commitment to the ban on images forbids him from furnishing either the workings of God's mind or the 'standpoint of redemption' with any positive determinations?

On first inspection, the answer to this question appears to lie in Adorno's use of the modal verb 'would': Kafka 'feigns' a standpoint that portrays the world as it *would* appear 'from the perspective of salvation' (hellish, mutilated, etc.).[227] This conditionality, for its part, has given rise to some enduring criticisms of Adorno's text. Jacob Taubes, for instance, argues that Adorno's aphorism reduces the 'standpoint of redemption' to a 'beautiful', albeit 'empty', fiction.[228] 'Think of *Minima Moralia*, the last part', 'Finale', he writes.[229] 'There you can tell (. . .) how the whole messianic thing becomes a *comme si* affair.'[230] This point is echoed some years later by Giorgio Agamben, who charges that 'Finale' amounts to little more than an 'aestheticisation of the messianic in the form of the *as if*, the *comme si*, the *als ob*:[231] a projection that can be pondered, even enjoyed, but never actualized. In other words, for Agamben (following Taubes), Adorno's remarks mean that philosophy is condemned to 'indefinitely contemplate the *appearance* of redemption',[232] which is to say that it is resigned to perpetual inaction. The invocation of 'redemption', understood here as a utopian ideal of sorts, is supposed to be merely regulative: it posits an imagined outcome, an 'Ende', that cannot be reached. Agamben generalizes Taubes's plaint, arguing that '[t]he whole of Adorno's philosophy is written' in this form – the 'as if' – conceived of as an 'intimate modality' at the heart of his thought.[233] Accordingly, philosophy may, indeed, have been realizing itself, as the famous opening lines of Negative Dialectics propose, but the moment of its realization was missed. 'The omission', Agamben argues, 'is at one and the same time absolutely contingent and absolutely irreparable, thus impotential. Redemption is consequently *only* a 'point of view',[234] a 'standpoint' or a 'perspective'.[235]

Given what was noted of the *intellectus archetypus*, it would appear that Taubes and Agamben thus read Adorno with a view to a related Kantian figure, namely the 'as if' ('*Als ob*'). It is true that, for Kant, the 'as if' means a maxim of regulative judgement, that is, a demand that we organize our thoughts and actions in certain ways even if the final consequence of this organization cannot be realized. However, Adorno, in fact, never uses this exact expression in the passages cited by Taubes and Agamben. An example of Kant's application of this figure occurs in the 'Transcendental Dialectic' of the *Critique of Pure Reason*. There Kant argues that reason demands of us that we seek to unify our conceptual scheme by aspiring to the ever-greater systematicity and differentiation of our concepts, even though a complete unity cannot – by definition – be achieved. As Howard Caygill notes,[236] such forms of analogical argument are ubiquitous in Kant's thinking, even if they are not systematically addressed as such: from his moral philosophy (e.g. to 'act *as if* your maxims were to serve at the same time as a universal law')[237] to his more pointedly theoretical reflections (e.g. to strive for 'the greatest possible empirical use of reason', namely to see 'all combinations' of a phenomenal manifold, '*as if* they were ordained by a highest reason' – an *intellectus archetypus* – 'of which our reason is only a weak copy').[238] As mentioned previously, humankind cannot *know* this 'highest reason'; but wherever it comes up against the limits of its legitimate theoretical and practical sphere of operation, it ought – at the very least – to aspire to it in the manner of a hypothetical 'as if'.

Moreover, and as Taubes and Agamben imply, the 'as if' also plays a distinctive role in the domain of aesthetics. For Kant, 'we approach objects aesthetically when we recognize with delight, wonder, and arrested attention the structural patterns of things; when, despite being unable to say, objectively, 'that they exhibit' something like 'purpose, we approach them *as if* they did'.[239] An example of this logic, which will prove central for the discussion of Adorno's aesthetics in Chapter 3, can be gleaned in §45 of the *Critique of the Power of Judgement*. There Kant notes that a work of art 'must (. . .) seem to be as free from all constraint by arbitrary rules *as if* it were a mere product of nature'.[240] As Eva Scharper explains, this is significant for the following reasons:

> Judging aesthetically, we have to use concepts as if they referred to objects of sense; but no schematic correspondences can be exhibited for them. Yet they are not 'empty' in the Kantian sense. For their indeterminate use specifies at the same time our delight, approval, dislike or aversion as if private subjectivity were all that mattered. But, as we offer aesthetic judgments as relevant to others who see the same objects, such feelings are not 'blind' sensations either. This is the Kantian As-If of aesthetics: aesthetic judgments proceed as if the concepts used in them had objective validity, and as if they described merely private feelings.[241]

In other words, the ostensibly 'private feelings' expressed in aesthetic judgements, in turn, are presented *as if* they had universal validity. In conceiving of this particular 'purposiveness without an end',[242] which, according to Kant, emerges in and through the operation of aesthetic judgements (including their in-built 'as if' character), we become conscious of our own powers, our 'capacity to transcend nature and to reach something beyond', namely morality.[243] Contrary to what Taubes and Agamben suggest, then, the judgements ostensibly under discussion here are not 'empty', in the Kantian sense, even if their determinacy is not the same as that of, say, cognitive–scientific or practical–ethical judgements; this is the manner in which judgements of taste approach a particular 'beyond'. Taubes and Agamben are right, of course, that such aesthetic judgements play an important role for Adorno, particularly, as we will find, in his discussion of natural beauty in *Aesthetic Theory* (1970); however, they do so only in the most qualified sense: through Adorno's account of art's language-like character and the related mode of what he calls 'judgementless' (*urteilslos*) judgements – a singular modification of Kant.[244]

We will return to these matters in Chapter 3. For now, though, it remains to note the following: Taubes and Agamben do not, in fact, characterize the supposed 'as if' character of Adorno's thinking with reference to Kant; rather, the quasi-subjunctive, hypothetical mood of 'Finale' is presented in terms of another source: *The Philosophy of 'As If'* (1911), a book by the neo-Kantian philosopher Hans Vaihinger. Vaihinger, for his part, is best remembered for developing a position that he describes as 'idealistic positivism':[245] a rejection of Kant's account of things in themselves, which posits, instead, that only sensations are real, and that all other facets of human cognition are, essentially, pragmatic fictions. Vaihinger's 'as if' philosophy is thus a kind of elaborate fictionalism; it proceeds by cross-reading aspects of Kant's epistemology (minus the thing in itself) with a broadly Darwinian evolutionary theory. Accordingly, the human mind is said to develop as a tool for survival. The functioning of this tool occurs within broadly Kantian limits with the difference that Vaihinger rejects the thought, still held by Kant, that there *is* a transcendent realm beyond these limits, even if we can know nothing of it. Where such a 'beyond' is nonetheless posited, it is only as a fiction useful for the preservation of the species. Vaihinger warns his readers 'not to confuse' such useful 'as if' 'fictions', including the supposition of things in themselves, 'with reality'.[246] Rather, every such fiction 'must *justify* itself by what it accomplishes for the progress of science'.[247]

Somewhat surprisingly, then, Agamben quotes the following passage from Vaihinger's book to illustrate a supposed similarity to Adorno's 'standpoint':

> The kingdom of truth will almost certainly never come, and in the final aim set before itself by the republic of scholars will, in all likelihood, never be attained. Nevertheless, the unquenchable interest in truth that burns in the breast of every thinking man will demand, for all eternity, that he should combat error with all his power and spread truth in every direction, i.e. behave exactly *as if* error must some day be completely extirpated and we might look forward to a time when truth will reign undisputed sovereignty. This indeed is characteristic of a nature like that of man, designed to be forever approximating to unattainable ideals (. . .). It is true that in all this you cannot scientifically demonstrate that it must be so. Enough that your heart bids you act *as if* it were so.[248]

According to Agamben, then, Adorno follows Vaihinger's full-blooded directive to act '*as if* God, the kingdom, truth, and so on existed', *qua* useful fictions, even if these ideals are deemed to be unattainable.[249] In this regard, the charge that Adorno conjures up an image of a divine 'standpoint' *as if* it were attainable, even if his negatively dialectical mode of reaching it is deemed to be 'impotential', suggests, first, that Adorno is committed to a continual progression towards such an ideal ('to be forever *approximating*' it); and, second, that he has a fully formed sense of what this ideal is, despite its fictional character ('to act as if *it were*', determinately, 'so'). However, this in unconvincing for several reasons. For one thing, Adorno only appears to be on record as commenting on Vaihinger once, in passing, in a 1959 lecture course on the *Critique of Pure Reason*, where he describes *The Philosophy of 'As If'* as being 'redolent of nineteenth-century flat-footedness'.[250] More importantly, the suggestion that the 'standpoint of redemption' is used regulatively as a useful fiction implies that Adorno's thinking proceeds according to a particular idea of progress – a view that is contradicted in his Kafka essay, where he notes that 'progress has', in fact, 'not yet begun'.[251] Adorno is emphatic on this point: '[N]o progress is to be assumed that would imply that humanity in general', that is, a humanity of the sort implied by Vaihinger's reference to a 'nature like that of man', 'already existed and therefore *could* progress'.[252] Adorno returns to this thought some years later, in an essay titled 'Progress' (1964), which speaks, obliquely, to the manner in which Vaihinger implicitly pre-empts the 'unattainable ideal' that his 'as if' philosophy seeks to gradually approximate: 'If humanity remains entrapped by the totality it itself fashions', the reified world of capitalist production, 'then, as Kafka said, no progress has taken place at all'.[253] True progress, in other words, 'would be the very establishment of humanity in the first place', namely *via negativa*, rather than by means of regulative judgements or useful 'as if' fictions – an 'establishment', in short, 'whose prospect opens up' only 'in the face of its' – that is, humanity's – 'extinction'.[254] This, Adorno notes, is the thought that 'animates' not only Kafka but also Benjamin, whose theses 'On the Concept of History' (1940) are presented as 'the most weighty critique of the idea of progress held by those who are reckoned in a crudely political fashion as progressives', including, arguably, Vaihinger himself.[255] Once more, the prospect of progress flashes up in 'the reverse image of the false',[256] in Kafka's 'photograph of earthly life', in which alone 'a condition can be envisaged (. . .) in which violence', epistemic or otherwise, 'might vanish altogether'.[257] Hence, Adorno's materialist 'utopia of cognition', which is supposed to emerge from an immanent critique of what he deems to be the false condition (the keyword here is surely 'extinction'), comes to coincide with the 'standpoint' of his 'inverse' theology.

This view can be rearticulated with reference to Kafka's novel fragment, *The Castle* (first published posthumously in 1926), thus allowing us to reprise the thematic arc that took us from Adorno's 'Sacred Fragment', at the beginning of this chapter, to his letter concerning Benjamin's essay on Kafka and, finally, to the question as to whether an 'inverse' theology entails a reversal of the fixed standpoints of humankind and God, respectively. Theologically inclined readers of Kafka – not least amongst them, Max Brod and Hans-Joachim Schoeps, to whom both Benjamin and Adorno are responding more or less directly – view *The Castle* in the following terms, condensed here for the sake of brevity: the castle represents the seat of divine grace, whereas the village at its foot represents the corrupt world of humankind. On this reading, castle and village are separated by an infinite qualitative distinction, manifested in the fact that Kafka's protagonist, the land-surveyor K, is, in fact, never admitted to the castle. By contrast – and this is decisive – for Adorno, this distinction is *collapsed*: 'Precisely that "infinite qualitative distinction" taught by Kierkegaard and Barth', whom Adorno repeatedly cites in connection with Kafka, 'is levelled off'; '*there is no real distinction (. . .) between town and castle*.'[258] That is to say, there is no transcendent seat of divine grace; there is only '[l]ife as it is lived in the village at the foot of the hill on which the castle is built', as Benjamin puts it in a famous letter to Scholem.[259] This maps onto the terms of our discussion thus far. The topographic, indeed, *tectonic* shifts discussed previously in terms of a dislocation of theology mean that the question as to how Adorno can legitimately reverse the standpoints of humanity and God (to speak *as if* he were occupying a fictional 'standpoint of redemption'), as it were, self-sublates. Put differently, if the putative polarity of village and castle is short-circuited, then so is the supposed distinction between the 'standpoints' of redemption and damnation. If 'perspectives' must, indeed, 'be fashioned that displace and estrange the world', then the 'messianic light' in which the world will 'one day' appear need not be progressively approximated; indeed, it need not shine from an outside source at all: it does not require a 'standpoint removed (. . .) from the (. . .) sphere of existence' by however little. Accordingly, Adorno cannot be seen as proposing to inhabit such a position as a fictive u-topos located in 'another world',[260] as Agamben and Taubes suggest. Instead, the 'messianic light' shines from *within* the world, through the 'rifts and crevices' of damaged life, or – as Adorno puts it in 'Notes on Kafka' – through the 'cracks and deformations of the modern age'.[261]

* * *

As I have sought to show, Adorno's singular adaptation of theological motifs can be read in terms of his critique of what, following Benjamin, was called a capitalist cult religion. In turn, the figure of Kafka – at the heart of the exchange between both authors – connects this critique with the ban on images. Both Benjamin and Adorno explicitly associate Kafka with the image ban: 'No other writer has obeyed the commandment "Thou shalt not make unto thee a graven image" so faithfully', Benjamin writes;[262] the mysterious character of Odradek, from Kafka's story 'The Cares of a Family Man' (1919), 'is the sole promise of immortality which the rationalist Kafka permits to survive the ban on images'.[263] This is because Odradek is '*himself* a sign of distortion', or, in our sense, of dislocation, *Entstellung*; 'and, precisely in his distortion', Peter E. Gordon notes, 'he (...) bears witness as a photographic negative to a happiness we have been denied.'[264] This is the sense in which, according to Adorno, 'he' – that is, Kafka – presents us with an inverted image of redemption.

In a different context, Kafka himself makes a striking reference to the image ban when he writes: 'Thou shalt no image –', the motto of the present chapter.[265] The conspicuous absence of the verb in this micro-parable can, I think, be taken to mean Kafka's own sense of the irreducibly self-transgressive character of the interdiction against image-making alluded to in the Prelude to the present study.[266] Accordingly, Werner Hamacher notes, '[t]he prohibition that the sentence is about to express intervenes' quite literally 'into this very sentence', thus making it 'into the fragment of a language that would correspond to the prohibition':[267] an instance of the imageless language spoken by the *intellectus archetypus*. 'By adhering to the prohibition', Hamacher continues, 'the only sentence' in which the prohibition 'could present itself as law', that is, as divine injunction, 'is interrupted'.[268] Accordingly, this auto-interruption of the image ban, which occurs at the level of its own articulation as law – as judgement, even – is presented as a kind of 'gesture': an elusive occurrence 'that opens up this law', and, indeed, *all* law, by interrupting and interceding in the very structure of judgement as such.[269] Such interruption, I argue, is akin to the manner in which Adorno seeks to intimate a mode of 'thinking', and, therefore, of judging that points beyond the sphere of mythic law, 'into *openness*':[270] a staging of the 'wholly other' effected from within without blueprints or guarantees.

3

Aesthetic negativity

Dem destruktiven Charakter schwebt kein Bild vor.[1]

Walter Benjamin

We have already seen some evidence that Adorno's aesthetic works – his texts on music, literature and the visual arts – abound with references to the Old Testament interdiction against image-making. Mahler and Schoenberg,[2] Hölderlin and Baudelaire,[3] Eichendorff and Corot[4] are all discussed in terms of their abidance by the image ban. However, the fullest articulation of Adorno's views concerning the aesthetic implications of this figure appears in his posthumously published *Aesthetic Theory* (1970). This is significant because by the late 1960s Adorno comes to view art as the last vestige of the very metaphysics with which he had declared his solidarity in *Negative Dialectics* at the time of its fall: '[A]rt (. . .), under the impress of its semblance' – *Schein* – is 'what metaphysics, which is without semblance, always wanted to be.'[5] Art, then, means the privileged zone in which resistance to the disenchanted world of capitalist exchange relations remains conceivable, if not positively presentable. Before proceeding to explore this matter further, however, it is worth calling to mind that Adorno's magnum opus remains emphatically unfinished. That is to say, the published version of the text is comprised of extensive notes and manuscripts left by the author and edited posthumously by his wife, Gretel Adorno, and his assistant Rolf Tiedemann. In the absence of a critical edition, however, *Aesthetic Theory* bears the mark of its editors almost as much as that of its author. Any attempt to interpret the work – including the one tendered here – must necessarily remain tentative and provisional.

With this in mind, a central passage from a chapter dedicated to the concept of natural beauty serves to frame the present investigation. Adorno writes:

> The Old Testament ban on images has an aesthetic as well as a theological dimension. That one should make no image, which means no image *of* anything whatsoever, expresses at the same time that it is impossible to make such an image. Through its duplication in art, what appears in nature is robbed of its being-in-itself, in which the experience of nature is fulfilled. Art holds true to appearing nature only where it makes landscape present in the expression of its own negativity. Borchardt's 'Verse bei Betrachtung von Landschaft-Zeichnungen geschrieben' [Verses Written While Viewing Landscape Drawings] (. . .) expressed this inimitably and shockingly. Where painting and nature seem happily reconciled – as in Corot – this reconciliation is keyed to the momentary: An everlasting fragrance is a paradox.[6]

In what follows I propose to approach this passage under two separate aspects. First, having discussed the way in which Adorno treats the 'theological dimension' of the ban on images, it now remains to ask how its ostensibly aesthetic element is to be understood. I take it that any effort to respond to this question will require some contextual groundwork. Accordingly, Part I of the present chapter will situate Adorno in a lineage of modern thinkers – ranging from Kant to Hegel and beyond – all of whom cite the image ban in their aesthetic writings, albeit with divergent emphasis. Given that Adorno was far better acquainted with this tradition than with any properly religious sources, reading him in these terms will provide a firmly non-theological – indeed *aesthetic* – account of how the image ban finds entry into his work, which supplements both the inversely theological derivation from Kafka and Benjamin and the critique of reflection theory.

Part II of this chapter, in turn, will interrogate what the supposed aesthetic dimension of the image ban says about the relationship between art, nature and beauty in capitalist modernity: another prism for figuring the 'wholly other'. In order to gain a clearer sense of what is at stake in the estimation that 'art holds true to appearing nature only where it makes landscape present in the expression of its own negativity', we must consider the polemical thrust of Adorno's decision to cite the image ban specifically in a passage on natural beauty. After all, as we will find, Kant for his part associates the image ban with the sublime rather than the beautiful in nature, whereas Hegel subordinates natural beauty to artistic beauty, the merely real to Spirit, *Geist*. Some questions raised by Rodolphe Gasché in a piece on the concept of natural beauty are instructive in this context. Gasché asks: Why is 'natural beauty the prime paradigm of the beautiful in Kant's aesthetics' to begin with?[7] Moreover, 'what is at stake for Hegel' – writing in the wake of Kant – 'in relegating the beautiful of nature to a secondary role in his aesthetics'?[8] And finally, 'what does Adorno hope to achieve by playing Kant and Hegel off against one another' by trying, we might add, to re-think natural beauty specifically under the aegis of the image ban?[9]

Perhaps one preliminary answer to this question could be phrased as follows: building on the accounts of image and imagelessness proffered in the opening chapter, Adorno's efforts are closely connected to his estimation that '[n]ature, as something beautiful, cannot be copied. For natural beauty as something that appears is itself image.'[10] That is to say the 'portrayal' of natural beauty 'is a tautology that, by objectifying what appears, eliminates it'.[11] And yet – Adorno seems to suggest – art 'holds true to appearing nature' precisely through the 'remembrance' of a reconciled condition, which 'probably never existed'.[12] Quite what is at stake in this confounding formulation will be explored over the course of the following pages.

Part I: Aesthetics

Let us begin by turning our attention to the contextual question raised at the outset: In what sense can Adorno be situated in a lineage of modern German thinkers, including Kant and Hegel, who cite the image ban in their aesthetic writings? In attempting to answer this question two distinct approaches will be taken. On the one hand, this will mean considering two historical sources which were well known to Adorno, and which feature prominently throughout *Aesthetic Theory*, namely Kant's *Critique of the Power of Judgement* (1790) and Hegel's lectures on *Aesthetics* (1835/1842). On the other hand, stock will be taken of a particular episode in the relatively recent reception of Kant's aesthetics during the 1980s, that is, some years after Adorno's death in 1969, namely the work of Jean-François Lyotard. Whereas the former serves to ground the subsequent discussion of Adorno's singular recovery of the seemingly antiquated concept of natural beauty, the latter serves – essentially – as a point of contrast. Although both Adorno and Lyotard aim to derive an orientation for art 'after Auschwitz' from the figure of the image ban, it will become apparent that their approaches differ markedly.

(i) Kant

The first example stems from Kant's *Critique of the Power of Judgement*, specifically from the closing section of the 'Analytic of the Sublime': the 'General Remark on the Exposition of Aesthetic Reflective Judgements'. There, Kant makes the following evocative claim: 'Perhaps there is no more sublime passage in the Jewish Book of the Law than the commandment: Thou shalt not make unto thyself any graven image, nor any likeness either of that which is in heaven, or on the earth, or yet under the earth etc.'[13] But what exactly does Kant mean when he aligns the image ban with the sublime?

The *Critique of the Power Judgement* is often viewed as Kant's attempt to bridge the realms of theoretical necessity and practical freedom (respectively associated with the faculties of understanding and reason), explored in the previous volumes of his critical trilogy: the *Critique of Pure Reason* (1781/1787) and the *Critique of Practical Reason* (1788). Accordingly, Kant emphasizes that 'the power of judgement' – *Urteilskraft* – 'provides the mediating concept between the concept of nature', treated in the first *Critique*, 'and the concept of freedom', treated in the second.[14] In this respect, Kant's third *Critique* rounds off his undertaking with a discussion of judgement as a fully fledged faculty in its own right.

In the most general sense, judgement for Kant means the capacity 'to subsume the particular under the general',[15] to distinguish between 'a' and 'b', 'this' and 'that'. However, as has already been indicated in the previous chapter, Kant differentiates between various different kinds of judgement. For instance, as is well known, for Kant, a 'determinate' judgement 'possesses' a concept which it then applies to 'a multiplicity of spatio-temporal appearances'.[16] By contrast, an 'indeterminate' judgement creates a concept at the same time as it determines whether a given thing is – in fact – 'a' or 'b', 'this' or 'that' and so on. Throughout the first two volumes of his trilogy, Kant's accounts of judgement range from seemingly simple functions, such as the ones cited earlier, to complex questions about the existence of God and the immortality of the soul, for example, in the case of regulative judgements or analogical 'as if' arguments. Hereby, Kant aims to delimit the sphere within which the judgements of philosophy can operate legitimately. Thus, he views himself as laying the ground on which to subsequently build his philosophical system.[17]

The *Critique of the Power of Judgement*, then, 'addresses what was taken for granted in the previous two critiques', namely 'that it was *possible*', without qualification, 'to make theoretical and practical judgements, and set about justifying the conditions for' their 'possibility' in the first place, as Howard Caygill notes.[18] That is to say, the third *Critique* 'inquires into the conditions of the possibility not of discrete theoretical or practical judgements' – what we can *know* and what we ought to *do* – 'but', rather, 'of judgement itself'.[19] Specifically, '[i]t does so by means of an analysis of two particularly problematic', liminal 'forms of judgement', that is, 'the aesthetic judgement of taste', on the one hand, and the so-called teleological judgement,[20] on the other. These judgements have a common peculiarity: they neither possess nor create a determining concept for a given thing. They are, in Kant's phrasing, 'reflective'.[21] One of the reasons that 'reflective' judgements are significant for Kant is that they throw the judging subject back onto its own resources; that is, they operate without reference to externally given concepts. In this regard, both aesthetic and teleological judgements say much about the judging subject's feelings of pleasure, displeasure and purpose, which, Kant wagers, harbour the *a priori* legislating principle of judgement in general. With regard to aesthetic judgements, in particular, then, Kant distinguishes between judgements of the beautiful and the sublime.

'Analytic of the Beautiful'

Kant's main account of beauty is contained in the twenty-two sections that comprise 'Book One' of the 'Analytic of Aesthetic Judgement', the 'Analytic of the Beautiful'. These sections are – in turn – grouped into four 'moments' ('quality', 'quantity', 'relation' and 'modality'), a division that echoes the table of categories from the *Critique of Pure Reason*. Kant assigns succinctly phrased formulae to each of these moments: the beautiful is that which pleases 'without any interest' (quality);[22] it is that which 'pleases universally without a concept' (quantity);[23] it is the 'form of the purposiveness of an object (. . .) without representation of an end' (relation);[24] and, finally, it is 'the object of a necessary satisfaction' that is 'cognised without a concept' (modality).[25] As will become clear, Kant's examples are overwhelmingly drawn from the realm of nature; it is only later in the book – specifically in the passages on 'Fine Art' and 'Genius', §§ 43–53 – that Kant discusses the possibility of an artificial beauty.

In the paragraphs dedicated to the first 'moment' – 'quality', §§ 1–5 – Kant argues that judgements of taste are 'disinterested'.[26] That is to say, they arise without any regard for fulfillable purposes or interests. In other words, if something is deemed to be beautiful, then – properly speaking – the object in question must be pleasing without appealing to any sensible, practical or intellectual 'interests'. The disinterestedness of aesthetic judgement is clarified by way of contrast with two other types of judgement: the 'agreeable' and the 'good'.[27] As Kant argues, the former merely pleases the senses and is thus no more than the expression of physiological 'interests'. Accordingly, such pleasures cannot legislate for an *a priori* (and, hence, universal) principle of judgement. With regard to judgements of the 'good', by contrast, Kant cites a political example: 'In true Rousseauesque style', he argues, 'I might vilify the vanity of the great who waste the sweat of the people' on building 'superfluous things', such as lavish palaces.[28] Indeed, I might expect that everyone should share in my disdain. However, as Kant contends, such judgements remain too closely tied to contingent, worldly concerns – however commendable they may be – to count as pure and thus disinterested.

In the second 'moment' – 'quantity', §§ 6–9 – Kant insists on the 'subjective universality' of aesthetic judgements.[29] Paul Guyer summarizes some of the salient issues running through this section. As he argues, Kant's central thought is 'that in a judgement of taste a person can claim inter-subjective' – indeed, *universal* – 'validity for the feeling of pleasure' that is experienced in response to a beautiful object.[30] This is because such feelings are 'produced, in an attitude of *disinterested contemplation*'; not 'by a practical concern for utility or advantage in the possession of an object' – interest – 'but by the free and harmonious play of the cognitive faculties of imagination and understanding that the beautiful object induces'.[31] Kant claims that our aesthetic judgements are universally valid since, ostensibly, we all share the same cognitive faculties, though this point, in particular, has been seriously (and, on the basis of Kant's own theory of knowledge, legitimately) contested by various standpoint epistemologies in the fields of Postcolonial Studies, Feminism, Disability Studies and so on. Nevertheless, he claims: '[E]veryone (. . .) who experiences an object that we find beautiful should' – at least in principle – 'experience the same pleasure in it that we do.'[32]

In the sections devoted to the third moment – 'relation', §§ 10–17 – Kant makes two claims. First, he asserts that judgements of taste occur strictly in the absence of a concept of an object (in this case, the concept of an object's utility or function). Truly beautiful objects are independent of use, that is, their beauty is 'free' rather than 'merely adherent'.[33] Second, he claims that despite the absence of such an 'objective purposiveness',[34] a beautiful object nonetheless appears to us *as if* it were, in fact, purposive. Hence, Kant famously describes beauty as evoking the paradoxical feeling of 'purposiveness without an end' – pure purposiveness, so to speak.[35] As Kant argues, we take pleasure in the *form* of an object, not in its content[36] – for instance, the play of shapes in a crystalline structure, but not its colour.[37] As Kant will later argue, the formal beauty of an object is testament to its pure purposiveness insofar as it satisfies 'our subjective purpose in cognition' – which is connected with 'our' moral vocation (though, again, the status of the implicit community of viewers remains contested) – but 'without serving any other, more concrete purpose'.[38] Kant cites an evocative example, characteristically taken from the natural world, to illustrate this point: 'Flowers are free natural beauties. Hardly anyone other than the botanist knows what sort of thing a flower is supposed to be; and even the botanist, who recognizes in it the reproductive organ of the plant, pays no attention to this natural end if he judges the flower by means of taste.'[39]

In the fourth and final moment of the 'Analytic of the Beautiful' – 'modality', §§ 18–22 – Kant attempts to substantiate his earlier claim that aesthetic judgements ought, in principle, to be agreed upon by all. To demonstrate this point he introduces the notion of 'common sense' (*Gemeinsinn*).[40] However, as it turns out, the putative necessity of common sense is, in fact, of a highly qualified sort, which Kant describes as 'exemplary' or 'conditioned'.[41] The point, here, is that, in the case of aesthetic judgements (rather than determinate ones), 'we do not have rules that we can mechanically follow, but at most examples that can, especially in the case of art, provide us with models not for imitation but for inspiration.'[42] That is to say, although genuine aesthetic judgements are necessary, they neither rest upon nor produce a *concept* of the beautiful, but rather stem from 'common sense': the universally communicable aspect of aesthetic feeling.

Against this backdrop, Gasché argues that, for Kant, '[t]he beautiful in nature becomes significant in view of the *duty* that man has to himself as a moral being.'[43] This 'duty', we are told, denotes a 'disposition (. . .) to love something (e.g. crystal formations, the indescribable beauty of plants) even apart from any intention to use it'.[44] As Gasché insists, the Kantian 'disposition' to love 'something that is of no use to us' (a clear echo of first moment from the 'Analytic of the Beautiful') denotes a 'sensible feeling that is beneficial' – if not definitive – for 'the formation of morality' and, hence, conducive to the fulfilment of a 'human being's destiny': the establishment of a moral world.[45] This is because, for Kant, beauty – and particularly *natural* beauty – is, in fact, an analogue (indeed, a 'symbol') for morality.[46]

Without wishing to detail the particularities of Kant's position, it is worth noting at least four parallels between beauty and morality outlined later in the book: (1) both please directly and irrespective of consequences or purposes; (2) both are without interest; (3) both entail the idea of a free conformity to law; and (4) both are grounded in a universal principle that does not involve the determining concepts of the understanding. Sidestepping the finer points of these supposed parallels, Gasché continues his questioning: but 'on what *basis* do beautiful things in (. . .) nature', rather than art, 'foster in us this' supposed 'love for things that we have no intention to use'?[47] After all, even if one were to concede Kant's association between beauty and morality, it might be objected that it is not at all clear why a natural phenomenon should be better suited to 'symbolize' morality than, say, a painting or a sculpture. Gasché describes this 'basis' by bringing certain precepts of, both, Kant's epistemology and his moral philosophy to bear upon the third *Critique*. As he recalls, 'only such things (. . .) for which we have no (determinate) concept can be found to be beautiful'.[48] Such things occur primarily in nature because, even where 'Genius' is able to channel the beautiful into art, these products remain mere echoes of beauty's proper place in nature. That is to say, for Kant, '[n]atural beauty' – far more than artificial beauty – is 'intimately tied to the indeterminacy of cognitively unfamiliar and undomesticated' objects.[49] However, it is not their 'indeterminacy' per se 'that makes natural things beautiful', but rather their *form* which 'raises them to the dignity of a thing and' thus 'makes them determinable', at least in principle;[50] and, according to Kant, the pleasure associated with the judgement that an 'undomesticated' thing is beautiful denotes precisely its conformity to our cognitive faculties. That is, the experience of beautiful things in nature 'is testimony to nature's conformity to reason even when no concepts of the understanding are at hand to determine them'.⁵¹ Thus, Gasché concludes, '[n]atural beauty is an index of nature's cognisability', and – inasmuch as Kant holds that 'it is our destiny to make nature knowable' – it thus 'becomes a moral issue'.⁵² In other words, Kant privileges natural beauty over artificial beauty because he views the former as affirming the primacy of reason – a primacy from which, he argues, humanity's moral 'duty', ultimately, stems.

Although Adorno's account of natural beauty will turn out to differ from Kant's in significant respects, his debt to the third *Critique* is clearly considerable. It concerns – above all – the extra-conceptual character of aesthetic judgement. Indeed, natural beauty is related to what Adorno calls the 'non-identical', that is, all that, which is repressed in the historical process. At the same time, Adorno will turn out to be critical of the fact that – on his reading, at least – Kant's account of natural beauty (like much else in his philosophy) ultimately stands to affirm the sovereign reign of reason over nature.⁵³ Bracketing the particularities of Adorno's ambiguous relation to Kant for the moment, it is worth noting that Adorno's particular use of the terms 'nature' and 'beauty' is, in fact, highly unusual. It points back to his cross-reading of Lukács and Benjamin under the aspect of 'second nature', noted earlier. This becomes especially clear in light of his considerations on Kant's 'Analytic of the Sublime', where the aforementioned reference to the image ban occurs.

'Analytic of the Sublime'

In 'Book Two' of the 'Analytic of Aesthetic Judgement', Kant details his thoughts on judgements of the sublime. Broadly speaking, the sublime means the experience of something awe-inspiring.⁵⁴ Specifically, Kant distinguishes between two variants of the sublime: the mathematical (§§ 25–27) and the dynamical (§§ 28–29). Whereas the former means a sense of awe experienced in the face of something 'absolutely great' in size,⁵⁵ the latter means a sense of awe experienced before something with great 'power'.⁵⁶ Kant cites two kinds of examples throughout this section: first, natural phenomena, including 'threatening cliffs, thunder clouds (. . .), flashes of lightning (. . .), volcanoes (. . .), hurricanes (. . .), the boundless ocean (. . .) etc.',⁵⁷ and, second, man-made phenomena, such as the Egyptian pyramids and St Peter's Basilica in Rome.⁵⁸ As will become apparent, however, Kant's examples are not in and of themselves sublime, but rather inspire in *us* a feeling of sublimity, which ultimately affirms 'the superiority of the rational', indeed moral 'vocation of' humankind's 'cognitive faculty' over nature.[59]

To begin with, Kant names three commonalities between the beautiful and the sublime. First, he argues that both are pleasing in their own right, that is, aside from any 'interest' (he cites the example of an awe-inspiring storm to illustrate this point). As Kant suggests, any struggle to save oneself from the 'real danger' posed by such a storm precludes this experience from qualifying as sublime.[60] This is because such an experience stems from a physiological interest in self-preservation, however understandable this impulse may be. As he argues, only if such a storm can be experienced from a position of relative 'safety' – that is, free from the constraints of self-interest – will its sublime force truly be felt.[61] To this extent, the sublime is indeed akin to the beautiful inasmuch as the latter, too, disqualifies judgements made on the basis of sensible, intellectual or, one might add, existential interests. Second, Kant suggests that, as in the case of the beautiful, judgements of the sublime are 'reflective' inasmuch as they concern experiences that exceed humankind's ability to sensibly determine them. And, third, like judgements of the beautiful, judgements of the sublime are said to demand universal assent. In other words, Kant claims that, at least in principle, the feeling of sublimity should be communicable to everyone, given that human beings apparently share the same set of cognitive faculties.

In turn, Kant cites two differences between the beautiful and the sublime. First, he argues that while beauty concerns the *form* of an object, the sublime concerns that which is 'form*less*'.[62] Kant appears to associate two characteristics with this term: on the one hand, he seems to mean phenomena whose appearance is erratic and unstable, for example, storms; on the other hand, he seems to mean phenomena that resist being comprehended in their totality, for example, the cosmos. Second, Kant claims that whereas judgements of the beautiful produce pleasure in the experience of an object's pure purposiveness (its determinability), the sublime – in fact – initially produces displeasure by frustrating our ability to sensibly determine a phenomenon. In other words, Kant claims that judgements of the beautiful stem from a playful and harmonious relationship between the faculties of imagination and understanding, whereas judgements of the sublime initially stem from a frustrated and dissonant relationship between the faculties of imagination and reason. However, his point – in turn – will be to demonstrate how this experience of frustration is recuperated as a certain kind of pleasure.

This conversion of frustration into pleasure, for its part, depends on the distinction Kant makes between the dynamical and the mathematical sublime. Kant initially defines the mathematically sublime as 'that which is absolutely great', that is, 'great beyond all comparison'.[63] Such judgements are occasioned by encounters with objects of an overwhelming size. Kant differentiates between two methods for judging the magnitude of such appearances: aesthetics and mathematics. With regard to the former, he argues that aesthetic judgements of size occur 'in mere intuition (measured by eye)'.[64] That is, judgements like 'this man is tall' do not follow from numerical measurements, but rather from our sense of 'the average magnitude of the people known to us'.[65] By contrast, the mathematical determination of an object's size requires us to employ a particular unit of measurement, that is, a calculation made 'by means of numerical concepts'.[66] Thus, mathematical determinations of size are directed by reason (rather than intuition). As Kant argues, '[f]or the mathematical estimation of magnitude' there is no single *'greatest'* figure, because 'the power of numbers goes to infinity'.[67] Even though the vast expanse of the cosmos exceeds our ability to fathom it intuitively, its parameters can nonetheless be expressed in terms of number – even if such sums defy our ability to imagine them.

Aesthetic judgements of size, by contrast, are limited. Encountering a monumental structure like St Peter's Basilica in Rome exceeds our ability to picture it as a totality. In Kant's view, thinking such a totality (in accord with the faculty of reason) would entail nothing less than determining the noumenal ground of its appearance. Thus, he describes experiences of overwhelmingly proportioned objects that make us aware of the inadequacy of our sensible cognition as 'absolutely great', that is, as 'an absolute measure, beyond which no greater is (. . .) possible', at least for 'the judging subject'.[68] However (and this is the clincher), the discussion of measure is significant because it demonstrates that the power of reason in fact *exceeds* the capacities of both the imagination and the understanding. As Kant writes, '[t]he very inadequacy of our faculty for estimating the magnitude of the things of the sensible world awakens the feeling of a supersensible faculty in us.'[69] That is to say, in Kant's view, mathematically sublime experiences produce a sense of 'respect' in us, which is only improperly attributed to natural phenomena (Kant calls this misattribution 'subreption').[70] The true object of reverence is our faculty of reason.[71] As Kant claims, this insight redeems our sense of dissatisfaction with the mathematically sublime and renders it pleasurable.

In the case of the dynamically sublime, by contrast, Kant observes an irresistible 'power' that apparently overwhelms our sense of free volition, that is, our will (specifically our sense of resistance).[72] To this end, Kant cites the following examples, already noted:

> Bold, overhanging, as it were threatening cliffs, thunder clouds towering up into the heavens, bringing with them flashes of lightning and crashes of thunder, volcanoes with their all-destroying violence, hurricanes with the devastation they leave behind, the boundless ocean set into a rage, a lofty waterfall on a mighty river, etc., make our capacity to resist into an insignificant trifle in comparison with their power.[73]

Kant seems to suggest that, just as our experience of the mathematically sublime begins by showing up the limits of our intuition, so the dynamically sublime initially proceeds by overpowering our sense of agency – our will. The point is as follows: as Kant argues, the dynamically sublime has a comparable relationship to *freedom* as the mathematically sublime has to *totality*. Amongst its other central functions, freedom, here, designates an independence from natural determination, signalling, instead, the rational institution of the moral law. Kant claims that what appears to us initially as an experience of overwhelming natural power, in turn, provokes in our minds an idea of freedom to which our will remains inadequate. This is analogous to the impossible demand for sensibly determining totality issued by our faculty of reason in the case of the mathematically sublime, for example, when encountering the pyramids. As seen previously, in that case the challenge causes us to realize reason's superiority over the merely sensible precisely at the limit of our aesthetic comprehension.

Similarly, in the case of the dynamically sublime, the very emergence of the idea of freedom – occasioned by phenomena that impinge on our will – recalls the fact that our faculty of reason is *super*-sensible, that is, that it is unfettered by natural determinations, however powerful they may be. Hence, Kant writes: '[W]e gladly call' storms, raging oceans and the like 'sublime' – although only improperly so, as noted previously – 'because they elevate the strength of our soul above its usual level, and allow us to discover within ourselves a capacity for resistance of quite another kind', namely resistance to the un-freedom of nature through recourse to our faculty of reason.[74] In this regard, Kant claims that nature's forces in fact have 'no dominion over us'.[75] More importantly, however, Kant views the dynamically sublime as the revelation of our moral nature – as that which, through transcending our sensible selves, seeks to become adequate to the idea of freedom. Reason's demand for the self-transcendence of the will thus relates directly to Kant's central philosophical ambition: attaining the freedom *to* obey the moral law.

Kant' reflections on our experience of the sublime as adumbrating the knowledge of our moral freedom are connected to his reference to the Jewish ban on images. As will be recalled, Kant writes: 'Perhaps there is no more sublime passage in the Jewish Book of the Law than the commandment: Thou shalt not make unto thyself any graven image, nor any likeness either of that which is in heaven, or on the earth, or yet under the earth etc.' In these lines Kant invokes the image ban in order to underwrite his portrayal of the sublime as being unintuitable. As Achim Geisenhanslüke helpfully elucidates, 'the true reason for the imagelessness of the sublime' lies in the fact that 'through the confrontation with a super-sensible power, the faculty of sensible presentation – the imagination – reaches a limit'.[76] As he continues, 'the limit of sensibility, which the sublime shows up by suspending the power of the imagination, becomes the guarantor for the infinite realm of reason', a realm with which Kant had associated the ideas of freedom, immortality and God.[77] As the experience of a certain limit, the sublime thus confronts humankind with its own finitude, not only as a 'negative pleasure',[78] as Kant emphasizes, but as a negative form of presentation (*Darstellung*). As Geisenhanslüke explains, '[w]hat appears in the sublime, the ideas of reason – freedom, immortality and God – eludes sensible form and yet, as something *de facto* unrepresentable, it is indirectly revealed as imageless.'[79]

This point was taken up during the 1980s by the French philosopher Jean-François Lyotard. Lyotard's reading of Kant, for its part, serves as an illuminating foil for the subsequent discussion of Adorno, insofar as he too foregrounds the importance of the image ban.

(ii) Lyotard

Lyotard's spearheading of a renewed interest in Kant's notion of the sublime is significant, in the present context, for the following reasons: (a) Lyotard relies specifically on Kant's citation of the image ban in order to bestow a certain ethical task upon contemporary art, namely to bear witness to the unrepresentable Other of thought (Lyotard is particularly interested in how this plays out in the work of the American painter Barnett Newman);[80] (b) Lyotard draws, for this purpose, on Adorno's much-maligned dictum, that '[t]o write poetry after Auschwitz is barbaric', thus situating himself squarely within the coordinates of the present investigation.[81] Lyotard seeks to transform the putative 'impossibility' of representing particular events – for example, Auschwitz, or, in Taubes and Agamben's terms, 'redemption' – into the grounds for 'an *art* of the unrepresentable'.[82] (Interestingly, Lyotard's enthusiastic reception of Adorno in his later writings comes off the back of an outright hostility towards his work during the 1970s.)[83] Whatever the cause of Lyotard's change of heart may be,[84] his late interest in both Kant and Adorno had an enduring influence on debates concerning what *can* and what *cannot*, in fact, be responsibly (re)presented in and by art. Without wishing to review these questions in their wider context, I take it that there are a number of difficulties associated with Lyotard's attempt to read Kant with Adorno. These difficulties are worth calling to mind before turning to a discussion of *Aesthetic Theory*, inasmuch as they show up, by way of contrast, the contours of Adorno's effort to derive an orientation for art from the Kantian image ban.

(a) In his well-known essay 'Newman: The Instant' (1985), Lyotard offers up an interpretation of the passage from the third *Critique*, which was treated earlier. As he writes,

> [o]ne cannot (. . .) represent the power of infinite might or absolute magnitude within space and time because they are pure ideas. But one can allude to them, or 'evoke' them by means of what he [Kant] baptises a 'negative presentation'. As an example of this paradox of a representation which represents nothing, Kant cites the Mosaic law which forbids the making of graven images.[85]

Indeed, Lyotard's observation resonates with our findings so far. However, he goes on to put a surprising spin on Kant's argument. As he suggests, the Kantian image ban prefigures an *artistic* manoeuvre, namely 'the minimalist and abstractionist solutions' that twentieth-century, Neo-Avant-Garde painters (above all, Barnett Newman) will employ 'to try to escape the figurative prison', which they are said to have inherited from tradition.[86]

Lyotard's verdict follows from his earlier claim that 'for the last century, the arts have not had the beautiful as their main concern, but something which has to do with the sublime'.[87] Whether or not this portrayal of the motivations behind 'minimalist and abstractionist' currents in post–Second World War painting is, in fact, art-historically sustainable cannot be decided here. Rather, we must limit ourselves to the following proviso: Lyotard appears to wilfully disregard the fact that, for Kant, works of art emphatically cannot be considered sublime.[88] The third *Critique* is clear on this point: even when the sublime is experienced in the face of man-made structures – for example, art – it strictly designates a feeling in *us*, not an objective quality of, say, St Peter's Basilica or the pyramids (to stick with Kant's examples). Such qualities appear *as if* they belonged, objectively, to a given structure in a manner that directs our thoughts and actions towards what ultimately counts: the universality of the moral law. This is what sets Kant apart from rationalist aestheticians like his forerunner, Christian Wolff. His point is that, in the experience of sublimity, 'we emerge from aesthetics proper and enter the realm of morality; we are led from the feeling of imagination's impotence to the feeling of humankind's destination in the supersensuous Kingdom – the province of Reason and Freedom – that would impose its rule over the power of Nature.'[89] Of course one must presume that Lyotard is aware of all this. Accordingly, it might seem 'pointless to argue *that*' he 'has misread Kant', as Jacques Rancière contends; rather, it warrants asking '*why* he reads Kant the way he does'.[90]

Answering this question hinges on the uncertain status of the object at the heart of Lyotard's estimation that 'for the last century, the arts have not had the beautiful as their main concern, but *something* which has to do with the sublime'. Without specifying what 'arts' he has in mind here, besides Newman's paintings, Lyotard begins to fill out this lacuna by revisiting Kant's prioritization of form over sensible content in the rendering of judgements of taste. On Lyotard's reading, Kant's notion of 'form' is to do with the 'form*ing*' of 'data' into mental representations – a task performed by the imagination.[91] This is taken to mean 'the most fundamental case of what (. . .) constitutes the property common to every mind: its capacity (. . .) to synthesise data, gather up the manifold (. . .) in general',[92] that is, its capacity for judgement. In the specific case of aesthetic judgements, this means the universal capacity of 'every mind' to derive pleasure from the recognition that – *qua* form – a given representation conforms, at least in principle, to our cognitive faculties (even if no concept is at hand to determine it). As Lyotard argues, the particular content of this 'data' is, then, 'presented as what is *par excellence* diverse, unstable and evanescent'.[93] This characterization raises an important question for Lyotard, which shifts his emphasis from the beautiful to the sublime. He asks: '[W]here does matter stand if', in the case of the sublime, 'the forms are no longer there to make matter' – which Lyotard foregrounds – '*presentable?*'[94] In other words, what is the status of the 'matter' that occasions our experience of the sublime, if it is seen as a mere catalyst for establishing the priority of reason *over* our capacity for sensible presentation (after all, as we have seen, the Kantian sublime concerns precisely that which is form*less*)?

Lyotard's response to this question takes the form of an indictment: the sublime 'signifies that the mind is lacking in nature, that nature is lacking for it', that is, that 'matter' falls by the wayside in the Kantian picture.[95] It signals that Kant's sublime is, in fact, 'nothing other than the sacrificial announcement of the ethical in the aesthetic field. Sacrificial in that it requires that (. . .) nature' – matter – 'must be sacrificed in the interests of practical reason.'[96] Kant's attempt to affirm the primacy of practical reason in the 'Analytic of the Sublime' is thus portrayed as entailing 'some specific problems for the *ethical* evaluation of the sublime sentiment' itself.[97] Hence, Lyotard's misgivings might be summed up in two ways: on the one hand, he argues that '[n]ature' – which is synonymous with matter – 'is "used", "exploited" by the mind according to a purposiveness that is not nature's';[98] on the other hand, he worries whether this 'slippage (. . .) leaves room for an aesthetic' at all.[99] Given these reservations, Lyotard sets out to devise an aesthetic of the sublime, whose ethical commitment is to 'matter', albeit in a highly unusual sense.

First of all, Lyotard focuses his efforts on 'matter in the arts', rather than nature.[100] Without elaborating on his reasons, he states: '[T]he aim for the arts, especially of painting and music, can only be that of approaching matter. Which means approaching presence without recourse to the means of presentation.'[101] This invites two terminological questions: first, what does Lyotard mean by 'presentation' (the Kantian *Darstellung*), and second what does he mean by 'presence'? With regard to the former, it seems that Lyotard means that which can be submitted to the law of the concept, the '*matter* of data'.[102] As he argues, we can determine colours and sounds conceptually, that is, 'in terms of vibrations, by specifying pitch, duration and frequency'.[103] With regard to the latter, by contrast, he appears to mean that which defies conceptual determination, namely 'timbre and nuance'.[104] As he explains,

> [n]uance and timbre are scarcely perceptible differences between sounds or colours which are otherwise identical in terms of the determination of their physical parameters. This difference can be due (. . .) to the way they are obtained: for example, the same note coming from a violin, a piano or a flute, the same colour in pastel, oil or watercolour.[105]

'Timbre and nuance' are thus placed on the side of 'presence', rather than 'presentation', because we register them as being distinct in spite of their identical 'physical parameters'; they are 'present', not in the sense of a 'here-and-now', which could be determined within the bounds of what, for Kant, can be experienced, but rather only to the extent that they proclaim *'that there is'* something.[106]

Registering this 'presence', however, demands that we suspend the 'active powers of the mind'.[107] That is to say, 'presence' (the sense *'that there is'* something) can only be experienced obliquely, 'if we suspend that activity of comparing and grasping, the aggressivity, the "hands-on" (. . .) and the negotiation that are the regime of mind'.[108] Only through such 'ascesis' would it be possible 'to become open to the invasion of nuances, passible to timbre'.[109] Hence, the 'aim of the arts' is to 'become open' to that aspect of 'matter', which defies conceptual presentation: the elusive 'presence' associated with nuance and timbre. The 'fundamental task' of art, in other words, is 'that of bearing (. . .) witness' to the 'inexpressible' 'presence' that proclaims *'that there is'* something, namely 'matter in its alterity'.[110] For Lyotard, finally, the experience of this 'singular, incomparable' quality of art causes a 'passion' in the mind: the sense of an 'obscure debt'.[111] But whose 'debt'? And to whom?

Rancière provides a compelling response to this question when he argues that, 'in Lyotard the tone or the nuance seems to play the same role as the pyramid or the stormy ocean in Kant. They induce a (. . .) break in the mind's capacity to take hold of its object.'[112] However, instead of affirming the *autonomy* of our reason in the face of natural forces, the 'aistheton' – 'matter in its alterity' – 'acts as a shock that induces in the mind the sensation of its radical dependence', its heteronomy.[113] This is the locus of the 'debt' that Lyotard invokes. It means that '[t]he soul comes into its existence dependent on the sensuous, thus violated, humiliated. The aesthetic condition is enslavement' – obligation – 'to the aistheton without which it is anaesthesia.'[114] In short: there is no aesthetic without a debt to the Other. Lyotard thus reverses Kant's terms. Instead of affirming the primacy and autonomy of the moral law, he emphasizes the 'enslavement to the law of alterity'.[115] As Rancière puts it, '[t]he law of ethics is here identified rigorously with a "debt" to an Other. It is the law of heteronomy, the enslavement to the mere, mute alterity of "the Thing" – the power inside the mind and prior to the mind that the mind ever tries to overcome, and never succeeds.'[116]

(b) It is at this juncture that Adorno's pronouncement regarding poetry after Auschwitz comes to bear on Lyotard's idiosyncratic reading of Kant. The hypothesis that art's task is to attend to the call of an un-presentable Other – derived from the interpretation of Newman – is applied to the question of how art can 'bear witness' to the horrific singularity of Auschwitz, on which both Adorno and Lyotard, in their respective ways, insist. As we are told, this attempt 'involves not so much recounting the event' – poetically or otherwise – 'as witnessing to a *there was*' that underlies it.[117] This 'there was' 'exceeds thought, not only through its (...) surplus' vis-à-vis the effort to 'recount' it (Auschwitz is seen as more than can be contained in, say, survivor testimony or historical research); rather, 'the peculiarity of the *there was*' is seen as being in excess of thought's scope *tout court* – it is, in a word, un(re)presentable.[118] Lyotard thus maps his thoughts on the possibilities of sublime art onto Adorno's question concerning the possibility of art after Auschwitz. After all, as has been noted, his emphasis on 'nuance and timbre' serves precisely to articulate a 'presence' that eludes the 'active powers of the mind' by bearing witness to the obscure sense *that there is* something. By the same token, art after Auschwitz is seen as bearing witness to an undetermined *there was* (the shift from present to past tense is striking here).

This view is underpinned by two further suppositions. First, in his book *Heidegger and 'the jews'* (1988), Lyotard associates the alleged debt to an un-presentable other – cited earlier – with a particular historical figure, namely that of 'the jews'.[119] (As will become apparent, this resonates closely with Hegel's association of the sublime with symbolic art and Judaism – a problematic and, by all accounts, unintentional coincidence for the Hegel-critic Lyotard.) Although we cannot presently concern ourselves with the peculiar re-imagining of Jewish history, which allows for this tenuous association, it is worth emphasizing that Lyotard thus credits 'the jews' (whoever that may mean in this context) with bearing witness to the same alleged 'enslavement to the law of alterity', which he otherwise locates in art. Rancière aptly summarizes this point: for Lyotard, '[s]ublime art is what resists the imperialism of thought forgetful' – anaesthetic – 'of the Other, just as the Jewish people is the one that remembers the forgetting.'[120] This analogy is important because – second – the attempted *extermination* of the Jewish people during the Shoah is taken to be the 'end-point of the process of a dialectical reason concerned to cancel from its core any alterity, to exclude it and, when it is a people, to exterminate it'.[121] (To be sure, this reading chimes with the characterization of Judaism proffered by Adorno and Horkheimer in *Dialectic of Enlightenment*. However, as remains to be seen, it ultimately serves a different argument.) It is thus incumbent upon art to interrupt this process, to testify 'not to the naked horror of the camps but to the original terror of the mind which the terror of the camps wishes to erase'.[122] Accordingly, for Lyotard, art 'bears witness not by representing heaps of bodies, but through the orange-coloured flash of lightning that traverses the monochrome of a canvas by Barnett Newman' or, indeed, through 'any other procedure whereby painting' (or another form of visual art) 'carries out an exploration of its materials when they are diverted from the task of representation.'[123]

It is at least debatable whether the 'orange-coloured flash of lightning', which traverses Newman's canvas, can really be called a 'nuance'. Arguably, by introducing the metaphor of lightning, Lyotard inadvertently restores the very mode of representation that he had sought to disavow. Herein lies a wider problem with respect to thinking the sublime artistically: How is one to avoid *representing* the sublime, and hence succumbing to the contradiction of, as it were, positively representing the unrepresentable? At any rate, the invocation of Newman poses a problem for Lyotard's cross-reading of Kant and Adorno:

> Lyotard's schema does quite the opposite of what it claims to do. It argues for some original unthinkable phenomenon resistant to any dialectical assimilation. But it itself becomes the principle of a complete rationalization. In effect it makes possible to identify the existence of a people with an original determination of thought and to identify the professed unthinkability of the extermination with a tendency constitutive of western reason. Lyotard radicalises Adorno's dialectic of reason by rooting it in the laws of the

unconscious and transforming the 'impossibility' of art after Auschwitz into an art of the unrepresentable.[124]

Following the direction of this reading, we can say that the key difference between Lyotard and Adorno appears to be this: whereas Lyotard's concern is essentially *ethical* – to institute art as the custodian of the Other, which can only ever say '*there was*' – Adorno's concern is fundamentally *critical* – to determine the complicity of art and barbarism in the present, while acknowledging that there are no other means for holding fast to the 'promise of happiness' contained in art.[125] Accordingly, it will become clear that Adorno's aesthetics hinge, not least, on his attempt to revive the seemingly outmoded notion of natural beauty (rather than sublimity), whose utopian orientation survives only negatively under the aegis of the image ban. For Adorno, art does not simply say '*there was*'; rather, it attests to the fact that 'art must be and wants to be Utopia (. . .); yet at the same time art may not be Utopia in order not to betray it by providing semblance and consolation'.[126] But before we can finally grapple with this paradoxical idea, it remains to ask how it is that – after Kant – the category of natural beauty (and its putative utopian promise) falls into such disrepute.

(iii) Hegel

Having thus established Lyotard's singular reading of Kant as a foil for the subsequent discussion of Adorno, we now return to the contextual question posed at the start: In what sense do Hegel's aesthetic writings (in addition to Kant's) inform Adorno's effort to rehabilitate the concept of natural beauty? After all, the Kantian themes of beauty and sublimity – as well as numerous references to the ban on images – re-emerge at prominent junctures in Hegel's works, albeit in marked contrast to their formulation in the third *Critique*. Inasmuch as it will be seen that, in the passages on natural beauty, Adorno plays off Hegel's aesthetics *against* Kant's (and vice versa), it remains to sketch the contours of the former in order to gain a clearer sense of what is at stake in this polemic.

Principally, the questions of beauty and sublimity are treated by Hegel in two sets of texts: first, in a highly condensed statement towards the end of his *Encyclopaedia of the Philosophical Sciences* (1817/1827/1830);[127] and second, in the collected transcripts of his extensive lecture series on aesthetics, particularly the edition published by his erstwhile student Heinrich Gustav Hotho (1835/1842).[128] What is of interest, presently, in this connection is (a) the manner in which Hegel prioritizes the beauty of art over that of nature, and (b) what he has to say on the relationship between sublimity and the image ban.

(a) It is worth calling to mind, at this juncture, that Hegel's lectures aim to give a dialectical account of beauty's historical development from its earliest instantiation in nature to its most sophisticated expression in art. All the while, the measure of this process is art's supposedly unique ability to give sensory expression to the central theme of Hegel's thought: the self-development of spirit.

In order to grasp what is at stake here, we must start by accounting for the general dynamic that governs the opening volume of Hegel's lectures. In Part I, Chapter II – on 'The Beauty of Nature' – Hegel gives the following definition: 'The beautiful is the idea as the immediate unity of the concept with its reality, the idea, however, only in so far as this its unity is present in sensuous and real appearance.'[129] Hegel thus aligns 'the beautiful' with 'the idea', that is, with the full actualization of a particular 'concept' in a 'sensuous and real appearance'. As he argues, 'the first existence of the idea is *nature*', that is, 'beauty begins as the beauty of nature'.[130] To the extent that Hegel's account 'begins' with the beauty of nature, however, it is positioned from the outset in view of its sublation into a higher, more thoroughly reflected stage. In other words, natural beauty is figured as part of a larger movement within which the idea becomes aesthetically actualized. Accordingly, '*natural* beauty not only suggests that there is an additional kind of beauty' (art) 'but also, since "first" means abstract, formal, limited, a beauty in which the idea finds a sensible appearance that is more appropriate' to its concept at this 'stage of its self-development', as Gasché writes of Hegel.[131]

Nevertheless, the concept of natural beauty also undergoes an internal transformation. The beauty of inorganic nature, for instance, is judged to be inferior to the beauty of organic nature, which – in turn – is seen as lesser than the beauty of animal life and so on. This progression follows the same dialectical logic that governs Hegel's work throughout. Starting with what is immediately at hand, observing consciousness discovers that what it initially deems to be beautiful is – in fact – deficient insofar as it turns out to be incommensurable with a more emphatic concept of beauty. Concept and appearance do not coincide. Instead, they contradict each other. However, by continually mediating between these contradictory terms, consciousness gradually discovers ever more adequate sensory expressions of the idea, most notably, in the form of classical Greek sculpture.[132] Dialectics, thus understood as the reflexive movement of consciousness through an exhaustive series of partial articulations, procures a series of aesthetic forms whose totality is conceived of as the comprehensive history of beauty – a history that reaches its highest articulation in certain historical forms of art, wherein the beauty of nature is finally fulfilled.

Bearing in mind this cursory account of the general dynamic that leads Hegel from the beauty of nature to the beauty of art, there are two points in need of further elaboration: first, in what sense *is* nature in fact beautiful, however momentarily, given that its eventual supersession has already been pre-empted? And, second, in what sense exactly is nature's beauty supposed to be deficient? As will become apparent, both questions hinge on Hegel's discussion of 'life' (*Leben*).

'The Idea as Life'

In the opening sections of Part I, Chapter II, 'life' is presented as the first instantiation of what Hegel calls the idea. Although elsewhere Hegel discusses this term at length,[133] I take it that – in this particular context – life means, above all, the proto-evolutionary development of biological processes towards the fulfilment of their concept. In other words, Hegel views life as a dialectical process of self-actualization. As he puts it, 'the power of life consists (. . .) in positing contradiction in itself, enduring it, and overcoming it.'[134] The beauty of life, in turn, depends on how successfully 'the harmony and unity' of these moments is expressed in sensual form. What is at stake here, then, is nothing less than the relationship between the spiritual and physical dimensions of life as such. Hegel discusses these in terms of the interplay between body and soul.[135] In Hegel's view, the soul – indeed, 'the Concept itself' – strives towards physical articulation *in* the body.[136] Insofar as they are adequate to one another, nature appears beautiful. As Hegel notes, it is 'at this point' – the first 'stage' of the idea's self-development – that 'we have (. . .) before us as the beauty of nature' an 'inherently ensouled harmony within the conceptually appropriate objectivity of natural productions'.[137] Judging how successfully body and soul harmonize within a given life form allows Hegel to distinguish between higher and lower kinds of beauty in nature. The details of these distinctions need not concern us here. Suffice it to note that animal life is presented as superior to vegetation and inorganic matter partly on account of its 'animation',[138] which is associated with self-determination and – hence – freedom. What interests us here, instead, is twofold. On the one hand, Hegel appears to view the soul as the agent of the creature's self-determination (the unifying principle of life), whereas – on the other hand – he concludes that 'the soul' (and therefore the idea) 'as such *cannot* make itself recognizable' in nature.[139] As he argues, 'when we look at natural forms that' appear to 'accord with the Concept' of life, 'such correspondence (. . .) is' – in fact – merely 'foreshadowed' but never truly actualized.[140] The beauty of nature thus appears deficient. 'The perception of nature as beautiful goes no further than this foreshadowing of the concept' because the immediate 'apprehension of nature remains purely indeterminate and abstract'.[141]

In order to grasp why, unlike Kant, Hegel thinks that the immediate apprehension of beauty in nature remains indeterminate and abstract it is worth considering a specific example. Gasché points to a revealing passage in the lectures, which succinctly captures Hegel's reservations:

> The living thing still lacks freedom, owing to its inability to bring itself into appearance as an individual point, i.e. as a subject (. . .). The real seat of the activities of organic life remains veiled from our vision; we see only the external outlines of the animal's shape, and this again is covered throughout by feathers, scales, hair, pelt, prickles or shells. Such covering does belong to the animal kingdom, but in animals it has forms drawn from the kingdom of plants. Here at once lies the chief deficiency in the beauty of animal life. What is visible to us in the organism is not the soul; what is turned outward and appears everywhere is not inner life, but forms drawn from a lower stage than that of life proper. The animal is living only within its covering, i.e. this 'insideness' is not itself real in the form of an inner consciousness and therefore this life is not visible over all the animal. Because the inside remains *just* an inside, the outside too appears *only* as an outside and not completely penetrated in every part by the soul.[142]

In the context of his aesthetics, at least, the 'freedom' that Hegel alludes to seems to mean a self-determined, animated, 'ensouled' expression of life that is not externally determined. However, as he argues, 'the living thing' – whose process of self-actualization is explored throughout Part I, Chapter II of the lectures – 'still *lacks* freedom', even at this relatively advanced stage of its development (animal life), 'owing to its inability to bring itself into appearance' as a 'subject'. In this context, 'subject' should thus be taken to mean the self-differentiated and self-specifying forms of life.

Accordingly, the beauty of 'animal life' is deficient vis-à-vis 'life proper' for at least two reasons: first, because it is unable 'to bring *itself* into appearance' as a harmonious and hence beautiful unity of diverse moments (i.e. it is not self-determining and, hence, un-free); second, because 'what is visible to us' when we encounter an organism – its 'appearance' – 'is not the *soul*'. Accordingly, 'the real seat of the activities of organic life' remains covered over, 'veiled from our vision'. All we can see are the 'external outlines of the animal's shape', not its 'inner life'. As Gasché observes, '[n]ature itself' thus turns out to be a 'medium in which life cannot unfold its full potential'.[143] This is why Hegel argues that 'the soul *as such*' cannot make itself recognizable in nature.

Although life in nature *is* beautiful at first glance, upon reflection it appears '*only* as an outside' because it is not 'completely penetrated in every part by the soul'. Insofar as body and soul do not coincide here, such nature is not truly beautiful. In other words, the apparent immediacy of the idea's actuality *qua* natural life means that it is beautiful only for others and not for itself. There is something incidental about natural beauty; it cannot be beautiful for itself because it is not the 'active agent of its own shining forth', as Gasché puts it.[144] Put differently, its beauty is not self-produced and consequently it lacks any relation to itself. Therefore, it is only beautiful for the consciousness that apprehends it. The chief deficiency of natural beauty (*qua* animal life) is hence presented as its inability to shine through the externality of its covering – 'feathers, scales, hair, pelt, prickles or shells'. Inasmuch as it cannot break through this covering, the beauty of nature remains abstract and indeterminate, that is, deficient.

However, as Hegel reminds us, the topic proper of his lectures on aesthetics is the beauty of *art*, not the beauty of nature. As he argues, only art is adequate to the idea of beauty. The treatment of nature – the primary existence of beauty – is thus only a preamble (albeit an important one): a first 'stage' in the processual unfolding of the idea, whose adequate sensory articulation occurs in art alone. In contrast to Kant, 'the intimate connection of beauty with life leads Hegel to find beauty first in animate nature, in order then to judge it deficient and to replace it with a higher beauty of man-made art':[145] a product *of* spirit *for* spirit, so to speak. In this regard, the Hotho-lectures in toto can be viewed as charting a comprehensive history of the aesthetic from the idea's most rudimentary articulation in nature to its most accomplished manifestations in art, including its apparent mis-steps, for example, in Romanticism.

Though it cannot be our task here to map out the whole of Hegel's wide-ranging art-historical considerations, we can nonetheless pre-empt that art too undergoes a complex processual development. It is of particular interest then that, following the denigration of natural beauty, Hegel's account comes to include some passages on what he calls Jewish art, which treat the ban on making graven images of God (and the corresponding priority of the word) in terms of the sublime.[146]

(b) Hegel discusses the role of the image ban in the art of Judaism in the following passage:

> [A]rt has above all to make the Divine the centre of its representations. But the Divine, explicitly regarded as unity and universality, is essentially only present to thinking and, as in itself imageless, is not susceptible of being imaged and shaped by imagination; for which reason, after all, the Jews and Mahometans are forbidden to sketch a picture of God in order to bring him nearer to the vision which looks around in the sensuous field. For visual art, which always requires the most concrete vitality of form, there is therefore no room here, and the lyric alone, in rising towards God, can strike the note of praise of his power and his glory.[147]

A detailed reading of these lines will be attempted in due course. To begin with, though, it suffices to note that Hegel anticipates here the subsequent identification of Jewish (and, indeed, Islamic) art with sublimity, rather than beauty. As he puts it later on in his lectures, 'sublimity in its first original character we find especially in the outlook of the Jews and in their sacred poetry. For visual art cannot appear here, where it is impossible to sketch any adequate picture of God; only the poetry of ideas, expressed in words, can.'[148] Accordingly, beauty and sublimity, poetry and the visual arts become the coordinates of Hegel's discussion. Their exact place is determined starting in Part II of the lectures: 'The Development of the Ideal into the Particular Forms of Art'.

The second part of Hegel's *Aesthetics* charts the history of art in terms of its dialectical development through three particular stages: the 'symbolic', the 'classical' and the 'romantic'.[149] Each of these stages is associated with a specific historical epoch and, moreover, with a string of cultures and civilizations whose particular means of relating the form and content of art are explored in some detail. Of these stages, the symbolic is of particular interest in the present context, as it is here that Hegel lays out his views on Jewish art. In order to account for the particular place of Jewish art in Hegel's schema, however, it is worth gaining a clearer sense of what motivates his tri-partite division first.

If Hegel's *Aesthetics* trace the processual unfolding of the idea *qua* sensory expression in art – that is, the harmonious coincidence of form and content – then the symbolic stage marks the earliest, most partial point of this development. In symbolic art, a particular content – the idea – unsuccessfully *seeks* adequate expression in an aesthetic form. (This adequate expression – beauty – is attained later in the classical stage.) There are two reasons for this alleged discordance. First, insofar as Hegel views symbolic art as proper to a particular moment in the self-development of spirit (manifest in certain cultures), and insofar as, according to Hegel, these cultures do not yet fully grasp themselves as free exponents of humanity, it follows that the content of their art – the idea – remains equally deficient. Notwithstanding Hegel's chauvinism on this point, this means – for instance – that the cult objects of various 'nature-religions'[150] *can*, supposedly, be called art to the extent that they seek to give material form to the idea; however, they purportedly fail as art because they *cannot* express this content adequately, since they have only a vague and indeterminate conception of it. Second, insofar as the consciousness under consideration is – in fact – credited with some degree of maturity (as in Hegel's assessment of Judaism),[151] it is said to be unable to express the idea artistically. As David James notes, this is because its 'inner thought' and its capacity for sensory expression have 'become independent of each other'.[152] Either way, instead of coming to a complete identification in the work of art, form and content produce a merely abstract harmony (albeit at various levels of accomplishment). The point in each case is that symbolic art – the standing-in of a form for a particular content – falls short of the concept of art as the self-produced, sensuous shining forth of the idea *in* material form.

'Judaism and Sublimity'

In a digression on Kant's 'Analytic of the Sublime', nested in the section on symbolic art, Hegel gives the following definition of sublimity: 'The sublime in general is the attempt to express the infinite' – the self-determined, unconditioned, absolute idea – 'without finding in the sphere of phenomena an object which proves adequate for this representation.'[153] The analogy with symbolic art is clear: both mark the frustrated effort to materially express an infinite content. In contrast to Kant, however, Hegel does not foreground the sublime feeling stirred by this impasse in *us*, whoever that may be. Rather, he emphasizes the futility of the efforts by the visual arts to materially express such content, which – due to its sheer indeterminacy – is incommensurable with any physical form. Hegel thus reads Kant in such a way as to suggest that sublimity is not so much an affectively experienced limit case of the imagination, as an impossible attempt to sensibly present the ideas of reason by finite means. At the lowest levels of symbolic art, Hegel characterizes these efforts as being unconscious of their own ineffectiveness (hence, Zoroastrianism, for instance, is said to lack the maturity to recognize the shortcomings of its tendency to identify light with divinity).

By contrast, Judaism is singled out as the genuine, that is, self-conscious, expression of the sublime because it renders explicit the relation between form and content that constitutes the essence of symbolic art, namely total discordance. Crucially for Hegel the marker of this schism is the ban on images itself. As James observes, 'Judaism's complete separation of the spiritual content from the sensory form in which it is presented is possible because this content is known independently of that which can be intuited by means of the senses.'[154] Judaism does not locate the divine in natural phenomena, nor does it put art objects in its stead; rather, the image ban marks Judaism's consciousness of the putative fact that the infinite content of art is essentially different from its finite articulation. 'Consequently, although we find in holy scripture and sacred poetry (i.e. the Psalms) a host of (. . .) images of God's greatness and glory, (. . .) the Jewish people were aware', or so Hegel claims, 'that these images could never adequately express the idea of the infinite or unconditioned which formed the true content of their religion.'[155] In this regard, Hegel perceives the Jewish conception of God as being highly advanced; but insofar as it is articulated in lieu of any material expression (besides 'symbolic' poetry), it remains abstract. How, then, is this reflected in the passages cited earlier?

If, as Hegel argues, 'art has above all to make the divine the centre of its representations', then symbolic art is characterized by a particular impasse: the infinite incommensurability of divine content and material form. Insofar as form and content do not harmonize in symbolic art, such art cannot truly be called beautiful. This discordance, in turn, is associated with sublimity (rather than beauty) because it is not susceptible to being imaged and shaped by the imagination. Given Hegel's view that the visual arts seek 'the most concrete vitality of form', expressed – for instance – in the beauty of Greek sculpture, it follows that the sublime formlessness of Jewish art may only appear in the form of poetry – as imageless language.

Notwithstanding the fact that the ritual objects of Judaism are hardly limited to the anti-ornamental, non-figurative kinds of works described by Hegel, his citation of the Psalms is consistent with the overall structure of his argument; it points forward to his ultimate prioritization of the spiritual over the sensory. Something of the ultimate truth of Hegel's system is already supposed to be partially contained at this relatively early stage. After all, at the end of his *Encyclopaedia*, religion and philosophy supersede art as the true exponents of absolute spirit. At the same time, though, the Jewish conception of God is deemed to be aesthetically deficient precisely because it is immaterial. In this respect, it is perhaps unsurprising that Hegel favours the idea of a Christian God made flesh.[156] Curiously, then, to the extent that Hegel identifies Kant with sublimity, he de facto portrays him as a kind of Jewish thinker – the proponent of a partial, abstract truth. Accordingly, we are led to the following preliminary conclusion: although Hegel credits Judaism with emancipating itself from the un-freedom of natural determination by displacing divine content from the physical realm into the super-sensible, he does not think that this is sufficient to make what he calls Jewish art truly beautiful. Only where form and content coincide is art seen as a genuine expression of the self-determined, unconditioned, absolute idea and hence of beauty, freedom and ethical life. Accordingly, Hegel claims, in Judaism, the move to the realm of freedom is not truly achieved, in spite of its radical break with nature.

* * *

In the present context, the salient lessons gleaned from Hegel's lectures on aesthetics are twofold: first, Hegel reverses Kant's prioritization of natural beauty over the beauty of art; second, he proceeds to outline a large-scale account of art's historical development, chronicled from the standpoint of beauty. As has been seen, Hegel's far-flung considerations contain some striking passages on what he describes as Jewish art, whose foremost feature is portrayed as the strict abidance by the biblical ban on making images of God. Hegel then claims that poetry is the only appropriate medium for such Jewish art. This is because the Psalms are supposed to be self-consciously 'symbolic' insofar as they acknowledge that the standing-in of an artistic form for a spiritual content is, in fact, lacking. After all, it was intimated previously, for Hegel art is beautiful only where form and content coincide, as in the case of classical sculpture. Since Hegel deems that the Psalms cannot do justice to God's sheer ineffability, he concludes that Jewish art is sublime rather than beautiful. His aesthetics thus pose a challenge to Kant, for whom sublimity served to affirm precisely those ideas of reason that – in Hegel's view – remain abstract in symbolic art: freedom, the immortality of the soul, God. We have already seen how an aspect of this tension lives on in Lyotard's particular contribution to the sublimity debate; it remains to see now how it plays out in Adorno's *Aesthetic Theory*.

Part II: Natural beauty

As has been seen, the Old Testament ban on making images of God is viewed by Kant, Hegel and, indeed, Lyotard as designating an ineffable sphere beyond (re)presentation – a moment in the relationship between thought and what is variously figured as the unconditioned, absolute, Other. For Adorno, too, the image ban signals something beyond the spellbound sphere of existence, namely the prospective reconciliation with 'that which surpasses all human immanence'.[157] In a word: nature. This utopian impulse is discernible not least in Adorno's singular recovery of the much-maligned notion of natural beauty, which – for its part – depends on the specific way that *Aesthetic Theory* pits certain precepts familiar from the works of Kant and Hegel against each other.

Broadly speaking, this means the following: on the one hand, Adorno plays off Hegel against Kant by arguing that the prioritization of art over nature is an 'immeasurable progress'.[158] (As he contends, pace Taubes and Agamben, Hegel frees art from the constraint of acting '*as if* it were a mere product of nature', thus ascribing a particular dignity to art.)[159] However, at the same time this progression is taken to signal an intensification of the domination of nature outlined in *Dialectic of Enlightenment*. Accordingly, the priority of art is double-coded with respect to Adorno's philosophy of history: art is at once a product of the domination of nature *and* a privileged medium for the critique of this condition. On the other hand, Adorno invokes Kant against Hegel by noting that '[w]hat Hegel chalks up as the deficiency of natural beauty – the characteristic of escaping from conceptual fixity – is', in fact, 'the substance of beauty itself', including the beauty of art.¹⁶⁰

This is significant because the opposition of art and nature appears here as an aesthetic re-articulation of the dialectical tension, explored at length in previous chapters, between the inherently coercive character of conceptual thought, on which we nonetheless depend, and the effort to intimate – immanently – 'a condition (. . .) in which violence', whether physical or epistemic, 'might vanish altogether'.¹⁶¹

It should also be noted that the title of *Aesthetic Theory* plays on the fact that Adorno views the possibility of theorizing the aesthetic as a contradiction in terms. This estimation draws on one of the central insights from Kant's *Critique of the Power of Judgement*, namely that one cannot theorize judgement. All one can do is delimit its sphere of application, its conditions of possibility and the limits of its legitimacy, in order, then, to account for the meaning of particular judgements. That is to say, for Kant, aesthetics is – in fact – a radically *non-*theoretical enterprise. The specificity of the aesthetic object exceeds the possibility of its full conceptualization.

Building on this insight, the contradiction expressed by the title of Adorno's book serves to articulate his position: on the one hand, there can be no *aesthetics* without theory; on the other hand, an aesthetic *theory* is not, in any obvious sense, a theory at all. For Adorno this means that neither aesthetics nor theory turn out to be adequate for an understanding of art. What he proposes instead is a reflection on the inadequacies of these approaches, particularly where they are thought together. In a duly negative-dialectical fashion, Adorno abstains from resolving these contradictions into a positive third term, for example, an ostensibly more suitable discourse about art. In short: for Adorno the significance of art lies precisely in the fact that it eludes theorization while, at the same time, demanding it.

This tension is further reflected in Adorno's analysis of the dynamics internal to works of art, for example, the tension between expression and construction, mimesis and rationality and so on. By confronting Hegel's prioritization of art, conceived of as the sensuous shining forth of the idea, with the extra-conceptual moment from Kant's theory of natural beauty,

Adorno seeks to circumscribe art's 'cognitive character':[162] the highly equivocal sense in which 'the most advanced works of any period'[163] model a particular relationship between nature and culture, subject and object, which were previously described in meta-epistemological terms as a 'Utopia of cognition'.[164] This modelling, however, occurs in the realm of semblance (*Schein*). Accordingly, Adorno writes, '[n]ature is beautiful in that it *appears* to say more than it is. To wrest this more' – 'that which surpasses all human immanence' – 'from that more's contingency, to gain control of its semblance, to determine it as semblance as well as to negate it as unreal: This is the idea of art.'[165]

Adorno's inquiry thus proceeds on several overlapping levels: a philosophy of history that plays out in his aesthetics, an aesthetics that bears the weight of his metaphysical concern with transcendence, and a metaphysics (or, indeed, an 'inverse' theology) that is compounded in a quasi-epistemological model which Adorno associates with the specific 'truth content' of art.[166] These matters will be explored in greater depth in due course. For now, it suffices to note that Adorno's confrontation of Kant and Hegel is more than a mere exercise in the history of philosophy. Rather, *Aesthetic Theory* stages an encounter between Adorno's own historical moment and the preceding 200 years of philosophical aesthetics in order to reappraise the dialectic between the beauty of art and the beauty of nature under the specific conditions of capitalist modernity (after all, *Aesthetic Theory* opens with the verdict that, under such conditions, '*nothing concerning art is self-evident anymore, not its inner life, not its relation to the world, not even its right to exist*').[167]

In the context of the present chapter, this means that if the aesthetic dimension of the image ban can be grasped neither as a limit case of the imagination (Kant), nor as a discordance between divine content and profane form (Hegel), nor – indeed – as an imperative to artistically attest to the forgetting of thought's irreducible Other (Lyotard), then the significance of this figure, for Adorno, might instead be seen as lying precisely in its 'cognitive character', that is, in the 'Utopia of cognition' that it intimates in art. To this end, the remainder of this chapter will consider (i) what motivates Adorno's return to the seemingly outmoded concept of natural beauty; (ii) the manner in which Adorno conceives of the relation between art, nature and beauty in capitalist modernity; and (iii) how Adorno figures the association between natural beauty and the image ban.

(i) In order to understand what motivates Adorno's singular recovery of the concept of natural beauty, it is worth locating his efforts in the wider context of his thought. The following passage from *Aesthetic Theory* is telling in that regard. As Adorno writes,

> Since Schelling, whose aesthetics is entitled the *Philosophy of Art*, aesthetic interest has centred on artworks. Natural beauty, which was still the occasion of the most penetrating insights in the *Critique of Judgment*, is now scarcely even a topic of theory. The reason for this is not that natural beauty was dialectically transcended, both negated and maintained on a higher plane, as Hegel's theory had propounded, but, rather, that it was repressed.[168]

Indeed, as was argued earlier, the emergence of speculative idealist aesthetics has lastingly displaced Kant's prioritization of natural beauty over the beauty of art (for the sake of brevity, we will sidestep Adorno's discussion of Schelling). Although Adorno also unequivocally foregrounds art, he rejects the claim (advanced by Hegel in particular) that the beauty of art has 'dialectically *transcended*' that of nature, both negating it and maintaining it 'on a higher plane'. Instead of attaining a greater degree of articulation in the beauty of art, Adorno argues that the beauty of nature falls prey to 'the hubris of a spirit that has exalted itself as an absolute'.[169] Natural beauty is, in a word, 'repressed'. The Freudian provenance of Adorno's phrasing indicates the general direction of his argument. After all, as has already been seen, one of the central tenets of Freud's thinking teaches that what is repressed must return elsewhere in a distorted form.[170]

Adorno thus brings one of the principal claims from *Dialectic of Enlightenment* to bear on his outwardly innocuous diagnosis concerning the supposed repression of natural beauty, namely that humankind's efforts to free itself from the overwhelming forces of nature tend to relapse into their opposite. As he argues, this dynamic is discernible in the works of Kant, Schiller, Hegel et al.: 'Natural beauty vanished from aesthetics as a result of the burgeoning domination of the concept of freedom and human dignity, which was inaugurated by Kant and then rigorously transplanted into aesthetics by Schiller and Hegel.'[171] To be sure, the references to 'freedom' and 'dignity' chiefly mean *humankind's* autonomy from natural determination, that is, 'freedom from the realm of causality'.[172] This is the sense in which Gasché notes that, in Adorno's view, the fully fledged 'terror that idealist aesthetics exercises by degrading natural beauty' (i.e. 'by depriving freedom from everything that is other than the subject') is part and parcel of the dialectic of reason.[173]

It is true, of course, that Adorno's idea of 'freedom' also has an aesthetic aspect, conceptualized in terms of artistic autonomy. According to Adorno, the autonomy of art has at least two facets: one formal, the other socio-historical. Whereas the former concerns his view that artworks function as ciphers for an emphatic kind of freedom by virtue of the immanent organization of their forms – a point that will resurface in due course – the latter means the institutional circumstances that allow for this function to unfold. Adorno thus narrates the socio-historical conditions of art's independence from traditional cultic functions and time-honoured relations of patronage. Inasmuch as he contends that these conditions follow from the emergence of capitalism, however, 'autonomous art' cannot be understood as being unfettered by its economic setting. As Stewart Martin observes, for Adorno autonomous art is thus 'both a commodity and not, both destroyed by and a product of capitalism, both its critique and its ideology. The artwork is presented as a contradiction produced by capitalism. Commodification is a condition of possibility of autonomous art as well as a condition of its impossibility.'[174] In other words, Adorno is concerned at once with 'the generation of art's autonomy from out of commodification' and with 'the refusal of commodification by a subversive mimesis of it'.[175]

However, in the present context it suffices to note that his concern with natural beauty is primarily motivated by a commitment to that which resists the purview of humankind's physical and intellectual domination over nature. The stakes are high. As Adorno wagers, '[t]he reorientation of aesthetic theory towards natural beauty' aims at nothing less than the 'vindication of what capitalism has oppressed: animal, landscape, woman'.[176] Indeed, as J. M. Bernstein emphasizes, Adorno views capitalism as the epitome of reason's sacrificial logic of exchange: '[T]echnological domination, which is at one with capital in demanding the fungibility of all individuals, is, most literally, mastery over nature (within and without).'[177] That is to say, '[b]ecause Adorno regards art as a counter movement to rationalised domination, he is sensitive to the traditional claims for natural beauty.'[178] Accordingly, the seemingly anachronistic emphasis on natural beauty gains currency in Adorno's rendering. Far from designating a simple opposition of 'good' nature versus 'bad' art or, indeed, 'good' art versus 'bad' capitalism, however, *Aesthetic Theory* seeks to dialectically short-circuit these antitheses: to interrupt the logic that sustains the opposition.

(ii) Adorno's estimation that 'nothing concerning art is self-evident anymore' leads him to conclude that the traditional connections between art, nature and beauty (laid out by Kant, Hegel, etc.) are no longer binding in their traditional forms. In *Aesthetic Theory*, he therefore aims to recast these relationships. As seen previously, Adorno does not share Hegel's view that the beauty of nature is sublated in the beauty of art. By the same token, he does not conceive of artworks as mere stand-ins for everything in nature that is supposed to escape the purview of reason. Nor, for that matter, does he think of 'nature' as a mere repository of authenticity, an original substratum, so to speak. Adorno follows Lukács on this point: 'a pure nature (. . .) that has not passed through social processes of mediation does not exist.'[179] Accordingly, he argues as follows:

> Wholly artifactual, the artwork seems to be the opposite of what is not made, nature. As pure antitheses, however, each refers to the other: nature to the experience of a mediated and objectified world, the artwork to nature as the mediated plenipotentiary of immediacy. Therefore, reflection on natural beauty is irrevocably requisite to the theory of art.[180]

Art and nature are entwined. The dialectic of art 'as the mediated plenipotentiary of immediacy' and nature as the mediate world of convention dissolves their putative antithesis. 'Like the experience of art', Adorno claims, 'the aesthetic experience of nature is that of images', that is, of thoroughly mediated re-presentations.'[181] This is because the notion of a 'pure nature' – an original presentation, so to speak – is seen as an illusion that is retroactively projected from the standpoint of culture. '[N]ature', in the emphatic sense, 'does not yet exist.'[182] Adorno illustrates this point with an implicit nod to the concept of a cultural landscape, a *Kulturlandschaft*:[183] 'The phenomenon of landscape' – an instance of 'beautiful' nature – 'is the result of a process of societal modernisation that includes the division of labour and the social division in labour and leisure time. It is only in leisure that we experience the landscape aesthetically, but this experience presupposes human mastery of nature.'[184] Nature, in short, is only experienced aesthetically as a function of its domination; its beauty follows from its repression. The effort to artistically effect reconciliation between humankind and 'that which surpasses all human immanence', then, does not constitute a *return* to nature conceived of as a storehouse of immediacy. Rather, artworks 'hold fast to the idea of reconciliation with nature by' – paradoxically – 'making themselves completely a *second* nature',[185] that is, by self-consciously laying bare the very artificiality that lies concealed in a phenomenon like landscape. (Interestingly, Adorno cites a number of slightly improbable works by Rudolf Borchardt and Jean-Baptiste-Camille Corot to illustrate this point.)

Adorno's view of the relationship between art and nature might thus be summarized as follows: although the ever-progressing domination of nature has irrevocably cemented the priority of art, art nonetheless 'stands in' for nature precisely where it bares itself as wholly artificial. As Adorno puts it, '[a]rt stands in for nature through its abolition in effigy'.[186] What is of particular interest here is the iconoclastic gesture of an 'abolition in effigy': a standing-in for something that does not yet exist and, hence, cannot be pictured, but which is, nonetheless, abolished.

Adorno's dialectical dissolution of the art–nature dyad recalls his early lecture on 'The Idea of Natural History' (1932). There, the traditional opposition of nature and history (later re-coded as that of nature and art) gives way to the chiasmus that all nature is historical and all history is natural. Adorno thus invites us '*to comprehend historical being in its most extreme historical determinacy, where it is most historical, as natural being, or if it were possible to comprehend nature as an historical being where it seems to rest most deeply in itself as nature*'.[187] On the one hand, this means that nature is rendered historical by dint of being transient (a point that harks back to Benjamin's account of baroque allegory in his ill-fated study on the *Origin of the German Trauerspiel*, 1928); on the other hand, it means that history is rendered natural by dint of being conventional (an allusion to the concept of a second nature from Lukács's *Theory of the Novel*, 1916). Adorno's question, in turn, is how to 'interpret' the 'alienated, reified, dead world' of second nature so as to break its spell.[188] In the present context this translates as: How are we to 'interpret' the aesthetic experience of nature (whose proper place is, paradoxically, in art) if the beauty of nature is a function of its domination? In other words, how can works of art, the 'mediated plenipotentiaries' of nature, hope to 'step outside of themselves' – 'into the open', as Adorno elsewhere puts it with a nod to Friedrich Hölderlin – if such a beyond (nature *qua* nature) 'does not yet exist'?[189]

The promise of natural beauty

There are three aspects of *Aesthetic Theory* that are helpful in formulating a possible response to the aforementioned question. They concern the following: (a) Adorno's notion of a *promise* of natural beauty, (b) his conviction that this promise is fulfilled through *remembrance* and (c) his particular view of the *language* in which this promise is supposed to be articulated. Clarifying these terms will provide a sense of how Adorno conceives of the relationship between art, nature and beauty in capitalist modernity, allowing us to finally revisit the passage concerning the aesthetic dimension of the image ban quoted at the start of the present chapter.

(a) First, then, Adorno argues that art throws into relief what the aesthetic experience of nature 'promises',[190] namely the aforementioned reconciliation with 'that which surpasses all human immanence'. In this respect, art is seen as paradoxically prefiguring 'Utopia as the harmony between humankind and nature', as Alfred Schmidt puts it.[191] As Adorno argues, art 'wants to keep nature's promise',[192] the unassailable *promesse du bonheur* once strikingly summoned by Stendhal;[193] however, it can do so only obliquely – 'by breaking that promise' – lest it betray the Utopia it presages.[194] After all, as already noted repeatedly, Adorno insists emphatically that 'one may not cast a picture of Utopia in a positive manner'; 'one can only talk about Utopia in a negative way.'[195] Instead of pleasing without interest, as it were, the promise of natural beauty 'rubs on a wound'.[196] It signals a 'longing for what beauty promises but never unveils'.[197] The experience of natural beauty, in other words, is eminently negative. Pace Kant and Hegel, its watchword is dissonance, not harmony. Dissonance – 'the technical term for (...) what aesthetics (...) calls ugly' – registers the discord between humankind and nature in capitalist modernity, just as suffering registers the non-identity between subject and object in *Negative Dialectics*.[198] Accordingly, the 'promise' of natural beauty – 'the harmony between humankind and nature' – appears *ex negativo* in those modern works of art that most obstinately refuse to yield to the dictate of harmony.

(b) The second point worth noting here is that, in Adorno's view, 'the reorientation of aesthetic theory towards natural beauty' is a labour of recovery: an 'attempt to do justice to that which falls victim to the ever-progressing (. . .) domination of nature'.[199] Such justice, Adorno asserts, is carried out 'symbolically';[200] its instrument is 'remembrance'.[201] But Adorno's quasi-Proustian appeal to memory is ambiguous. On the one hand, he writes that 'humanity becomes aware in art of what rationality has erased from memory',[202] that is, all that is affective, somatic and (apparently, at least) irrational. In this regard, Adorno appears to come close to Lyotard for whom art is precisely 'what resists the imperialism of thought forgetful of the Other'; but unlike Lyotard, Adorno does not locate art's task primarily in the ethical imperative to bear witness to this forgetting; nor does the Other positively predate the dialectic of enlightenment in a way that invites fantasies of returning to it. Insofar as Adorno deems that 'art must be and wants to be Utopia', his notion of 'remembrance' is paradoxically both retrospective and prospective. To be sure, art 'recollects a world without domination'; however, as he contends, such a world 'probably never existed'.[203] Simon Jarvis puts this in the following terms:

> Adorno, in effect, is speculatively rewriting the oldest maxim of aesthetics. Art imitates nature: but nothing like 'nature' exists as yet: art imitates what does not yet exist. For Adorno it can be said that all authentic art is a mimesis of Utopia – yet this mimesis can be carried out only negatively. Art cannot provide an explicit image of Utopia. The possible 'nature' which does not yet exist can only be imitated by the determinate negation of the falsely naturalised culture which does exist.[204]

The 'vindication of what capitalism has oppressed', then, lies not so much in bearing witness to the forgetting of an immemorial Other in a gesture of imagined homecoming as it lies in the conviction that even past injustices can be redeemed through criticism of the present – a criticism carried out for the sake of the future whose contours remain uncertain. To this extent, Adorno's thought evinces distinctly messianic traits.

(c) Finally, the third point worth noting here is to do with what was previously signposted as art's 'cognitive character'. In a striking passage from a lecture dated 2 December 1958, Adorno writes that what 'becomes audible in works of art is the *voice* of the victim', which might be taken to mean the voice of nature.[205] It is no coincidence, perhaps, that the notion of the voice recalls another prominent vocal metaphor from elsewhere in Adorno's work, namely the scream. As he writes, '[p]erennial suffering has as much right to expression as a tortured man has to scream.'[206] Although the metaphor of the voice, as a figure of embodiment, sits somewhat uneasily alongside Adorno's more sight-based assertion that nature appears in the form of images, it is nonetheless significant to the extent that it designates what he describes as art's 'language-like' character,[207] which – in turn – is connected to its 'logicality'.[208] Artworks *speak*. They seek to express 'what has become opaque to humans in the language of nature';[209] but insofar as nature 'does not yet exist', that which becomes audible in works of art cannot be grasped as a simple summoning-forth of the 'voice of the victim', as though it resounded – however diffusely – through the recesses of memory. Rather, as previously, such remembrance means paradoxically projecting forward the utopian model of a 'nonconceptual, nonrigidified significative language', a particular mode of judgement, in terms of which something like nature may yet become conceivable.[210] As Adorno stipulates, such a language – the language of art – would be 'incommensurable with all communicative language';[211] it would be, in a word, 'mute'[212] or 'pure', to borrow Benjamin's term.[213] We are thus faced with two contrasting conceptions of language: one 'communicative', that is, propositional, declarative and conceptual, the other artistic, that is, 'nonconceptual', non-significational and 'mute'. Adorno's paradoxical claim thus appears to be that the muteness of art is 'the single medium through which nature speaks'.[214] Such a 'medium', in turn, is not supposed to subject what it names to the operations of a language that violently subsumes difference under larger conceptual rubrics.[215] In this respect the two divergent modes of language, in fact, designate two divergent modes of thought: one connected with the ills of conceptual cognition, which Adorno associates with the domination of nature (what he calls 'identity-thinking');[216] the other connected with the metaphysical 'gesture of stepping out into the open' – into a realm where nature and culture could conceivably be reconciled.[217] Bracketing the former for a moment, Adorno frames the latter by use of a syntactical analogy: the work of art becomes 'like language in the development of the connection of its elements, a wordless *syntax*'.[218] Adorno puts this in Kantian terms: insofar as works of art are quasi-syntactical, they bear a structural likeness to certain forms of judgement. As Bernstein explains,

> [A]rtworks are synthetic wholes; they synthesise a manifold. (. . .) This unifying endeavour is the work of reason in art, art's logicality and

conceptuality, and hence the sense in which artworks are judgement-like. Nonetheless, artworks are not judgements and this is in part because their syntheses occur through the medium of artistic 'form' rather than through concepts, propositions and syllogisms. (. . .) For Adorno everything turns on form's proximity to conceptuality in terms of its synthesising function, and its distance from conceptuality, in its restraint, its not subsuming the elements of a work in it or under it, and hence its not providing for conceptual determinacy or closure.[219]

Art, in other words, is *like* the philosophical language of judgement insofar as it 'synthesises a manifold' of materials *qua* form; however, it is *unlike* the philosophical language of judgement insofar as its syntheses do not subsume their compositional materials in a manner that curtails their irreducible particularity. Formally accomplished works of art 'speak' in terms of 'judgementless'[220] (*urteilslos*) judgements, which model a relationship between their elements that might be described as the 'state of differentiation without domination'[221] invoked at the beginning of the present study. Put differently, they are the paradoxical expressions of an 'uncoercive gaze', to borrow Gerhard Richter's term.[222] That is to say, art enacts Utopia negatively and in full awareness of its un-reality. Adorno explains this in the following terms: 'The question of the truth of something made' – art – 'is indeed none other than the question of semblance', *Schein*,

> and the rescue of semblance as the semblance of the true. Truth content cannot be something made. Every act of making in art is a singular effort to say what the artefact itself is not and what it does not know: precisely this is art's spirit. This is the locus of the idea of art as the idea of the restoration of nature that has been repressed and drawn into the dynamic of history. Nature, to whose imago art is devoted, does not yet in any way exist; what is true in art is something nonexistent.[223]

What remains unclear, however, is how Adorno negotiates the relationship between these two divergent cognitive–linguistic registers. If 'what becomes audible in works of art is' indeed 'the voice of the victim' and if this 'victim' is in fact nature; if, in turn, art is the 'medium through which nature speaks' (even though nothing like nature exists as yet) and the language of art is, 'judegementless', 'mute'; and if – finally – this muteness intimates a form of 'wordless syntax' that 'symbolically' models a prospective reconciliation between nature and culture as self-conscious semblance, then the following question arises: How can Adorno invoke such a Utopia without transgressing against the ban on positively schematizing it?

Adorno's response to this question directs us back to the beginning of the present chapter. It follows from his estimation that 'nature is beautiful in that it appears to say more than it is'. As he writes:

> Artworks become artworks in the production of this more; they produce their own transcendence, rather than being its arena, and thereby they once again become separated from transcendence. The actual arena of transcendence in artworks is the nexus of their elements. By straining toward, as well as adapting to, this nexus, they go beyond the appearance that they are, though this transcendence may be unreal. (...) Their transcendence is their eloquence, their script, but it is a script without meaning or, more precisely, a script with broken or veiled meaning.[224]

Notwithstanding the increasingly dense cluster of metaphors with which Adorno frames art's enigmatic emanations – image, voice, script – his argument follows a familiar pattern: artworks hold true to the promise of natural beauty where they break this promise; they do justice to what is oppressed in nature by standing-in for it in effigy; they render audible the voice of nature by falling silent and so on. The relationship between the two cognitive–linguistic models under discussion here is no exception. Insofar as the 'actual arena of transcendence in artworks is the nexus of their elements', and insofar as these elements are resolutely of this world, the 'more' that artworks intimate does not require them to be removed – 'even though by a hair's breadth'[225] – from the scope of existence. 'Transcendence', once again, is intimated negatively. Its 'arena' is aesthetic immanence.

(iii) With all the requisite tools in place, it is now finally possible to revisit the passage cited at the outset of this chapter, where Adorno speaks of the 'aesthetic dimension' of the image ban. As will be recalled, Adorno writes the following:

> The Old Testament ban on images has an aesthetic as well as a theological dimension. That one should make no image, which means no image *of* anything whatsoever, expresses at the same time that it is impossible to make such an image. Through its duplication in art, what appears in

nature is robbed of its being-in-itself, in which the experience of nature is fulfilled. Art holds true to appearing nature only where it makes landscape present in the expression of its own negativity. Borchardt's 'Verse bei Betrachtung von Landschaft-Zeichnungen geschrieben' ['Verses Written Whilst Contemplating Landscape Drawings'] expressed this inimitably and shockingly. Where painting and nature seem happily reconciled – as in Corot – this reconciliation is keyed to the momentary: An everlasting fragrance is a paradox.

As already noted, Adorno's assertion that 'the Old Testament ban on images has an aesthetic ... dimension' is borne out by the fact that this motif appears repeatedly throughout the history of German philosophical aesthetics, not least in the works of Kant and Hegel. Against this backdrop, the commandment that one *should* not make an image 'of anything whatsoever' (least of all God) might appear as a variant of an old art-philosophical question concerning mimesis: By what means can 'anything' be represented? But Adorno's phrasing is more emphatic. It points beyond a concern with mere representational commensurability. 'That one should make no image ... *of* anything whatsoever, expresses at the same time that it is impossible to make such an image.' Adorno proceeds to narrow his focus. The alleged impossibility of making any image 'whatsoever' is measured against the specific sense in which art depicts nature. As Adorno writes, 'through its duplication in art what appears in nature is robbed of its being-in-itself.' At first glance this verdict appears to chime with Adorno's earlier assertion that nature itself appears in the form of 'images', that is, that art's 'duplication' of nature amounts to little more than a mere tautology. However, upon closer examination this view is complicated by Adorno's claim that 'nature, to whose imago art is devoted, does not yet in any way exist'. Adorno thus appears to present two contrasting views of the mimetic relation between art and nature: one based on duplication, the other on a kind of projection.[226]

With regard to the former, it is striking that Adorno emphasizes 'what *appears* in nature'. This appearance – '[w]as an Natur er*schein*t' – is of particular interest inasmuch as 'appearing' (*erscheinen*) already contains the very notion of *Schein* (semblance) that Adorno associates with art's paradoxical claim to transcendence, its projection of a nature that 'probably never existed'.[227] (The echoes of both Kant and Hegel's distinctive uses of the terms *Schein, scheinen, Erscheinung* and the like are unmistakable here.) The 'experience of nature'

– its fulfilment, no less – hinges on the indeterminate 'what' at the heart of this formulation. 'What' appears *in* (or, rather, *of*) nature is 'robbed' of its 'being-in-itself' through duplication, which signals closure and a prematurely declared state of self-identity rather than openness. With regard to the latter, in turn, Adorno argues that 'art holds true to appearing nature only where it makes landscape present in the expression of its own negativity'.[228] He provides the context for this line by citing Borchardt's 'Verses'[229] and Corot's landscape paintings. His conceit appears to be that Borchardt and Corot's respective renditions of 'landscape' (be they poetic, graphic or painterly) 'hold true' to that which appears in nature – its promise, its voice, its script – through an expression of their own 'negativity': melancholic muteness.

This is curious, not least in light of Adorno's characterization of 'landscape' as a cultural construct: *Kulturlandschaft*. What does it mean, then, for art to 'make landscape present in the expression of its own negativity'? Adorno gives some indication hereof in the following lines: '[P]erhaps the most profound force of resistance stored in the cultural landscape is the expression of history that is compelling, aesthetically, because it is etched by the real suffering of the past.'[230] Landscape is thus placed under the banner of Adorno's idea of 'natural history': 'The cultural landscape, which resembles a ruin even when the houses still stand, embodies a wailful lament that has since fallen mute.'[231] That is to say, art's immanent organization of forms – its 'wordless syntax' – gives a voice to nature's mute lament by appearing to say 'more than it is', even if the impression of this 'more' is necessarily both fleeting and illusory. The 'profound force of resistance' that allows Adorno to associate the image ban with natural beauty (rather than sublimity), in turn, is memorably described in a lecture, dated 18 November 1958. Herein Adorno writes,

> In this feeling of resistance against mere existence lies the Utopia that this existence doesn't have the last word. And this imageless image of Utopia, this expression of a Utopia that does not pronounce itself, but which rather appears only through the sense that something is stronger (. . .) than the world as it is: this (. . .) is one of the categories of which I should like to think that it is characteristic for the beautiful in general.[232]

Accordingly, 'the profound force of resistance' that Adorno ascribes to certain artistic renditions of landscape lies in their particular ability to negatively intimate an 'imageless image of Utopia' as something beautiful. To be sure, the sense that there is 'something stronger . . . than the world as it is' recalls a central tenet of the Kantian sublime – the affirmation of humankind's supersensible reason vis-à-vis the overwhelming force of nature. However, Adorno's point here is precisely not to affirm the sovereign reign of reason over nature, but rather to challenge it through a feeling of resistance. To encounter Corot's painting or Borchardt's poetic rendering of a 'natural' scene; to experience this scene as beautiful in the highly qualified sense described earlier; to heed the self-conscious artificiality of this beauty as an expression of 'negativity'; to sense that this 'negativity' – the landscape's 'wailful lament' – awakens a 'feeling of resistance' against the ills of enlightenment reason: this and nothing less is what Adorno hopes to accomplish by the seemingly innocuous manoeuvre of tying the image ban to beauty, rather than sublimity. The 'imageless image of Utopia', which is 'characteristic for the beautiful', thus appears as the nodal point of his philosophy: an inversely theological materialism of the suffering body whose subversive workings are borne out in art.

Reprise

'Zum Ende'

'Ein Zeichen sind wir, deutungslos,
Schmerzlos sind wir und haben fast
Die Sprache in der Fremde verloren.'[1]

Friedrich Hölderlin

One could conceivably repeat the argument outlined in the preceding chapters *ad libitum* – for instance, with reference to Adorno's nascent ethics, say, or his philosophy of language: to push, from within, against the boundaries of an established discourse in the hope that the order of knowledge in question may overreach in such a way that its terms collapse under the weight of critical scrutiny, namely in a manner that allows for their radical reconfiguration. In each case, the particular outcome of this operation cannot be pre-empted; and nonetheless, the general movement of Adorno's dialectic is, in the first instance, *prospective*. Once stripped of its theological associations, the image ban is significant, in this respect, because it marks a space for something categorically different to appear; not as a fully-formed incursion from a transcendent beyond, but as a surplus bursting forth from the sum of immanently unworked parts, or – put differently – from what remains when a historical form of reason is found lacking vis-à-vis its own emphatic concept. For this reason, Adorno's references to the image ban often occur at the end of his disquisitions, when the internal contradictions in a given set of terms are supposed to have been shown up, and the conditions for the emergence of something else are thus presumed to have been delineated – however provisionally.

What Adorno intimates at these junctures seems to be something like Utopia, variously figured as a 'state of differentiation without domination',[2] as 'harmony between humankind and nature',[3] as 'undeluded happiness, including bodily pleasure'[4] and so on. However, for the Adorno of the 1960s, the utopian actualization of philosophy in this manner is historically 'blocked off'.[5] Hence, the Utopia in question is of the most qualified sort: it appears only obliquely. In other words, Adorno's Utopia has no positive content; it is not waiting, ready-made, elsewhere. Consequently, the prefix *u*, which is supposed to render the location of Utopia uncertain, is, in fact, still too positive. Adorno's position is better characterized as an *a*-topia, and, hence, not as a regulative ideal to which thought is always underway, because Utopia already exists elsewhere. To change the historical conditions at the heart of his much-maligned diagnosis of a 'blockage' that prevents humankind from reaching this topos, Adorno assumes a methodological self-consciousness akin to that of the young Marx: a practice based on the 'ruthless criticism of all that exists', not least of all philosophy itself.[6] It is true that, in the end, Adorno places the burden of this task not on philosophy, as such, but on autonomous works of art, which perform the labours of philosophy in a different register. Art is, ultimately, said to model, negatively, in the mode of a paradoxical remembrance, what philosophy *ought* to yield: a way of apprehending and inhabiting the world that would finally be free from violence and coercion. In this regard, Adorno's dialectic is *retrospective*: it seeks the *restitutio ad integrum* of something that has never existed. The paradoxically prospective–retrospective temporality of the non-space intimated by Adorno thus appears as follows: 'Not forward: under the law of the present', as Adorno puts it in a discussion of Hölderlin's *Mnemosyne* (1803), which, he argues, entails a 'taboo against abstract utopia (. . .) in which the theological ban on graven images (. . .) lives on'; '[n]ot backwards: because of the irretrievability of something once overthrown'.[7] Adorno's writings thus seek to stage this paradoxical movement at the level of its own presentation: as an interruption of what merely is. This much, I hope, has become clear.

* * *

I take it, then, that this description of Adorno's project also applies to what might be termed his 'politics'. Politics, in this connection, does not principally mean the narrow sphere of governance or administration, nor even the more emphatic sphere of commitments to particular struggles, of which Adorno surely had many (in addition to his critique of Nazism, his remarks on the Vietnam War, South African Apartheid and the European Student movements come to mind). Rather, politics, here, means a manner of delineating the epistemic, ethical and aesthetic conditions under which a life free from domination might become conceivable – in the caesura (to borrow Hölderlin's term) opened up through the labour of critique.[8] These conditions, once more, cannot be pre-empted; they do not mark the anticipatable *telos* of an Adornian politics. Rather, they must emerge tacitly from the immanent recalibration of 'everything that exists' – from the subject–object relation to the nature–culture dyad. Adorno's politics, in other words, is coterminous with his un-working of existing philosophical positions, say, the manner of subsuming particulars under universals in thought, which is supposed to be at one with the operations of capitalist exchange, the putative mastery over internal and external nature and so on. Ultimately, anything short of disrupting this nexus – however desirable the short-term outcomes may be – perpetuates the status quo and, hence, falls into the domain of a certain pseudo-praxis. This circumstance, in turn, has consequences, both, for the reception of Adorno's writings and for their actuality.

With regard to the former, the most enduring criticism of Adorno's politics concerns his supposed resignation, that is, his presumed turn away from what is variously presented as viable forms of praxis or normatively justifiable modes of argumentation. For all their differences – and surely there are many – this view is common to some of Adorno's most prominent critics: from representatives of the German student movement (above all, his erstwhile student, Hans-Jürgen Krahl) to second-generation Frankfurt school thinkers (notably, Habermas), and latter-day political theologians (not least amongst them, Taubes and Agamben). After all, Krahl argues that Adorno's critical theory 'moved more and more away from historical praxis', for example from the concrete struggles embodied by the student movement, towards 'traditional forms of contemplation', inaction, 'which', Krahl argues, 'could hardly be justified'.[9] Adorno's politics is thus seen as lacking because it does not – apparently – make the all-important transition to revolutionary action. Likewise, for Habermas, speaking from a very different position, Adorno's mode of contemplation forfeits the prospect of 'emancipation'[10] because his account of reason's 'self-destruction' is taken to be total; that is, for the purposes of its own exposition, 'it still has to make use of the critique that has been declared dead.'[11] Accordingly, Habermas presents the whole of Adorno's mature thought as a 'continuing explanation of why we have to circle about within this *performative contradiction*'[12] instead of entering into the arena of politics, conceived of as the well-reasoned ground of inter-subjective communication. Adorno's politics is thus seen as lacking because it suffers from a normative deficit. Finally, and in spite of their evident distance from both Krahl and Habermas, Taubes and Agamben, too, view Adorno's philosophy as being radically 'impotential',[13] 'Shmontses',[14] because his account of a 'wholly other' is supposed to be *merely* regulative, thus, apparently, rendering his idea of emancipation constitutively unattainable. On this reading, then, his politics appear utopian in the pejorative sense: empty.

With this in mind, I'd like to conclude with the following thought on the political actuality of Adorno's thinking. There is a sense, I think, in which Adorno's negative dialectic is, both, *less* and *more* political than his critics suggest – at least if one views politics in the terms that they propose: as the activist modification of the status quo through the use of ostensibly just means for the attainment of desired ends, for example, though strike action for the improvement of working conditions (Krahl); as the negotiation of such modifications in a public sphere through recourse to the supposed power of the better argument, for example, through parliamentary debate for the attainment of cross-factional consensus (Habermas); or as the gradual approximation of an unknowable form of divine community, for example, through recourse to regulative modes of judgement for acting 'as if' the kingdom of God were at hand (following the characterization of Adorno's position by Taubes and Agamben).

Adorno's 'standpoint' is *less* political than these examples demand because it neither contains a blueprint for revolutionary action or inter-subjective communication, nor – indeed – for the approximation of a fully formed (political) ideal.[15] At the same time, Adorno's 'standpoint' is *more* political than his critics allow because the transformations it entails are, in fact, of the most emphatic sort. Herein, I argue, lies the actuality of Adorno's thinking. Politics, in this regard, means nothing less than, paradoxically, seeking to present the un-presentable topos on which the re-articulation of *all* existing relations might yet become possible. It means thinking what 'would have to be done so as to (...) think thinking differently', as Jacques Derrida put it in reference to Adorno:[16] to think, from the inside out, the conditions of possibility for 'synthesis of a different kind', not least as this might apply to a different kind of *polis*.[17] Hence, Adorno's remark that politics would be 'the realization of universality in the reconciliation of differences'.[18] Such reconciliation, finally, would be the 'vindication' of what historical forms of identity thinking have 'oppressed', in Adorno's terms: 'animal, landscape, woman'.[19] Such a conception of politics, however, hinges, in the first instance, on its own mode of presentation; and if, as I have argued, the figure of the image ban is Adorno's formula for this point from which 'what would finally be different' might yet erupt into the present, then it faces quite a different threat than that of melancholic resignation, namely the threat of ossifying into a mere image, an idol.[20]

Notes

Prelude

1 'The children have no future. They are afraid of the whole world. They do not make themselves an image of it; they only picture hopscotch squares, for they can be delimited in chalk.' Ingeborg Bachmann, 'Jugend in einer österreichischen Stadt', in *Werke, Bd. 2: Erzählungen*, ed. Christine Koschel, Inge von Weidenbaum and Clemens Münster (Munich: Piper, 1980), 86–7; my translation.
2 Schoenberg composed the first two acts of his opera between 1930 and 1932 before his re-conversion to Judaism and his forced emigration to the United States in 1933. Schoenberg reportedly omitted the second 'a' in his spelling of Aron because the amount of letters in the title would have otherwise tallied thirteen – a bad omen, in his view. The English translators of Schoenberg's libretto apparently did not share his concern. Cf. Allen Shaw, *Arnold Schoenberg's Journey* (Cambridge, MA: Harvard University Press, 2002), 148.
3 Adorno, 'Sacred Fragment: Schoenberg's "Moses und Aron"', in *Quasi Una Fantasia: Essays on Modern Music*, trans. Rodney Livingstone (London: Verso, 1992), 225.
4 Cf. Barton Bryg, 'Musical Modernism and the Schoenberg Films', in *Landscapes of Resistance: The German Films of Danièle Huillet and Jean-Marie Straub* (Berkeley: University of California Press, 1995), 139–63.
5 Exod. 31.18.
6 Arnold Schoenberg, 'Moses and Aaron (Act Two, Scene Two)', in *Schoenberg's 'Moses and Aaron', with the Complete Libretto in German and English*, ed. Karl Wörner, trans. Paul Hamburger (London: Faber & Faber, 1963), 161.
7 Ibid.
8 Ibid.; my emphasis.
9 Ibid., 169; original emphasis.
10 Ibid., 173; original emphasis.
11 Ibid., 174; original emphasis.
12 Ibid., 177; original emphasis.
13 Ibid; original emphasis.

14 Ibid., 179; original emphasis.
15 Exod. 32.19-20.
16 Exod. 32.31.
17 Schoenberg, 'Moses und Aron (Act Two, Scene Five)', 187.
18 Ibid., 189.
19 Adorno, 'Sacred Fragment', 226.
20 Ibid., 225.
21 I derive this point from a talk by Andrew Benjamin titled 'Images, Iconoclasm and the Founding of the Law', held at Kingston University on 27 October 2015.
22 Adorno, 'Sacred Fragment', 230.
23 Exod. 20.4.
24 Exod. 20.5.
25 Rebecca Comay, 'Materialist Mutations of the *Bilderverbot*', in *Sites of Vision*, ed. David Michael Levin (Cambridge, MA: MIT Press, 1997), 342; my emphasis. Sigmund Freud observes an analogous mechanism in animistic practices. Cf. Sigmund Freud, *Totem & Taboo: Some Points of Agreement between the Mental Lives of Savages and Neurotics*, trans. James Strachey (London: Routledge, 1966).
26 Moshe Halbertal and Avishai Margalit, *Idolatry*, trans. Naomi Goldblum (Cambridge, MA: Harvard University Press, 1998), 2; my emphasis.
27 Ibid.
28 Adorno, 'Sacred Fragment', 225.
29 Comay, 'Materialist Mutations of the *Bilderverbot*', 344.
30 Cf. Hermann Cohen, *Religion of Reason Out of the Sources of Judaism*, trans. Simon Kaplan (Oxford: Oxford University Press, 1995).
31 Theodor W. Adorno and Max Horkheimer, *Dialectic of Enlightenment*, trans. Edmund Jephcott, ed. Gunzelin Schmid Noerr (Stanford: Stanford University Press, 2002), 17.
32 Ibid., xviii.
33 Martin Heidegger, *Nietzsche, Vol. 1: The Will to Power as Art*, trans. D. F. Krell (London: Routledge & Kegan Paul, 1981), 10. On the remarkable commonalities between Heidegger and his self-avowed antipode Adorno, see Alexander García Düttmann, *The Memory of Thought: An Essay on Heidegger and Adorno*, trans. Nicholas Walker (London: Continuum, 2002).
34 Cf. Plato, 'Book VII (514a-517a)', *The Republic*, trans. Allan Bloom (New York: Basic Books, 1968), 193–6.
35 Cf. Friedrich Nietzsche, '"Reason" in Philosophy' & 'How the "Real World" at Last Became a Myth', in *Twilight of the Idols & The Anti-Christ*, trans. R. J. Hollingdale (London: Penguin Classics, 1989), 45–9 and 50–1; Friedrich

Nietzsche, 'Of the Afterworldsmen', in *Thus Spoke Zarathustra*, trans. R. J. Hollingdale (London: Penguin Classics, 1969), 58–60.

36 Cf. Alain Besançon, *The Forbidden Image: An Intellectual History of Iconoclasm*, trans. Jane Marie Todd (Chicago: University of Chicago Press, 2000); Horst Bredekamp, *Image Acts: A Systematic Approach to Visual Agency*, trans. Elizabeth Clegg (Berlin: De Gruyter, 2018); Marie-Jose Mondzain, *Image, Icon, Economy: The Byzantine Origins of the Contemporary Imaginary* (Stanford: Stanford University Press, 2004); Carlos M. N. Eire, *War against the Idols: The Reformation of Worship from Erasmus to Calvin* (Cambridge: Cambridge University Press, 1986).

37 Cf. Dermot Moran, 'Neoplatonism and Christianity in the West' & Sarah Pessin 'Islamic and Jewish Neoplatonism', in *The Routledge Handbook of Neoplatonism*, ed. Svetla Slaveva-Griffin and Paulina Remes (London: Routledge, 2014), 508–24 and 541–58.

38 Cf. Stefan Müller-Doohm, *Adorno: A Biography*, trans. Rodney Livingstone (Cambridge: Polity Press, 2009), 19.

39 Adorno, 'Theses Upon Art and Religion Today', in *Gesammelte Schriften, Bd. 11: Noten zur Literatur* (Frankfurt am Main: Suhrkamp, 1974), 647.

40 Adorno, 'Theologie, Aufklärung und die Zukunft der Illusion', in *Frankfurter Adorno Blätter VIII*, ed. Rolf Tiedemann (Munich: Edition Text + Kritik, 2003), 235; my translation.

41 Adorno, *Negative Dialectics*, trans. E. B. Ashton (London: Routledge, 1973), 19; translation altered.

42 Ibid., 3.

43 Alfred Schmidt, 'Der Begriff des Materialismus bei Adorno', in *Adorno Konferenz 1983*, ed. Ludwig v. Friedenburg and Jürgen Habermas (Frankfurt am Main: Suhrkamp, 1984), 25; my translation.

44 Simon Jarvis, 'Adorno, Marx, Materialism', in *The Cambridge Companion to Adorno*, ed. Tom Huhn (Cambridge: Cambridge University Press, 2004), 80.

45 Theodor W. Adorno and Ernst Bloch, 'Something's Missing: A Discussion Between Ernst Bloch and Theodor W. Adorno on the Contradictions of Utopian Longing (1964)', in *The Utopian Function of Art and Literature*, trans. Jack Zipes and Frank Mecklenburg (Cambridge, MA: MIT Press, 1988), 9.

46 Comay, 'Materialist Mutations of the *Bilderverbot*', 348.

47 Adorno and Horkheimer, *Dialectic of Enlightenment*, xi.

48 Asaf Angermann, ed., *Briefe und Briefwechsel, Band 8: "Der Liebe Gott wohnt im Detail": Theodor W. Adorno & Gershom Scholem, 1939-1969*, (Frankfurt am Main: Suhrkamp, 2015), 414; my translation.

49 Adorno, *Nachgelassene Schriften, Abteilung IV: Vorlesungen, Bd. 3: Ästhetik (1958/59)*, ed. Eberhard Ortland (Frankfurt am Main: Suhrkamp, 2009), 52; my translation.
50 Adorno, *Negative Dialectics*, xx.
51 Adorno, *Metaphysics: Concept and Problems*, trans. Edmund Jephcott, ed. Rolf Tiedemann (Cambridge: Polity Press, 2000), 68; original emphasis.
52 Karl Marx and Friedrich Engels, *Marx & Engels Collected Works, Vol. 3: 1843–1844* (London: Lawrence & Wishart, 1975), 142.

Chapter 1

1 'Whatever the value and penetrative power of an explanation, the thing being explained is still and always the most real, and within its reality figures precisely the mystery that we have been trying to dissipate.' Paul Valéry, *Valéry's Oeuvres, Vol. II*, ed. Jean Hytier (Paris: Gallimard, 1960), 738; my translation.
2 Comay, 'Materialist Mutations of the *Bilderverbot*', 339.
3 For a useful history of the term 'Western Marxism', see Perry Anderson, *Considerations on Western Marxism* (London: Verso, 1976).
4 For an influential overview of the theological streak running through the works of Bloch, Benjamin et al., see Michael Löwy, *Redemption & Utopia – Jewish Libertarian Thought in Central Europe*, trans. Hope Heaney (London: Athlone Press, 1992).
5 Adorno, *Negative Dialectics*, 207; translation altered.
6 Adorno, 'The Actuality of Philosophy', trans. Benjamin Snow, *Telos*, no. 31 (Spring 1977): 120.
7 Jarvis, 'Adorno, Marx, Materialism', 96; my emphasis.
8 Adorno views Lukács's defence of 'reflection theory' in his account of literary realism as an extension of this problem. However, for reasons of brevity this issue will be sidestepped here. Cf. Georg Lukács, *Realism in Our Time: Literature and the Class Struggle*, trans. John and Necke Mander (New York: Harper and Row, 1964); Adorno, 'Extorted Reconciliation: On Georg Lukács' Realism in Our Time', in *Notes to Literature, Vol. 2*, trans. Shierry Weber Nicholsen (New York: Columbia University Press, 1992), 216–40.
9 Adorno, *Negative Dialectics*, 206.
10 Ibid., 204.
11 Ibid., 205–6.
12 Adorno, *Philosophische Terminologie, Bd. 2* (Frankfurt am Main: Suhrkamp, 1974), 200; my translation.

13 Ibid., 203; my emphasis. Despite his misgivings about the concept of Utopia, Jacques Derrida's discussion of the forfeiture of the emancipatory impulse underlying Marx's thought, especially in the context of Francis Fukuyama's declaration of 'the end of history' in 1989, appears to chime with Adorno's considerations. Cf. Jacques Derrida, *Specters of Marx: The State of the Debt, the Work of Mourning and the New International*, trans. Peggy Kamuf (London: Verso, 1993).
14 Adorno, *Negative Dialectics*, 10; translation altered.
15 Schmidt, 'Der Begriff des Materialismus bei Adorno', 25; my translation.
16 Comay, 'Materialist Mutations of the *Bilderverbot*', 342.
17 Schmidt, 'Der Begriff des Materialismus bei Adorno', 25; my translation.
18 Adorno and Bloch, 'Something's Missing', 9.
19 It goes beyond the remit of the present chapter to outline the differences between Marx's and Engels's respective approaches. Suffice it to note that the de facto identity of their positions was assumed by many Soviet readers, not least amongst them Lenin. An important discussion of this theme can be found in the doctoral thesis of Alfred Schmidt, which was written under the supervision of Adorno and Horkheimer. Cf. Alfred Schmidt, *The Concept of Nature in Marx*, trans. Ben Fowkes (London: New Left Books, 1971).
20 For a compact and illuminating discussion of these issues, see Ingo Elbe, 'Between Marx, Marxism and Marxisms – Ways of Reading Marx's Theory', *Viewpoint Mag*, last altered October 2013. Available online: https://viewpointmag.com/2013/10/21/between-marx-marxism-and-marxisms-ways-of-reading-marxs-theory/#rf43-2941 (accessed 20 October 2015).
21 Friedrich Engels, *Dialectics of Nature*, trans. Clemens Dutt (London: Lawrence & Wishart, 1940), 34.
22 Elbe, 'Between Marx, Marxism and Marxisms'.
23 Cf. G. W. F. Hegel, *Philosophy of Nature*, trans. A. V. Miller (Oxford: Oxford University Press, 2004).
24 J. B. S. Haldane, 'Preface', in Friedrich Engels, *Dialectics of Nature*, ed. J. B. S. Haldane (London: Lawrence & Wishart, 1940), vii; my emphasis.
25 Elbe, 'Between Marx, Marxism and Marxisms'; my emphasis.
26 Ibid; my emphasis.
27 Karl Marx and Friedrich Engels, *Selected Correspondence* (Moscow: Progress Publishers, 1975), 520.
28 Schmidt, *The Concept of Nature in Marx*, 52.
29 Ibid., 55–6; my emphasis.

30 Karl Marx, 'Theses on Feuerbach', in *Marx & Engels Collected Works, Vol. 5: 1845–1847* (London: Lawrence & Wishart, 1976), 3; original emphasis.
31 Engels, *Dialectics of Nature*, 27.
32 Schmidt, *The Concept of Nature in Marx*, 56.
33 Elbe, 'Between Marx, Marxism and Marxisms'.
34 Adorno, *Philosophische Terminologie, Bd. 2*, 179; my translation and emphasis.
35 Vladimir Ilyich Lenin, *Collected Works, Vol. 14: Materialism and Empirio-Criticism* (Moscow: Foreign Languages Publishing House, 1961), 252.
36 Ibid., 258.
37 Mach's presence at this juncture opens up another, more speculative avenue of inquiry in connection with the so-called imageless thought controversy surrounding Oswald Külpe – a psychologist whose theories drew extensively on both Mach and Husserl. Cf. Oswald Külpe, *Outlines of Psychology, Based Upon the Result of Experimental Investigation*, trans. Edward Bradford Titchener (London: Swann, Sonnenschein & Co., 1901).
38 Ernst Mach, *The Analysis of Sensations and the Relation of the Physical to the Psychical*, trans. C. M. Williams and Sydney Waterlow (New York: Dover, 1959), 29.
39 David G. Rowley, 'Bogdanov and Lenin: Epistemology and Revolution', *Studies in East European Thought*, no. 48 (1996): 5.
40 Ibid.
41 Ibid; original emphasis.
42 Ibid.
43 Ibid.
44 Lance Byron Richey, 'Editor's Introduction – Pannekoek, Lenin and the Future of Marxist Philosophy', in *Lenin as Philosopher: A Critical Examination of the Philosophical Basis of Leninism*, ed. Anton Pannekoek (Milwaukee: Marquette University Press, 2003), 43.
45 Ibid.
46 Lenin, *Materialism and Empirio-Criticism*, 51. Recent works on both Mach and Bogdanov have pointed out the ways in which Lenin misreads these authors. Cf. David G. Rowley, 'Introduction', in Alexander Alexandrovich Bogdanov, *The Philosophy of Living Experience*, ed. David G. Rowley (Leiden: Brill, 2016), 1–41; James White, *Red Hamlet: The Life and Ideas of Alexander Bogdanov* (Leiden: Brill, 2019); Erik C. Banks, *The Realistic Empiricism of Mach, James, and Russell: Neutral Monism Reconceived* (Cambridge: Cambridge University Press, 2014). I am grateful to Cat Moir for these references.

47 Ibid., 267; my emphasis.
48 Ibid., 69; original emphasis.
49 Ibid., 129.
50 Richey, 'Editor's Introduction', 53.
51 For an influential defence of Lenin's 'scientific' materialism, see Louis Althusser, 'Lenin and Philosophy', in *Lenin and Philosophy and Other Essays*, trans. Ben Brewster (New York: Monthly Review Press, 2001), 23–67.
52 Adorno and others commonly attribute this line to Hegel, although to the best of my knowledge it does not appear anywhere in Hegel's writings. Cf. Adorno, 'Aspects of Hegel's Philosophy', in *Hegel: Three Studies*, trans. Shierry Weber Nicholsen (Cambridge, MA: MIT Press, 1993), 31.
53 Adorno, *Negative Dialectics*, 204.
54 Ibid., 204–5.
55 Ibid., 205.
56 Ibid.
57 Adorno, *Philosophische Terminologie, Bd. 2*, 215; my translation.
58 G. W. F. Hegel, *Phenomenology of Spirit*, trans. A. V. Miller (Oxford: Oxford University Press, 1977), 56.
59 Ibid.; my emphasis.
60 Ibid.
61 Cf. G. W. F. Hegel, *Lectures on the History of Philosophy, Vol. III*, ed. Robert F. Brown, trans. Robert F. Brown, J. M. Stewart and H. S. Harris (Berkeley: University of California Press, 1990), 263.
62 Hegel, *Phenomenology of Spirit*, 47; translation altered.
63 Adorno, *Negative Dialectics*, 206.
64 Adorno, *Philosophische Terminologie, Bd. 2*, 215; my translation.
65 Adorno, *Against Epistemology – A Metacritique: Studies in Husserl and the Phenomenological Antinomies*, trans. Willis Domingo (Oxford: Blackwell Publishing, 1982), 27; my emphasis. The English translation of *Zur Metakritik der Erkenntnistheorie* as *Against Epistemology* obfuscates Adorno's intention to provide an immanent reworking of epistemological categories, a meta-critique, by suggesting a simple relation of opposition ('against').
66 Ibid; my emphasis.
67 Adorno, *Negative Dialectics*, 205.
68 Adorno, *Philosophische Terminologie, Bd. 2*, 213–14; my translation.
69 Ibid.; my translation.
70 Cf. Eduard Zeller, *A History of Greek Philosophy: From the Earliest Period to the Time of Socrates*, trans. Sarah Frances Alleyne (London: Longmans, Green, and Co., 1881); Cf. Frederick Albert Lange, *History of Materialism and Criticism of*

Its Present Importance, trans. Ernest Chester Thomas (London: Trubner & Co., 1877); Cf. Karl Marx, 'The Difference Between the Democritean and Epicurean Philosophy of Nature', in *Marx & Engels Collected Works, Vol. 1: 1835–1843* (London: Lawrence & Wishart, 1974), 25–7.
71 Adorno, *Philosophische Terminologie, Bd. 2*, 190–1; my translation.
72 Lange, *History of Materialism*, 25.
73 Ibid., 17.
74 Adorno, *Philosophische Terminologie, Bd. 2*, 210; my translation.
75 Ibid., 191; my translation.
76 Lange, *History of Materialism*, 19; original emphasis.
77 Ibid., 22; original emphasis.
78 Ibid., 20; original emphasis.
79 Ibid., 27; original emphasis.
80 Ibid., 106.
81 Ibid.
82 Ibid.
83 Adorno, *Philosophische Terminologie, Bd. 2*, 212; my translation.
84 Ibid.; my translation.
85 Ibid.; my translation.
86 Ibid.; my translation.
87 Ibid., 214; my translation and emphasis.
88 Ibid.; my translation and emphasis.
89 Karl Marx and Friedrich Engels, *Marx & Engels Collected Works, Vol. 35: Capital, Vol. 1* (London: Lawrence & Wishart, 1996), 81.
90 Schmidt, 'Der Begriff des Materialismus bei Adorno', 18; my translation.
91 For a useful overview of the genesis of 'speculative realism' and the diverse theoretical positions that have come to be collected under this banner – from Graham Harman's 'object-oriented-ontology' to Iain Hamilton Grant's 'neo-vitalism' – see Levi Bryant, Nick Srnicek and Graham Harman, 'Towards a Speculative Philosophy', in *The Speculative Turn: Continental Materialism and Realism* (Melbourne: re.press, 2011), 1–18.
92 Cf. Quentin Meillassoux, *After Finitude: An Essay on the Necessity of Contingency*, trans. Ray Brassier (London: Continuum, 2008).
93 Slavoj Žižek, *Less Than Nothing: Hegel and the Shadow of Dialectical Materialism* (London: Verso, 2012), 625. See also Ray Brassier, *Nihil Unbound: Enlightenment and Extinction* (New York: Palgrave MacMillan, 2007), 246; Nathan Brown, 'The Speculative and the Specific: On Hallward and Meillassoux', in *The Speculative Turn: Continental Materialism and Realism*

(Melbourne: re.press, 2011), 156; Adrian Johnston, 'Empiricism', in *The Meillassoux Dictionary*, ed. Peter Gratton and Paul J. Ennis (Edinburgh: Edinburgh University Press, 2015), 62.
94 Peter Hallward, 'Anything Is Possible: A Reading of Quentin Meillassoux's *After Finitude*', in *The Speculative Turn: Continental Materialism and Realism* (Melbourne: re.press, 2011), 141.
95 Brown, 'The Speculative and the Specific', 163.
96 For an interesting Adornian critique of Meillassoux, see Daniel Spaulding, 'Inside Out', *Mute Magazine*, last altered 20 December 2015, Available online: http://www.metamute.org/editorial/articles/inside-out-0 (accessed 27 November 2015).
97 Despite Meillassoux's evident debt to his teacher, Alain Badiou, the outwardly a-political tenor of his writing has not gone unnoticed. Cf. Svenja Bromberg, 'The Anti-Political Aesthetics of Object Worlds and Beyond', *Mute Magazine*, last altered 25 July 2013. Available online: http://www.metamute.org/editorial/articles/anti-political-aesthetics-objects-and-worlds-beyond (accessed 27 November 2015).
98 Adorno, *Negative Dialectics*, 215.
99 Hallward, 'Anything Is Possible', 130.
100 Quentin Meillassoux, 'Speculative Realism', *Collapse: Philosophical Research and Development* 3 (2007): 393; my emphasis.
101 Hallward, 'Anything Is Possible', 131.
102 Meillassoux, *After Finitude*, 5; my emphasis.
103 Ibid., 38.
104 Immanuel Kant, *Critique of Pure Reason*, trans. Paul Guyer and Allen W. Wood (Cambridge: Cambridge University Press, 1998), 507.
105 Hallward, 'Anything Is Possible', 135.
106 Kant, *Critique of Pure Reason*, 110.
107 Ibid.
108 Meillassoux, *After Finitude*, 118.
109 For a biting account of certain problems in Meillassoux's critique of Kant, see Andrew Cole, 'Those Obscure Objects of Desire', *Artforum*. Available online: https://artforum.com/inprint/issue=201506&id=52280 (accessed 7 January 2016).
110 Meillassoux, *After Finitude*, 9–10. As Meillassoux is surely aware, Kant does not require one to witness an occurrence first-hand for its material remnants to be accounted for.
111 Ibid., 38.

112 Hallward, 'Anything Is Possible', 136; my emphasis.
113 Meillassoux, *After Finitude*, 53; my emphasis.
114 Ibid., 52.
115 Hallward, 'Anything Is Possible', 136.
116 Ibid.
117 Meillassoux, *After Finitude*, 90.
118 Ibid.
119 Ibid., 91.
120 Hallward, 'Anything Is Possible', 132; my emphasis.
121 Ibid., 133.
122 Quentin Meillassoux, 'Spectral Dilemma', *Collapse: Philosophical Research and Development* 4 (2008): 274.
123 Meillassoux, *After Finitude*, 126.
124 Reconstructing Meillassoux's foray into Cantorian set theory exceeds the scope of the present chapter. Suffice it to note that, in his view, Cantor allows him to challenge our belief in the stability of natural laws by arguing that they stem from an untenable 'probabilistic' calculation.
125 Ibid., 138; my emphasis.
126 Ibid.
127 Ibid.
128 Alberto Toscano, 'Against Speculation, or, a Critique of Critique: A Remark on Quentin Meillassoux's *After Finitude* (After Colletti)', in *The Speculative Turn: Continental Materialism and Realism* (Melbourne: re.press, 2011), 91.
129 Hallward, 'Anything Is Possible', 140.
130 Ibid.
131 Adorno, 'Marginalia on Theory and Praxis', in *Critical Models: Interventions and Catchwords*, ed. Henry W. Pickford (New York: Columbia University Press, 1998), 26.
132 To be sure, Adorno's concept of the image cannot be reduced to its adverse association with Soviet reflection theory. For one thing, the tension between image and imagelessness is closely connected with Adorno's great debt to a mode of thinking in images detailed in Benjamin's ill-fated *Habilitationsschrift* on the *Origin of the German Trauerspiel*, 1928. For an in-depth account of Adorno's application of Benjamin's philosophy of the image, see Peter Fenves, 'Image and Chatter: Adorno's Construction of Kierkegaard', *Diacritics* 22, no. 1 (Spring 1992): 99–114.
133 The question of Adorno's politics has long been the cause of heated debate, not least in light of his ambiguous relationship with the German student

movement of the 1960s. See Wolfgang Kraushaar, ed., *Frankfurter Schule und Studentenbewegung: Von der Flaschenpost zum Molotowcocktail, 1946–1995*, 3 Vols. (Hamburg: Rogner & Bernhard, 1998–2004); Adorno, 'Resignation', in *Critical Models*, trans. Henry W. Pickford (New York: Columbia University Press, 1998), 289–94.

134 A fascinating document of Adorno's interest in the mode of non-hierarchical, constellational thinking outlined in the Benjamin's *Origin of the German Trauerspiel* can be found in the notes accompanying his *Privatissimum* on Benjamin's book from the summer of 1932. Cf. Adorno, 'Protokolle vom Seminar über Benjamins *Ursprung des deutschen Trauerspiels*, Sommersemester 1932', in *Frankfurter Adorno Blätter. Bd. IV*, ed. Rolf Tiedemann (Munich: Edition Text + Kritik), 52–77.

135 Walter Benjamin, *Origin of the German Trauerspiel*, trans. Howard Eiland (Cambridge, MA: Harvard University Press), 4.

136 Ibid., 9.

137 Ibid., 2–3.

138 Walter Benjamin, 'Critique of Violence', in *Selected Writings, Vol. 1: 1913–1926*, ed. Marcus Bullock and Michael W. Jennings (Cambridge, MA: The Belknap Press of Harvard University Press, 1996), 247.

139 Axel Honneth, *Pathologies of Reason: On the Legacy of Critical Theory*, trans. James Ingram et al. (New York: Columbia University Press, 2009), 50.

140 For a interesting account of 'inversion' as a literary–philosophical device in a wider context, see Manfred Frank and Gerhard Kurz, 'Ordo Inversus. Zu einer Reflexionsfigur bei Novalis, Hölderlin, Kleist und Kafka', in *Geist und Zeichen: Festschrift für Arthur Henkel*, ed. Herbert Anton (Heidelberg: Carl Winter, 1977), 75–97.

141 Karl Marx, *Capital, Vol. 3: Critique of Political Economy*, trans. David Fernbach (London: Penguin Classics, 1991), 2073.

142 For a discussion of how this bears on Adorno's notion of an 'inverse' theology, see pp. 94–103 of the present study.

143 'The true is the index of itself and of that which is false.' Benedict Spinoza, *On the Improvement of the Understanding / The Ethics / Correspondence*, trans. R. H. M. Elwes (London: Dover Books, 1955), 417; translation altered.

144 'The false is the index of itself and of that which is true.' Adorno and Bloch, 'Something's Missing', 11. Both Adorno and Marx play on this maxim elsewhere. Cf. Adorno, 'Notes on Kafka', in *Prisms*, trans. Samuel Weber and Shierry Weber (Cambridge, MA: MIT Press, 1981), 246; Karl Marx, 'Comments on the Latest Prussian Censorship Instruction', in *Marx & Engels*

Collected Works, Vol. 1: 1835–1843 (London: Lawrence & Wishart, 1974), 112.

145 Adorno, *Minima Moralia: Reflections on a Damaged Life*, trans. Edmund Jephcott (London: Verso, 1974), 247; translation altered.
146 Adorno, 'The Actuality of Philosophy', 126.
147 Adorno and Horkheimer, *Dialectic of Enlightenment*, 18. Given the quasi-Judaic provenance of Adorno's philosophy of imagelessness, it is noteworthy that he asserts a primacy of the scriptural.
148 Gershom Scholem, ed., *The Correspondence of Walter Benjamin and Gershom Scholem 1932–1940*, trans. Gary Smith and Andre Lefevere (New York: Schocken Books, 1989), 84.
149 Cf. Søren Kierkegaard, *Either/Or, Pt. I*, trans. Howard V. Hong and Edna H. Hong (Princeton: Princeton University Press, 1987), 354.
150 Adorno, *Kierkegaard: Construction of the Aesthetic*, trans. Robert Hullot-Kentor (Minneapolis: University of Minnesota Press, 1989), 42.
151 Susan Buck-Morss, *The Origin of Negative Dialectics: Walter Benjamin, Theodor W. Adorno and the Frankfurt Institute* (New York: Free Press, 1977), 114.
152 Ibid.
153 Ibid., 116.
154 Kierkegaard, *Either/Or*, 354; translation altered.
155 Adorno, *Kierkegaard*, 42.
156 Ibid.
157 Ibid.
158 Ibid, 27.
159 Ibid, 29.
160 Ibid, 39.
161 Karl Marx, 'The German Ideology', in *Marx & Engels Collected Works, Vol. 5: 1845–1847* (London: Lawrence & Wishart, 1976), 36.
162 Adorno, *Minima Moralia*, 247.
163 Elizabeth Pritchard, 'Bilderverbot Meets Body in Theodor W. Adorno's Inverse Theology', *The Harvard Theological Review* 95, no. 3 (July 2002): 307.
164 Adorno, *Minima Moralia*, 39; translation altered.
165 Adorno and Horkheimer, *Dialectic of Enlightenment*, 18.
166 Hegel, *Phenomenology of Spirit*, 51.
167 Ibid.
168 Adorno, *Negative Dialectics*, 158.
169 Ibid., 159–60; my emphasis.
170 Adorno, 'The Experiential Content of Hegel's Philosophy', in *Hegel: Three Studies*, trans. Shierry Weber Nicholsen (Cambridge, MA: MIT Press, 1993), 80.

171 For a discussion of Hegel's treatment of the image ban, see pp. 129–32 of the present study.
172 Adorno, *Negative Dialectics*, 3.
173 Adorno, 'Marginalia on Theory and Praxis', 265; original emphasis.
174 Walter Benjamin, 'The Destructive Character', in *Selected Writings, Vol. 2.2: 1931–1934*, ed. Howard Eiland, Michael W. Jennings and Gary Smith (Cambridge, MA: The Belknap Press of Harvard University Press, 1999), 541–2.
175 Jarvis, 'Adorno, Marx, Materialism', 80.
176 Adorno, *Negative Dialectics*, 5.
177 Ibid.
178 Ibid., 10.
179 The palpable parallels between Adorno and Derrida have often been noted, not least of all by Derrida himself. Cf. Jacques Derrida, 'Fichus: Frankfurt Address', in *Paper Machine*, trans. Rachel Bowlby (Stanford, CA: Stanford University Press, 2005), 164–81.
180 Adorno, *Negative Dialectics*, 3.
181 Above all, Adorno cross reads Kant and Marx in terms that are familiar from the work of Alfred Sohn-Rethel. Adorno and Sohn-Rethel engaged in a lively correspondence from the mid-1930s onwards. In particular, they discuss Sohn-Rethel's view of a structural correspondence between Kant's transcendental subject and the money form of value. Cf. Alfred Sohn-Rethel, *Intellectual and Manual Labour: A Critique of Epistemology*, trans. Martin Sohn-Rethel (London: Macmillan, 1978); Christoph Gödde, ed., *Theodor W. Adorno & Alfred Sohn-Rethel: Briefwechsel, 1936–1969* (Munich: Edition Text + Kritik, 1991).
182 Adorno, *Negative Dialectics*, 183.
183 Adorno, 'On Subject and Object', in *Critical Models: Interventions and Catchwords*, ed. Henry W. Pickford (New York: Columbia University Press, 1998), 245.
184 Ibid. To be sure, Adorno's emphasis on the autonomy of individual subjects brings his project into the orbit of a certain kind of liberalism, in the sense that much here hinges on the concept of individual freedom. For a useful discussion of these questions, see Espen Hammer, *Adorno and the Political* (London: Routledge, 2006).
185 Adorno, 'On Subject and Object', 249.
186 Ibid., 253.
187 For a fuller account of *Dialectic of Enlightenment*, see pp. 62–4 of the present study.
188 Georg Lukács, *Theory of the Novel: A Historico-Philosophical Essay on the Forms of Great Epic Literature*, trans. Anna Bostock (London: Merlin Press, 1988), 63.

189 Adorno, 'Marginalia on Theory and Praxis', 262.
190 Adorno, 'On Subject and Object', 246.
191 Ibid., 254.
192 Cf. Georg Lukács, *History and Class-Consciousness: Studies in Marxist Dialectics*, trans. Rodney Livingstone (London: Merlin Press, 1971), 83.
193 Adorno, 'On Subject and Object', 246.
194 *Adorno & Sohn-Rethel: Briefwechsel*, 24; my translation. The crucial difference between Adorno and Sohn-Rethel is that for the former the constitution of subjectivity is an aspect of the domination of nature, whereas for the latter it follows from the principle of exchange itself. In both cases, though, these principles are problematically projected back into a kind of conjectural prehistory of humankind.
195 Adorno, 'On Subject and Object', 247.
196 Ibid., 246.
197 Ibid., 247; my emphasis.
198 Adorno, *Negative Dialectics*, 192.
199 Ibid.
200 Ibid.
201 Ibid., 193.
202 Ibid.
203 Adorno, *Philosophische Terminologie, Bd. 2*, 187; my translation. Incidentally, Adorno vigorously contests the Christological connotations of this formulation. Instead, he cites the *Wisdom of Solomon* as his source.
204 Adorno, *Nachgelassene Schriften, Abteilung IV: Vorlesungen, Bd. 3: Ästhetik (1958/59)*, ed. Eberhart Ortland (Frankfurt am Main: Suhrkamp, 2009), 52; my translation.
205 Adorno, *Negative Dialectics*, 202; translation altered.
206 For an account of Adorno's concept of a negative universal history, see pp. 146–7 of the present study.
207 As has been noted by numerous commentators, Adorno was apparently planning a major tome on ethics, which was to follow his *Aesthetic Theory*. Although this final contribution to Adorno's systematically anti-systematic philosophy never got off the ground, his ethical concerns can nonetheless be gleaned from his lecture series on the *Problems of Moral Philosophy*, 1963. Cf. Adorno, *Problems of Moral Philosophy*, ed. Thomas Schröder, trans. Rodney Livingstone (Cambridge: Polity Press, 2000); See also: J. M. Bernstein, *Adorno: Disenchantment and Ethics* (Cambridge: Cambridge University Press, 2001).
208 Adorno, *Negative Dialectics*, 203; translation altered.

209 Ibid., 203–4; original emphasis.
210 Adorno, 'Theses on Need', trans. Keston Sutherland, *Quid*, no. 16 (2005): 43.
211 Ibid; my emphasis.
212 Adorno, 'Towards a Portrait of Thomas Mann', in *Notes to Literature, Vol. 2*, trans. Shierry Weber Nicholsen (New York: Columbia University Press, 1992), 18; my emphasis.
213 René Buchholz, *Zwischen Mythos und Bilderverbot: Adornos Philosophie als Anstoß zu einer kritischen Fundamentaltheologie im Kontext der späten Moderne* (Frankfurt am Main: Peter Lang, 1991), 144; my translation.
214 Adorno, *Minima Moralia*, 140.
215 Adorno, *Philosophische Terminologie, Bd. 2*, 198; my translation.
216 Ibid.; my translation.
217 Walter Benjamin, 'On the Concept of History', in *Selected Writings, Vol. 4: 1938–1940*, ed. Howard Eiland and Michael W. Jennings (Cambridge, MA: The Belknap Press of Harvard University Press, 2003), 390.

Chapter 2

1 'Thou shalt no image –' Franz Kafka, *Nachgelassene Schriften und Fragmente II*, ed. Jost Schillemeit (Frankfurt am Main: Fischer Verlag, 2002), 360; my translation.
2 My exposition hinges on a distinction between religion and theology that is treated at some length later. To begin with, however, it is worth noting the following: 'religion', commonly held to stem from the Latin *religare* (to bind), is generally taken to mean submitting to a traditionally imparted authority derived directly from God. By contrast, 'theology' – from the Greek *theos* (God) and *logos* (divine word, order of knowledge) – is conventionally viewed as a reasoned discourse *about* God. With respect to our present focus on Judaism and Christianity (the coordinates of Adorno's presentation) this means, above all, a reasoned discourse about scripture.
3 Adorno, 'Theses Upon Art and Religion Today', in *Noten zur Literatur* (Frankfurt am Main: Suhrkamp, 1974), 647.
4 Adorno, 'Theologie, Aufklärung und die Zukunft der Illusion', 235; my translation.
5 Adorno, 'Sacred Fragment', 229.
6 Ibid., 228.
7 Ibid.

8 Ibid., 226–7; my emphasis.
9 Ibid., 226.
10 Ibid.; my emphasis. Adorno's point, in turn, will be that the success of Schoenberg's piece lies, precisely, in distancing itself from any kind of *personal* expression. The work itself speaks.
11 Ibid.
12 Ibid., 227.
13 Ibid., 228.
14 Ibid.
15 Ibid., 236.
16 Cf. Walter Benjamin, 'Capitalism as Religion', in *Selected Writings, Vol. 1: 1913–1926*, ed. Marcus Bullock and Michael W. Jennings (Cambridge, MA: The Belknap Press of Harvard University Press, 1996), 288–91.
17 For an illuminating discussion of this figure in the context of Adorno's philosophy of existence, see Peter E. Gordon, *Adorno and Existence* (Cambridge, MA: Harvard University Press), 194–200.
18 Cf. Walter Benjamin, 'Franz Kafka: On the Tenth Anniversary of His Death', in *Selected Writings, Vol. 2.2: 1931–1934*, ed. Howard Eiland, Michael W. Jennings and Gary Smith (Cambridge, MA: The Belknap Press of Harvard University Press, 1999), 794–818.
19 Henri Lonitz, ed., *Theodor W. Adorno & Walter Benjamin: The Complete Correspondence, 1928–1940*, trans. Nicholas Walker (Cambridge, MA: Harvard University Press, 2001), 66–7; translation altered.
20 Adorno, 'Mahagonny', in *Gesammelte Schriften 17: Musikalische Schriften IV*, ed. Rolf Tiedemann et al. (Frankfurt a.M.: Suhrkamp), 114. I am grateful to Jacob Bard-Rosenberg for this reference.
21 Adorno, *Minima Moralia*, 247.
22 Adorno, 'Notes on Kafka', 243–72.
23 Adorno, *Minima Moralia*, 247.
24 Cf. Löwy, *Redemption & Utopia*, 16; original emphasis.
25 *Theodor W. Adorno & Walter Benjamin: The Complete Correspondence*, 143.
26 For a useful summary of the disagreement over dialectics in Adorno and Benjamin's 1935 correspondence, see Susan Buck-Morss, 'The Adorno-Benjamin Debate, Part 1: The Issues', in *The Origin of Negative Dialectics: Theodor W. Adorno, Walter Benjamin and the Frankfurt Institute* (New York: The Free Press, 1979), 136–50.
27 Cf. Evelyn Wilcock, 'Negative Identity: Mixed German Jewish Descent as a Factor in the Reception of Theodor Adorno', *New German Critique*, no. 81 (Autumn 2000): 169–87.

28 The fact that Adorno toyed with the idea of a conversion to Catholicism in his youth – as documented in his correspondence with Ernst Krenek – is of little consequence here as he quickly dismissed his plans as impossibly romantic. Cf. Wolfgang Rogge, ed., *Theodor W. Adorno & Ernst Krenek: Briefwechsel* (Frankfurt am Main: Suhrkamp, 1974). See also Stefan Müller-Doohm, 'Family Inheritance: A Picture of Contrasts', in *Adorno: A Biography*, trans. Rodney Livingstone (Cambridge: Polity Press, 2009), 3–66.

29 Cf. Detlev Claussen, *Theodor W. Adorno: One Last Genius*, trans. Rodney Livingstone (Cambridge, MA: Harvard University Press, 2010).

30 Cf. Wolfgang Schopf, ed., *Theodor W. Adorno & Siegfried Kracauer: Correspondence, 1923–1966*, trans. Susan Halstead (Cambridge: Polity, 2020).

31 Adorno, 'Brief an Leo Löwenthal, 22.08.1923', in *Das Utopische soll Funken schlagen – zum 100. Geburtstag von Leo Löwenthal*, ed. Peter-Erwin Jansen (Frankfurt am Main: Gesellschaft der Freunde der Stadt- und Universitätsbibliothek, Frankfurt am Main, 2000), 45; my translation.

32 Adorno, *The Jargon of Authenticity*, trans. Knut Tarnowski and Fredric Will (London: Routledge, 1973), 16; translation altered.

33 Cf. Wolfgang Schivelbusch, *Intellektuellendämmerung: Zur Lage der Frankfurter Intelligenz in den zwanziger Jahren* (Frankfurt am Main: Suhrkamp, 1985).

34 Hermann Deuser, *Dialektische Theologie: Studien zu Adornos Metaphysik und zum Spätwerk Kierkegaards* (Munich and Mainz: Kaiser Verlag, 1980), 284; my translation. Benjamin, in turn, is generally seen as owing his knowledge of Judaism in good measure to the relationship with his lifelong friend, the renowned Kabbalah scholar Gershom Scholem. Scholem, for his part, recounts a meeting with Adorno in the following terms: '[t]he good spirit that prevailed in the meetings between Adorno and me was due not so much to the cordiality of the reception as to my considerable surprise at Adorno's appreciation of the continuing theological element in Benjamin.' Gershom Scholem, *Walter Benjamin: The Story of a Friendship*, trans. Harry Zohn (London: Faber & Faber, 1982), 15.

35 Christoph Gödde and Henri Lonitz, ed., *Briefe und Briefwechsel, Bd. 1: Theodor W. Adorno & Max Horkheimer, 1927–1937* (Frankfurt am Main: Suhrkamp, 2003), 52; my translation.

36 Hent De Vries, *Minimal Theologies: Critiques of Secular Reason in Adorno and Levinas*, trans. Geoffrey Hale (Baltimore: Johns Hopkins University Press, 2005), xvii.

37 Cf. Adorno, 'The Actuality of Philosophy', 120–33; Adorno, 'The Idea of Natural History', trans. Robert Hullot-Kentor, *Telos*, no. 57 (Fall 1983): 111–24; Adorno, *Kierkegaard: Construction of the Aesthetic*, trans. Robert Hullot-Kentor

(Minneapolis: University of Minnesota Press, 1989); Adorno and Horkheimer, *Dialectic of Enlightenment*; Adorno, 'World Spirit and Natural History', in *Negative Dialectics*, trans. E. B. Ashton (London: Routledge, 1973), 300–60.
38 Adorno, *Negative Dialectics*, 320.
39 Adorno, *History and Freedom: Lectures 1964–1965*, trans. Rodney Livingstone (Cambridge: Polity Press, 2006), 80.
40 On Adorno's account, Hegel himself overstates his case when he suggests that history turns contingent events into necessary ones according to their providential *telos*. It is, at the very least, debatable, however, whether Hegel *is*, in fact, suggesting this.
41 Adorno, *History and Freedom*, 82.
42 Cf. Benjamin, 'On the Concept of History', 389–400.
43 Adorno, *History and Freedom*, 87.
44 Adorno, *Negative Dialectics*, 320.
45 Ibid., 319.
46 Adorno, *History and Freedom*, 91; my emphasis.
47 Ibid.
48 Ibid.
49 Adorno, *Minima Moralia*, 247; translation altered. See pp. 37–40 of the present study.
50 Adorno and Horkheimer, *Dialectic of Enlightenment*, xviii.
51 Ibid., 35.
52 Ibid.
53 Ibid., 205.
54 Ibid., 3; my emphasis. Adorno and Horkheimer's entire exposition must be taken *cum grano salis*. Their account of animism, for example, is certainly not concerned with, say, questions of empirical anthropology. Rather, these sections serve to illustrate a wider, speculative point about the formation of subjectivity. This is not to suggest, of course, that Adorno and Horkheimer's glaring Eurocentrism is immune to criticism; only that this is not our current focus.
55 Adorno, *Kierkegaard*, 119.
56 For an illuminating reading of these passages from *Dialectic of Enlightenment*, see Rebecca Comay, 'Adorno's Siren Song', *New German Critique*, no. 81 (Autumn, 2000): 21–48.
57 Adorno and Horkhemimer, *Dialectic of Enlightenment*, 43.
58 Adorno, 'Reason and Revelation', in *Critical Models: Interventions and Catchwords*, trans. Henry W. Pickford (New York: Columbia University Press, 1998), 138.

59 Adorno, 'Über Tradition', in *Gesammelte Schriften, Bd. 10: Kulturkritik und Gesellschaft*, ed. Rolf Tiedemann et al. (Frankfurt am Main: Suhrkamp, 1977), 310; my translation.
60 Freud, *Totem & Taboo*, 77.
61 Adorno and Horkheimer, *Dialectic of Enlightenment*, 13.
62 See p. 4 of the present study. Scholem, with whom Adorno corresponded on these matters, outlines a damning critique of the identification of Judaism with reason. The problem with such a conflation, he argues, is that it ignores the mystical, 'irrational' strands of Judaism contained in the Zohar, the Lurianic Kabbalah and elsewhere. Cf. Gershom Scholem, 'The Science of Judaism – Then and Now', in *The Messianic Idea in Judaism* (New York: Schocken Books, 1995), 304–13.
63 Adorno and Horkheimer, *Dialectic of Enlightenment*, 145; my emphasis.
64 Ibid.; my emphasis.
65 Ibid., 136.
66 The text was first presented at a roundtable discussion between Adorno and the historian Eugen Kogon, held in Münster in 1957, and broadcast by the *Westdeutscher Rundfunk*. Transcripts of both Adorno's and Kogon's presentations (as well as their ensuing discussion) were published in two parts in 1958 under the heading 'Offenbarung oder autonome Vernunft' in a journal co-edited by Kogon, titled *Frankfurter Hefte*. Cf. Theodor W. Adorno and Eugen Kogon, 'Offenbarung oder autonome Vernunft (i)', *Frankfurter Hefte: Zeitschrift für Kultur und Politik* 13, no. 6 (June 1958): 392–402; 'Offenbarung oder autonome Vernunft (ii)', *Frankfurter Hefte: Zeitschrift für Kultur und Politik* 13, no. 7 (June 1958): 484–98.
67 Adorno, 'Reason and Revelation', 136.
68 Ibid.
69 Ibid.; my emphasis.
70 Although Adorno does not mention Heidegger in 'Reason and Revelation', he is on record as saying the following in the discussion with Kogon that followed his initial presentation of the text: 'I believe (...) that the blame' or, we might add, the cause for the developments described in 'Reason and Revelation', 'does not lie primarily in *intellectual* – but rather in *societal* developments. Or, rather, inasmuch as it is to do with intellectual forces, philosophy today is more to blame than positive religion. And I am indeed of the opinion that Mr. Heidegger's name should be stressed at this point as one of the main culprits'. Ibid., 137; original emphasis.
71 Adorno and Kogon, 'Offenbarung oder autonome Vernunft [ii]', 497; my translation and emphasis.

72 Adorno, 'Reason and Revelation', 138.
73 For two very different readings of Adorno's own relationship to nominalism – a term that plays a significant role in *Aesthetic Theory* – see Robert Hullot-Kentor, 'Title Essay: Baroque Allegory and "The Essay as Form"', in *Things Beyond Resemblance: Collected Essays on Theodor W. Adorno* (New York: Columbia University Press, 2008), 125–35; Fredric Jameson, 'Nominalism', in *Late Marxism: Adorno or the Persistence of the Dialectic* (London: Verso, 1990), 157–64.
74 Adorno and Kogon, 'Offenbarung oder autonome Vernunft (ii)', 496; my translation.
75 Ibid.; my translation.
76 Ibid.; my translation.
77 Adorno, 'Reason and Revelation', 136; original emphasis.
78 Ibid; original emphasis.
79 Ibid.
80 Ibid., 137.
81 Ibid., 139–40.
82 Ibid., 140.
83 It has, in fact, been widely acknowledged that Luther was, indeed, lastingly influenced by his study of a form of logical nominalism that was widespread amongst a generation of older Catholic thinkers, including Gabriel Biel and William of Ockham. Cf. Graham White, *Luther as Nominalist: A Study of the Logical Methods Used in Martin Luther's Disputations in the Light of their Medieval Background* (Helsinki: Luther-Agricola-Society, 1994); Heiko A. Oberman, *Man Between God and the Devil* (New Haven: Yale University Press, 2006). Oberman argues that Luther became well acquainted with the works of Biel and Ockham during his studies at Erfurt. Accordingly, he suggests that Luther remains indebted to their logical frameworks even where he seems to denounce them.
84 Adorno, 'Reason and Revelation', 139.
85 Ibid., 137.
86 Ibid., 136.
87 Ibid., 138.
88 Ibid.
89 Ibid., 136.
90 In the Christian tradition, apophatic theology is associated with figures including Pseudo-Dionysius the Aeropagite and Meister Eckhart. In the Jewish tradition, notable exponents include Philo of Alexandria and

Moses Maimonides. Cf. Ilse N. Bulhof and Laurens ten Kate, 'Echoes of an Embarrassment – Philosophical Perspectives on Negative Theology', in *Flight of the Gods: Philosophical Perspectives on Negative Theology*, ed. Ilse N. Bulhof and Laurens ten Kate (New York City: Fordham University Press, 2000), 1–57.

91   Christopher Craig Brittain, *Adorno and Theology* (London: Continuum, 2010), 92.
92   Ibid., 91.
93   Ibid., 89–90.
94   Jürgen Habermas, 'The Primal History of Subjectivity', in *Philosophical-Political Profiles*, trans. Frederick G. Lawrence (Cambridge, MA: MIT Press, 1983), 170. Max Horkheimer describes the figure of the 'wholly other' in the following terms: 'Both Adorno and I (. . .) no longer spoke of God but of the "yearning for the wholly other". In the Bible it says "You shall not make yourself an image of God." You cannot represent what is absolutely good. The pious Jew avoids the word "God" where possible (. . .). By the same token, Critical Theory too carefully calls the absolute "the other"'. Max Horkheimer, 'Was wir Sinn nennen wird verschwinden – Spiegel Gespräch mit dem Philosophen Max Horkheimer', *Der Spiegel* (5 January 1970): 81; my translation.
95   Adorno and Horkheimer, *Dialectic of Enlightenment*, 18.
96   James Gordon Finlayson, 'On not Being Silent in the Darkness: Adorno's Singular Apophaticism', *The Harvard Theological Review* 105, no. 1 (January 2012): 2.
97   Ibid.
98   Habermas, 'The Primal History of Subjectivity', 185–6; my emphasis.
99   Finlayson, 'On Not Being Silent in the Dark', 4; my emphasis.
100 Raymond Geuss, 'A Republic of Discussion: Habermas at Ninety', *The Point Mag*, last altered 18 June 2019. Available online: https://thepointmag.com/politics/a-republic-of-discussion-habermas-at-ninety/ (accessed 21 December 2019).
101 Jürgen Habermas, *The Theory of Communicative Action, Vol. 1: Reason and the Rationalization of Society*, trans. Thomas McCarthy (Boston, MA: Beachon Press, 1987), 25.
102 The following passage from Geuss's criticism of Habermas – conducted, I would argue, in Adorno's spirit – is worth citing here: 'there is good reason to be skeptical about the main thesis Habermas proposes in this context: that the main contemporary problem is a deficit of legitimacy for social institutions, and that this can be remedied by developing a theory of communication. First of all, as has been mentioned previously, it is a Kantian prejudice that "legitimation" is the basic problem of philosophy or even the basic problem of philosophy

in the modern era. It is even less plausible to think that it is the basic social problem of the modern world. Then, Habermas's conception of "discourse-without-domination"' – the 'ideal speech situation' – 'makes no sense: communication has no stable, invariant structure, certainly not one that would allow us to infer from it criteria for a universally valid set of norms, and for the identification and criticism of all forms of domination. In other words, there is no communication, at any rate in the following sense: there is no rule-governed form of linguistic behaviour that is necessarily oriented to universal norms that are implicit in it, can be anticipated and are always presupposed by those who participate in that form of behaviour.' Geuss, 'A Republic of Discussion'.

103 Adorno, *Minima Moralia*, 80.
104 Habermas, 'The Primal History of Subjectivity', 106–7.
105 Geuss, 'A Republic of Discussion'.
106 Adorno, *Metaphysics*, 7.
107 Adorno, *Minima Moralia*, 50; translation altered.
108 Adorno, *Metaphysics*, 7; translation altered.
109 Adorno, *Negative Dialectics*, 397.
110 Adorno, *Metaphysics*, 4.
111 Ibid., 7.
112 Adorno, *Negative Dialectics*, 408.
113 Adorno, 'Aberglaube aus zweiter Hand', in *Gesammelte Schriften, Bd. 8: Soziologische Schriften I*, ed. Rolf Tiedemann et al. (Frankfurt am Main: Suhrkamp, 1972), 174; my translation.
114 Adorno, *Gesammelte Schriften, Bd. 2: Kierkegaard – Konstruktion des Ästhetischen*, ed. Rolf Tiedemann et al. (Frankfurt am Main: Suhrkamp, 2003), 261; my translation.
115 Cf. Nietzsche, 'Of the Afterworldsmen', 58–60.
116 As noted in the previous chapter, an early articulation of this view appears in Adorno's inaugural lecture on 'The Actuality of Philosophy', 1931: '[w]hoever chooses philosophy as a profession today must first reject the illusion that earlier philosophical enterprises began with: that the power of thought is sufficient to grasp the totality of the real.' Adorno, 'The Actuality of Philosophy', 120.
117 Adorno, *Negative Dialectics*, 372; my emphasis. In one sense, Adorno sees Kant's effort to scientifically ground metaphysics as resigning him to rigid and immutable forms of cognition and experience. Indeed, Adorno argues that Kant 'equates the subjective side of Newtonian science with cognition, and its objective side with truth. The question how metaphysics is possible as a science must be taken precisely: whether metaphysics satisfies the criteria of a cognition

that takes its bearings from the ideal of mathematics and so-called classical physics.' Adorno, *Negative Dialectics*, 386–7.
118 Lukács, *Theory of the Novel*, 41.
119 For an illuminating account of Adorno's effort to think the particularity of historical suffering in terms of proper names, see Düttmann, *The Memory of Thought*.
120 Indeed, one of Adorno's twelve Meditations is dedicated specifically to the question of nihilism, which serves only as a diagnosis, not as a sustainable philosophical standpoint: 'nihilism implies the contrary of *identification* with nothingness'; rather, the negation of the 'created world (. . .) is the chance of another world that is not yet'. Adorno, *Metaphysics*, 104; my emphasis.
121 Adorno, *Negative Dialectics*, 381; my emphasis.
122 Adorno, *Metaphysics*, 68; original emphasis.
123 See pp. 48–50 of the present study.
124 Adorno, *Negative Dialectics*, 203.
125 Peter Osborne, 'Adorno and the Metaphysics of Modernism: The Problem of a "Postmodern" Art', in *The Problems of Modernity: Adorno and Benjamin*, ed. Andrew Benjamin (London: Routledge, 1989), 23.
126 Adorno, *Metaphysics*, 406.
127 Ibid., 363.
128 de Vries, *Minimal Theologies*.
129 Adorno, 'Reason and Revelation', 142.
130 Benjamin, 'Capitalism as Religion', 288; my emphasis. Cf. Max Weber, *The Protestant Ethic and the Spirit of Capitalism*, trans. Talcott Parsons (London: Routledge, 1992). To be sure, Benjamin's reading of Weber is, in some respects, unsatisfactory. After all, for Weber, it is the chance and not the teleological meeting between the rationality of predestination in Calvinism and commercial instrumentality that provides the occasion for capitalism's emergence. Weighing up this matter in due detail, however, exceeds the scope of the present inquiry.
131 Cf. Werner Hamacher, 'Guilt History: Benjamin's Sketch "Capitalism as Religion"', trans. Kirk Wetters, *Diacritics* 32, no. 3/4 (Autumn–Winter, 2002): 81–106.
132 Ernst Bloch, *Thomas Münzer als Theologe der Revolution* (Frankfurt am Main: Suhrkamp, 1962), 123, cited in: Hamacher, 'Guilt History', 88.
133 Hamacher, 'Guilt History', 88.
134 Cf. Uwe Steiner, 'Kapitalismus als Religion', in *Benjamin Handbuch, Leben – Werk – Wirkung*, ed. Burkhardt Lindner (Stuttgart & Weimar: Verlag J.B. Metzler, 2011), 167–74.

135 Steiner speculates that 'Abbau der Gewalt' may be identical with the only finished piece from the projected series, namely Benjamin's essay, 'Critique of Violence' (1921).
136 To my knowledge this piece has not been translated into English.
137 Cf. Uwe Steiner, 'The True Politician: Walter Benjamin's Concept of the Political', *New German Critique*, no. 83, Special Issue on Walter Benjamin (Spring–Summer 2001): 43–88.
138 Samuel Weber, *Benjamin's Abilities* (Cambridge, MA: Harvard University Press, 2010), 253.
139 Benjamin, 'Capitalism as Religion', 288; translation altered. The translators of Benjamin's *Selected Writings* have dropped the term *unmittelbar* – immediately – from their translation.
140 Ibid., 290.
141 Ibid.
142 Ibid. In the 1930s Benjamin elaborates this idea with a view to Marx. In the notes comprising his unfinished *Arcades Project*, for instance, he describes the shopping arcades of *fin-de-siècle* Paris as 'temples of commodity capital'. In this early fragment, however, Benjamin remains critical of Marx, echoing Landauer's claim that capitalism cannot produce socialism out of itself. Cf. Walter Benjamin, *The Arcades Project*, ed. Rolf Tiedemann, trans. Howard Eiland and Kevin McLaughlin (Cambridge, MA: The Belknap Press of Harvard University Press, 1996), 37.
143 Weber, *Benjamin's Abilities*, 254.
144 Ibid.
145 Ibid.
146 Ibid.
147 Benjamin, 'Capitalism as Religion', 288; translation altered. As Steiner argues, Benjamin's original formulation, 'sans rêve et sans merci', without dream or mercy, is probably the result of a confusion on his part. The allusion is in all likelihood to Charles Baudelaire's poem 'Le Crépescule du Soir', which is contained in the *Tableaux Parisiens* (1857), which Benjamin translated.
148 Ibid.
149 Weber, *Benjamin's Abilities*, 256; my emphasis.
150 Benjamin, 'Capitalism as Religion', 288.
151 Ibid., 289; translation altered.
152 Ibid.
153 Ibid.
154 Hamacher, 'Guilt History', 90.
155 Benjamin: 'On the Concept of History', 395.

156 Hamacher, 'Guilt History', 81.
157 Ibid.
158 Ibid.
159 Ibid., 85.
160 Ibid., 98.
161 Benjamin, 'Capitalism as Religion', 289.
162 Friedrich Nietzsche, *On the Genealogy of Morals*, trans. Walter Kaufmann and R. J. Hollingdale (New York: Vintage Books, 1989), 92.
163 Ibid. I consciously bracket Benjamin's discussion of Nietzsche's *Übermensch*, which opens up a strand of his fragment that need not concern us at present.
164 Hamacher, 'Guilt History', 98.
165 Walter Benjamin, 'Fragment 65', in *Gesammelte Schriften VI: Fragmente Vermischten Inhalts / Autobiographische Schriften*, ed. Rolf Tiedemann and Hermann Schweppenhäuser (Frankfurt am Main: Suhrkamp, 1985), 92; my translation.
166 Hamacher, 'Guilt History', 84.
167 Walter Benjamin, 'Fate and Character', in *Selected Writings, Vol. 1: 1913–1926*, ed. Marcus Bullock and Michael W. Jennings (Cambridge, MA: The Belknap Press of Harvard University Press, 1996), 204; translation altered.
168 Samuel Weber, 'Guilt, Debt and the Turn to the Future: Walter Benjamin and Hermann Levin Goldschmidt' (A Foray into Economic Theology), *Dialogik*, last altered December 2012. Available online: http://www.dialogik.org/wp/wp-content/uploads/2010/12/Sam-Weber-Turn-to-the-Future1.pdf (accessed 18 July 2014).
169 Weber, *Benjamin's Abilities*, 259.
170 Benjamin, 'Fate and Character', 204; translation altered. In recent years, Giorgio Agamben has adopted the idea of 'bare life' in his work on the *homo sacer*. Cf. Giorgio Agamben, *Homo Sacer: Sovereign Power and Bare Life*, trans. Daniel Heller-Roazen (Stanford: Stanford University Press, 1998).
171 Sami Khatib, 'Towards a Politics of "Pure Means": Walter Benjamin and the Question of Violence', *Anthropological Materialism*, last altered March 2014. Available online: http://anthropologicalmaterialism.hypotheses.org/1040 (accessed 18 July 2014).
172 Weber, 'Guilt, Debt and the Turn to the Future'.
173 Benjamin, 'Critique of Violence', 239. For an in-depth exploration of Benjamin's concept of historical time and the prospects of its interruption time, see Werner Hamacher, 'Now: Walter Benjamin and Historical Time', in *Walter Benjamin and History*, ed. Andrew Benjamin (London: Continuum, 2005), 38–68.

174 Adorno and Horkheimer, *Dialectic of Enlightenment*, 145.
175 Adorno, *Negative Dialectics*, 207; my emphasis.
176 M. F. Connell, 'Through the Eyes of an Artificial Angel: Secular Theology in Theodor W. Adorno's Freudo-Marxist Reading of Kafka and Walter Benjamin', in *Trajectories of Mysticism in Theory and Literature*, ed. P. Leonard (London: Palgrave Macmillan, 2000), 198.
177 For an illuminating account of the relationship between Adorno and Blumenberg, see Christian Voller, 'Kommunikation verweigert. Schwierige Beziehungen zwischen Blumenberg und Adorno', *Zeitschrift für Kulturphilosophie*, no. 2 (2013): 381–405. Voller discusses the brief correspondence between Adorno and Blumenberg in light of their respective contributions to the Seventh German Philosophers' Congress in Münster (1962). The focus of this event was the concept of progress in the philosophy of history. (Blumenberg's presentation formed the basis for the first part of *The Legitimacy of the Modern Age*, whereas Adorno's presentation was reworked into an essay titled 'Progress'. Both papers were first published in a volume containing the papers presented at the conference.) Reconstructing Voller's detailed cross-reading exceeds the scope of the present chapter. Suffice it to note that Blumenberg's critique of the concept of secularization allows for an interesting perspective on Adorno's intentions.
178 Hans Blumenberg, *The Legitimacy of the Modern Age*, trans. Robert M. Wallace (Cambridge, MA: MIT Press, 1983), 92.
179 Ibid., 3.
180 Stephen A. McKnight, 'The Legitimacy of the Modern Age: The Löwith-Blumenberg Debate in Light of Recent Scholarship', *The Political Science Reviewer*. Available online: http://www.mmisi.org/pr/19_01/mcknight.pdf (accessed 26 August 2014).
181 Cf. Fredric Jameson, 'The Vanishing Mediator: Narrative Structure in Max Weber', *New German Critique*, no. 1 (Winter 1973): 52–89. As has already been suggested, this claim runs through *The Protestant Ethic and the Spirit of Capitalism*, where Weber argues that capitalism first usurps and then effaces the religious sources from which it emerges.
182 Carl Schmitt, *Political Theology*, trans. Georg Schwab (Chicago: University of Chicago Press, 1985), 36. As Blumenberg points out, Schmitt's wholesale identification of political sovereignty with divine sovereignty is axiomatic for his book *Political Theology* (1922). I consciously bracket here both Blumenberg's and Benjamin's (not to mention Taubes's and Agamben's) relationship to Schmitt.

183 Cf. Karl Löwith, *Meaning in History: The Theological Implications of the Philosophy of History* (Chicago: University of Chicago Press, 1949).
184 Robert M. Wallace, 'Secularisation and Modernity: The Löwith-Blumenberg Debate', *New German Critique*, no. 22 (Winter 1981): 64.
185 Ibid.
186 Blumenberg, *The Legitimacy of the Modern Age*, 9.
187 Agamben, 'In Praise of Profanation', 73.
188 Ibid.
189 Ibid.
190 Ibid., 74.
191 Ibid.
192 Ibid., 76.
193 Ibid., 75; my emphasis.
194 Ibid., 76.
195 Ibid.
196 Ibid.
197 Cf. Giorgio Agamben, *The Kingdom and the Glory: For a Theological Genealogy of Economy and Government*, trans. Lorenzo Chiesa and Matteo Mandarini (Stanford: Stanford University Press, 2011); Giorgio Agamben, *The State of Exception*, trans. Kevin Attell (Chicago: University of Chicago Press, 2004).
198 Alberto Toscano, 'Divine Management: Critical Remarks on Giorgio Agamben's *The Kingdom and the Glory*', *Angelaki: Journal of the Theoretical Humanities* 3, no. 16 (November 2011): 128.
199 Toscano, 'Divine Management', 129.
200 The term *Entstellung* is somewhat inopportunely rendered only as 'distortion' in the standard English-language edition of Freud's works. This rendering obfuscates the term's dynamic and topographical connotations, which are better captured by the word 'dislocation'. The term initially appears in the first part of Freud's *The Interpretation of Dreams*. Sigmund Freud, 'Distortion in Dreams', *The Standard Edition of the Complete Psychological Works of Sigmund Freud, Vol. IV: The Interpretation of Dreams (First Part)*, ed. James Strachey, Anna Freud, Alex Strachey and Alan Tyson, trans. James Strachey (London: Hogarth Press, 1953), 134–63.
201 Sigmund Freud, *Moses and Monotheism*, trans. Katherine Jones (New York: Vintage Books, 1955), 52.
202 Cf. Jean-Luc Nancy, 'Ré-fa-mi-ré-do-si-do-ré-si-sol-sol (le peuple souverain s'avance)', in *La démocratie à venir*, ed. Marie-Louise Mallet (Paris: Galilée, 2004), 348; my translation.

203 Samuel Weber, *Return to Freud: Jacques Lacan's Dislocation of Psychoanalysis*, trans. Michael Levine (Cambridge: Cambridge University Press, 1991), xvii.
204 Sami Khatib, *'Teleologie Ohne Endzweck': Walter Benjamins Ent-Stellung des Messianischen* (Marburg: Tectum, 2013), 37; my translation.
205 Ibid., 39; my translation.
206 Ibid.; my translation.
207 Ibid., 41. Admittedly, this very literal reading is open to certain criticisms. As Samuel Weber argues, there is no original 'location' that precedes the 'dislocation' of the unconscious. With a view to Lacan, Weber gives the problem a linguistic framing by characterizing the 'language of the unconscious' in terms of the 'unconscious *as* language'. He continues: '[w]hat distinguishes this particular linguistic form is that it never simply speaks directly (…) but rather misspeaks itself [*verspricht sich*], concealing, denying, disavowing.' As Weber explains, '[i]n this way the unconscious forms a language of representation that is not constituted by what it designates (…), a translation without an original or, as Freud would say, another scene.' Weber, *Return to Freud*, 1–2.
208 For a critical account of Adorno's reading of Benjamin's piece, see Sigrid Weigel, 'Zu Franz Kafka', in *Benjamin Handbuch, Leben – Werk – Wirkung*, ed. Burkhardt Lindner (Stuttgart & Weimar: Verlag J.B. Metzler, 2011), 539–42. A brief note on Benjamin and Adorno's place in the history of Kafka reception: both authors reject two dominant interpretative strands from the 1930s, which they describe as 'natural' and 'supernatural', respectively. While the former refers to authors such as Hellmuth Kaiser, whose book *Kafkas Inferno* (1931) attempts a psychological account of Kafka's texts, the latter means – above all – Kafka's editor Max Brod, who emphasizes the religious weighting of his friend's work (see *Theodor W. Adorno & Walter Benjamin: The Complete Correspondence*, 67). As Brod insists, Kafka's concern with guilt, grace, judgement and redemption indicates a positive commitment to God in the face of existential despair. In this respect, he asserts that Kafka's Judaism is equally decisive as his affinity for heterodox Christian thinkers like Kierkegaard. This view is taken up by Brod's erstwhile collaborator Hans-Joachim Schoeps, who goes one step further by arguing that Kafka must be read in light of Karl Barth's dialectical theology. As Schoeps suggests, both Barth and Kafka honour Kierkegaard's verdict about the infinite qualitative distinction between humankind and God: only the inward turn to faith – away from the corrupt institution of the church – can bring about humanity's redemption. Cf. Hellmuth Kaiser, *Kafkas Inferno: Eine psychologische Deutung seiner Strafphantasie* (Vienna: Psychoanalytischer Verlag, 1931); Max Brod, *Franz Kafkas Glauben und Lehre* (Düsseldorf: Onomato, 2011);

Max Brod and Hans-Joachim Schoeps, *Im Streit um Kafka und das Judentum* (Frankfurt am Main: Jüdischer Verlag, 1985). For a sharp rebuke of Schoeps's position, see Gershom Scholem, 'Open Letter', in *Gershom Scholem: Kabbalah and Counter-History* (Cambridge, MA: Harvard University Press, 1982), 130. On the connection to Barth, see Margarete Kohlenbach, 'Kafka, Critical Theory, Dialectical Theology: Adorno's Case Against Hans-Joachim Schoeps', *German Life and Letters* 63, no. 2 (April 2010): 146–65; see also Hent de Vries, 'Inverse versus Dialectical Theology: The Two Faces of Negativity and the Miracle of Faith', *Cornellcast Video*, last altered September 2012. Available online: http://www.cornell.edu/video/inverse-versus-dialectical-theology (accessed 26 August 2014). Regarding Kafka's connection to Kierkegaard: Adorno changes his mind on this point. Early on he describes Kafka as Kierkegaard's 'student'. Adorno, *Kierkegaard*, 25; later on he describes him as his 'critic'. Adorno, 'Notes on Kafka', 267.

209 This text is thought to have been lost.
210 Cf. Carolin Duttlinger, *Kafka and Photography* (Oxford: Oxford University Press, 2007).
211 For a useful account of Adorno's reading of Kafka, see Sonja Dierks, 'Kafka-Lektüre' in *Adorno Handbuch, Leben – Werk – Wirkung*, ed. Richard Klein, Johann Kreuzer and Stefan Müller-Doohm (Stuttgart & Weimar: Verlag J.B. Metzler, 2011), 210–13. Although Adorno frequently refers to Kafka, his 1953 essay is the only sustained engagement with the author.
212 Adorno, *Minima Moralia*, 247; translation altered, my emphasis.
213 Cf. Gershom Scholem, *Major Trends in Jewish Mysticism* (Jerusalem: Schocken Books, 1941).
214 Adorno, 'Notes on Kafka', 268.
215 Ibid.
216 Ibid.
217 Cf. Kant, *Critique of Pure Reason*, 618.
218 Cf. Immanuel Kant, *Critique of the Power of Judgement*, ed. Paul Guyer, trans. Paul Guyer and Eric Matthews (Cambridge: Cambridge University Press, 2000), 277.
219 Ibid.
220 Ibid.
221 Kant, *Critique of Pure Reason*, 606.
222 Kant, *Critique of the Power of Judgement*, 277.
223 Ibid.
224 Ibid.

225 Ibid., 274.
226 Kohlenbach, 'Kafka, Critical Theory, Dialectical Theology', 159–60.
227 Ibid.; my emphasis.
228 Jacob Taubes, *The Political Theology of Paul*, trans. Dana Hollander (Stanford: Stanford University Press, 2003), 74. Curiously, this objection is anticipated in Taubes's earlier critique of Alexandre Kojève: Cf. Jacob Taubes, 'Ästhetisierung der Wahrheit im Posthistoire', in *Alexandre Kojève: Überlebungsformen*, ed. Andreas Hiepki (Berlin: Merve Verlag, 2007), 39–57.
229 Taubes, *The Political Theology of Paul*, 74.
230 Ibid.
231 Giorgio Agamben, *The Time That Remains: A Commentary on the Letter to the Romans*, trans. Patricia Dailey (Stanford: Stanford University Press, 2005), 35.
232 Ibid., 38; my emphasis.
233 Ibid.
234 Ibid.; my emphasis.
235 Agamben appears to be referring to the opening passage from *Negative Dialectics*, where Adorno famously claims that '[p]hilosophy, which once seemed obsolete, lives on because the moment to realise it was missed' (Adorno, *Negative Dialectics*, 3). As is well known, Adorno plays here on Marx's view of communism as the becoming-socially-actual of philosophical universality in practice. Pending this actualization, however, Adorno views philosophy as having a suspended life, a kind of posthumous existence. He accepts Marx's materialist critique of philosophy, whereby philosophers have only interpreted the world, whereas the point would be to change it, albeit with the proviso that history has cast serious doubt on the possibility of such a practical overcoming in the present. As was noted in the previous chapter, *Negative Dialectics* thus continues with the philosophical critique of philosophy because Adorno deems that these efforts have not been sufficient. The critique of philosophy must continue on the understanding that the Marxian actualization of philosophy may yet occur. For Agamben, however, Adorno's arrest in the moment of critique means that he retreats to a realm of semblance – '[a]esthetic beauty' as *schöner Schein* – conceived of as a 'chastisement' for 'philosophy's having missed its moment' (Agamben, *The Time That Remains*, 37).
236 Howard Caygill, *A Kant Dictionary* (Oxford: Blackwell Publishing, 2000), 86.
237 Immanuel Kant, *Groundwork of the Metaphysics of Morals*, trans. Mary Gregor (Cambridge: Cambridge University Press, 1997), 45; my emphasis.
238 Kant, *Critique of Pure Reason*, 609; my emphasis.
239 Eva Schaper, 'The Kantian "As If" and Its Relevance for Aesthetics', *Proceedings of the Aristotelian Society, New Series* 65 (1964–1965): 227; original emphasis.

240 Kant, *Critique of the Power of Judgement*, 185; my emphasis.
241 Schaper, 'The Kantian "As If" and Its Relevance for Aesthetics', 232.
242 Kant, *Critique of the Power of Judgement*, 112.
243 Ibid., 233.
244 Adorno, *Aesthetic Theory*, ed. Rolf Tiedemann and Gretel Adorno, trans. Robert Hullot-Kentor (London: Continuum, 2002), 123; translation altered.
245 Hans Vaihinger, *The Philosophy of 'As If'*, trans. C. K. Ogden (London: Kegan Paul, Tench, Trubner & Co., 1935), xii.
246 Ibid., 105.
247 Ibid.; original emphasis.
248 Vaihinger, *The Philosophy of 'As If'*, 322, cited in: Agamben, *The Time That Remains*, 36–7.
249 Agamben, *The Time That Remains*, 37.
250 Adorno, *Kant's Critique of Pure Reason*, ed. Rolf Tiedemann, trans. Rodney Livingstone (Stanford: Stanford University Press, 2001), 111.
251 Adorno, 'Valéry's Deviations', in *Notes to Literature, Vol. 2*, trans. Shierry Weber Nicholsen (New York: Columbia University Press, 1992), 157; my emphasis.
252 Adorno, 'Progress', in *Critical Models: Interventions and Catchwords*, trans. Henry W. Pickford (New York: Columbia University Press, 1998), 145.
253 Ibid.
254 Ibid.
255 Ibid.
256 Ibid., 151.
257 Ibid., 153.
258 Adorno, 'Notes on Kafka', 258; my emphasis.
259 Walter Benjamin, *The Correspondence of Walter Benjamin 1910–1940*, ed. Theodor W. Adorno and Gershom Scholem, trans. Manfred R. Jacobson and Evelyn M. Jacobson (Chicago: University of Chicago Press, 1994), 453.
260 Agamben, *The Time That Remains*, 30–1.
261 Adorno, 'Notes on Kafka', 259; translation altered.
262 Benjamin: 'Franz Kafka', 808.
263 Adorno, 'Notes on Kafka', 270.
264 Gordon, *Adorno and Existence*, 179; original emphasis.
265 Kafka, *Nachgelassene Schriften und Fragmente II*, 360; my translation.
266 See p. 3 of the present study.
267 Werner Hamacher, 'The Gesture in the Name: On Benjamin and Kafka', in *Premises*, trans. Peter Fenves (Cambridge, MA: Harvard University Press, 1996), 336.
268 Ibid.

269 Ibid.
270 Adorno, *Metaphysics*, 7; original emphasis. I am conscious of the fact that the Adorno-critic, Hamacher, would almost certainly not have endorsed this view.

Chapter 3

1 'The destructive character sees no image before him.' Walter Benjamin, 'Der destruktive Charakter', in *Gesammete Schriften IV: Kleine Prosa / Baudelaire-Übertragungen*, ed. Tillmann Rexroth (Frankfurt am Main: Suhrkamp, 1991), 397; my translation.
2 Adorno, 'Mahler', in *Quasi Una Fantasia: Essays on Modern Music*, trans. Rodney Livingstone (London: Verso, 1992), 110; Adorno, 'Sacred Fragment', 243.
3 Adorno, 'Parataxis: On Hölderlin's Late Poetry', in *Notes to Literature, Vol. 2*, trans. Shierry Weber Nicholsen (New York: Columbia University Press, 1992), 142; Adorno, *Aesthetic Theory*, 21.
4 Adorno, *Aesthetic Theory*, 67.
5 Ibid., 344.
6 Ibid., 67; original emphasis.
7 Rodolphe Gasché, 'The Theory of Natural Beauty and Its Evil Star: Kant, Hegel, Adorno', *Research in Phenomenology* 32, no.1 (2002): 104.
8 Ibid.
9 Ibid.
10 Adorno, *Aesthetic Theory*, 67.
11 Ibid.
12 Ibid., 65–6.
13 Kant, *Critique of the Power of Judgement*, 156. It seems probable that Kant's reference to the image ban follows from his exchange with the pre-eminent philosopher of the Jewish Enlightenment, Moses Mendelssohn. Cf. Ingrid Lohmann, 'Das Motiv des Bilderverbots bei Moses Mendelssohn', *Das Achtzehnte Jahrhundert – Zeitschrift der Deutschen Gesellschaft für die Erforschung des achtzehnten Jahrhunderts* 36, no. 1 (2012): 33–42.
14 Kant, *Critique of the Power of Judgement*, 81–2.
15 Ibid., 9.
16 Ibid., 54.
17 Incidentally, Kant has often been charged with failing to realize this ambition. Hegel, for instance, famously criticizes Kant's effort to lay a comprehensive

groundwork for any future philosophy by likening it to learning to swim before getting into the water. Cf. Hegel, *Lectures on the History of Philosophy*, 263.
18 Caygill, *A Kant Dictionary*, 140; my emphasis.
19 Ibid.
20 Ibid.
21 Kant, *Critique of the Power of Judgement*, 43. As Caygill highlights, despite prevalent commonplaces, it is, in fact, far from self-evident what exactly Kant means by a 'reflective' judgement. '[T]he principle of reflective judgement remains undetermined, although it clearly involves pleasure, the enhancement of life, communication through common sense and tradition, and hints of a supersensible harmony.' Caygill, *A Kant Dictionary*, 55. See also Howard Caygill, *The Art of Judgement* (Oxford: Blackwell Publishing, 1989).
22 Kant, *Critique of the Power of Judgement*, 96.
23 Ibid., 104.
24 Ibid., 120.
25 Ibid., 124.
26 Ibid., 89.
27 Ibid., 91–2.
28 Ibid., 90. For an interesting account of Kant's views on the French Revolution, see Dieter Henrich, 'The French Revolution and Classical German Philosophy: Toward a Determination of Their Relation', in *Aesthetic Judgement and the Moral Image of the World* (Stanford: Stanford University Press, 1992), 85–99.
29 Ibid., 97.
30 Guyer, 'Editor's Introduction', xvii.
31 Ibid.; my emphasis.
32 Ibid., xxix; my emphasis.
33 Kant, *Critique of the Power of Judgement*, 114. Kant discusses both 'perfect' and 'ideal' kinds of beauty as exceptions to this rule. The details of his account need not concern us here. Suffice it to note that Kant postulates an ideal of beauty as something that is adequate to the idea of the moral law, which – in turn – governs humankind's highest and final purpose.
34 Ibid., 111.
35 Ibid., 112.
36 Cf. Rodolphe Gasché, 'On Mere Form', in *The Idea of Form: Rethinking Kant's Philosophy* (Stanford: Stanford University Press, 2003), 60–88.
37 It is not immediately plain to see how Kant distinguishes between the legitimate pleasure derived from the form of an object and the illegitimate gratification

derived from its sensory aspect. In fact, this difficulty has repeatedly earned Kant the charge of a certain formalism. As Caygill summarizes, '[b]y distinguishing beauty from any content, whether rational or sensible', Kant is sometimes seen as having 'severely limited' the 'scope' of beauty. 'If sensible content were to play any part, then the object would not be beautiful but only agreeable; if a concept were involved, then the beautiful would be too easily convertible with the rational. If they could exist, such beauties would be "dependent" and contrasted with the "free" beauties which "represent nothing" and cannot strictly speaking even be artefacts. Consequently, Kant appeared to many critics as unduly privileging the beauty of nature over the beauty of art, even on those occasions when he attempts to rescue the beauty of art by insisting that it appear as if it were natural.' Caygill, *A Kant Dictionary*, 92.
38 Guyer, 'Editor's Introduction', xxix; my emphasis.
39 Kant, *Critique of the Power of Judgement*, 114.
40 Ibid., 122.
41 Ibid., 123.
42 Guyer, 'Editor's Introduction', xxx.
43 Gasché, 'The Theory of Natural Beauty and Its Evil Star: Kant, Hegel, Adorno', 108; my emphasis.
44 Immanuel Kant, *The Metaphysics of Morals*, trans. Mary J. Gregor (Cambridge: Cambridge University Press, 1996), 237.
45 Gasché, 'The Theory of Natural Beauty and Its Evil Star: Kant, Hegel, Adorno', 106.
46 Kant, *Critique of the Power of Judgement*, 225. The question of the symbol will resurface in our discussion of Hegel.
47 Gasché, 'The Theory of Natural Beauty and Its Evil Star: Kant, Hegel, Adorno', 107; my emphasis.
48 Ibid., 108.
49 Ibid.
50 Ibid.
51 Ibid., 108–9.
52 Ibid., 109.
53 Cf. Adorno, *Kant's Critique of Pure Reason*.
54 As is well known, the sublime became a central philosophical concern during the eighteenth century, particularly in Britain, where it was theorized extensively by the likes of Edmund Burke and David Hume – authors with whose work Kant was well acquainted. The term itself dates back to Longinus's tract *On the Sublime*, thought to have been written between AD 100 and 300.

For an interesting overview of philosophies of the sublime, see Andrew Ashfield and Peter de Bolla, eds, *The Sublime: A Reader in British Eighteenth-Century Aesthetic Theory* (Cambridge: Cambridge University Press, 1996).
55 Kant, *Critique of the Power of Judgement*, 131.
56 Ibid., 143.
57 Ibid., 144.
58 Ibid., 136.
59 Ibid., 141.
60 Ibid., 136.
61 Ibid., 144.
62 Ibid., 128; my emphasis.
63 Ibid., 131–2.
64 Ibid., 134.
65 Ibid., 133.
66 Ibid., 134.
67 Ibid., 135; my emphasis.
68 Ibid.
69 Ibid., 134.
70 Ibid., 141.
71 Ibid.
72 Ibid., 143.
73 Ibid., 144.
74 Ibid., 144–5.
75 Ibid., 143.
76 Achim Geisenhanslüke, 'Bilderverbot: Kant – Lyotard – Kafka', in *Der Bildhunger der Literatur – Festschrift für Günter E. Grimm*, ed. Dieter Heimböckel and Uwe Werlein (Würzburg: Königshausen + Neumann, 2005), 37; my translation.
77 Ibid.
78 Kant, *Critique of the Power of Judgement*, 129.
79 Geisenhanslüke, 'Bilderverbot: Kant – Lyotard – Kafka', 37–8; my translation.
80 Cf. Jean-François Lyotard, 'Newman: The Instant', in *The Inhuman: Reflections on Time*, trans. Geoffrey Bennington and Rachel Bowlby (Cambridge: Polity Press, 1991), 78–88; Jean-François Lyotard, 'The Sublime and the Avant-Garde', in *The Lyotard Reader*, ed. Andrew Benjamin, trans. Geoffrey Bennington and Marian Hobson (Oxford: Blackwell Publishing, 1989), 196–211. For an interesting account of the ethical commitments underlying Lyotard's philosophy, see Martin Jay, 'The Ethics of Blindness and the Postmodern

Sublime: Levinas and Lyotard', in *Downcast Eyes: The Denigration of Vision in Twentieth-Century French Thought* (Berkeley: University of California Press, 1993), 543–86.

81 Adorno, 'Cultural Criticism and Society', in *Prisms*, trans. Samuel Weber and Shierry Weber (Cambridge, MA: MIT Press, 1981), 34.
82 Jacques Rancière, 'Are Some Things Unrepresentable?', in *The Future of the Image*, trans. Gregory Elliott (London: Verso, 2007), 134; my emphasis.
83 Cf. Jean-François Lyotard, 'Adorno as the Devil', *Telos*, no. 19 (Spring 1974): 127–37.
84 Lyotard's wider interest in Adorno is spelled out in the following texts: Jean-François Lyotard, *The Different: Phrases in Dispute*, trans. Georges Van Den Abbeele (Manchester: Manchester University Press, 1988); 'Discussions, or Phrasing "after Auschwitz"', in *The Lyotard Reader*, ed. Andrew Benjamin, trans. Geoffrey Bennington and Marian Hobson (Oxford: Blackwell Publishing, 1989), 360–92.
85 Lyotard, 'Newman: The Instant', 246.
86 Ibid.
87 Jean-François Lyotard, 'After the Sublime, the State of Aesthetics', in *The Inhuman: Reflections on Time*, trans. Geoffrey Bennington and Rachel Bowlby (Cambridge: Polity Press, 1991), 135.
88 To be sure, Lyotard is not alone in associating the sublime with art. Following Hegel, Adorno, too, explores this possibility (albeit to different ends). See especially the closing sections in *Aesthetic Theory* entitled 'Truth Content Is Historical: The Sublime in Nature and Art' and 'The Sublime and Play'.
89 Jacques Rancière, 'The Sublime from Lyotard to Schiller – Two Readings of Kant and Their Political Significance', *Radical Philosophy*, no. 126 (July–August 2004): 8.
90 Rancière, 'The Sublime from Lyotard to Schiller', 10; my emphasis.
91 Lyotard, 'After the Sublime, the State of Aesthetics', 136; my emphasis.
92 Ibid.; my emphasis.
93 Ibid.; translation altered.
94 Ibid.; original emphasis.
95 Ibid.; 137.
96 Ibid.
97 Ibid.; original emphasis.
98 This view comes close to the central precept of Critical Theory, namely the notion of instrumental reason. Cf. Max Horkheimer, *Critique of Instrumental Reason*, trans. Matthew J. O'Connell (New York: Seabury Press, 1974).

99 Lyotard, 'After the Sublime, the State of Aesthetics', 136.
100 Ibid., 138.
101 Ibid., 139.
102 Ibid., 138; original emphasis.
103 Ibid., 139.
104 Ibid.
105 Ibid., 140.
106 Ibid.; original emphasis.
107 Ibid.
108 Ibid., 139.
109 Ibid.
110 Rancière, 'The Sublime from Lyotard to Schiller', 8.
111 Lyotard, 'After the Sublime, the State of Aesthetics', 141.
112 Rancière, 'The Sublime from Lyotard to Schiller', 9.
113 Ibid., 10.
114 Jean-François Lyotard, 'Anima Minima', in *Postmodern Fables*, trans. Georges van den Abbeele (Minneapolis: University of Minnesota Press, 1999), 243.
115 Rancière, 'The Sublime from Lyotard to Schiller', 10.
116 Ibid.
117 Rancière, 'Are Some Things Unrepresentable?', 111; original emphasis.
118 Ibid.
119 Lyotard qualifies his use of the lower case as follows: 'I write "the jews" this way neither out of prudence nor lack of something better. I use lower case to indicate that I am not thinking of a nation. I make it plural to signify that it is neither a figure nor a political (Zionism), religious (Judaism), or philosophical (Jewish philosophy) subject that I put forward under this name. I use quotation marks to avoid confusing these 'jews' with real Jews.' Jean-François Lyotard, *Heidegger and 'the Jews'*, trans. Andreas Michel and Mark Roberts (Minneapolis: University of Minnesota Press, 1990), 3. I resist the temptation of asking quite which 'jews' Lyotard does mean.
120 Rancière, 'Are Some Things Unrepresentable?', 133.
121 Ibid.
122 Ibid., 134.
123 Ibid. In *Heidegger and 'the jews'*, Lyotard devotes some lengthy passages to Claude Lanzmann's path-breaking documentary film *Shoah* (1985).
124 Ibid.
125 Adorno, *Aesthetic Theory*, 136.
126 Ibid., 32.

127 Cf. G. W. F. Hegel, *Philosophy of Mind: Being Part Three of the Encyclopaedia of Philosophical Sciences*, trans. William Wallace (Oxford: Clarendon Press, 1971). See especially the passages on 'Art' in the section on 'Absolute Spirit' (§§ 556–563).

128 A collection of transcripts from Hegel's numerous lecture series on aesthetics, held in Heidelberg and Berlin between 1820 and 1829, was edited and published by his student Heinrich Gustav Hotho in 1835 (a second, expanded edition followed in 1842). Hotho's volume is supposed to have been based on a manuscript by Hegel; however, the original text has long since been lost. Although the lectures are generally viewed as the fullest articulation of Hegel's aesthetics – at any rate, they are Adorno's source – it should be noted that Hotho's edition has increasingly come under fire for its heavy-handed editorial interventions. Annemarie Gethmann-Siefert, for instance, argues that there is evidence to suggest that Hegel's aesthetics are not as systematic as Hotho would have us believe. The wider implications of this claim are only gradually beginning to emerge as more reliable transcripts of Hegel's lectures are becoming available. Cf. Annemarie Gethmann-Siefert, *Einführung in Hegels Ästhetik* (Munich: Wilhelm Fink Verlag, 2005); Annemarie Gethmann-Siefert, 'Phänomen versus System', in *Phänomen versus System: zum Verhältnis von philosophischer Systematik und Kunsturteil in Hegels Berliner Vorlesungen oder Philosophie der Kunst*, ed. A. Gethmann-Siefert (Bonn: Bouvier, 1992), 9–40; G. W. F. Hegel, *Philosophie der Kunst oder Ästhetik. Nach Hegel. Im Sommer 1826. Mitschrift Carl Hermann Victor von Kehler*, ed. A. Gethmann-Siefert and B. Collenberg-Plotnikov (Munich: Wilhelm Fink Verlag, 2004); G. W. F. Hegel, *Philosophie der Kunst. Vorlesung von 1826*, ed. A. Gethmann-Siefert, J. I-Kwon and K. Berr (Frankfurt am Main: Suhrkamp, 2004); G. W. F. Hegel, *Vorlesung über Ästhetik. Berlin 1820-21. Eine Nachschrift*, ed. H. Schneider (Frankfurt am Main: Peter Lang, 1995); G. W. F. Hegel, *Vorlesungen über die Philosophie der Kunst*, ed. A. Gethmann-Siefert (Hamburg: Felix Meiner Verlag, 2003).

129 G. W. F. Hegel, *Aesthetics: Lectures on Fine Arts*, trans. T. M. Knox (Oxford: Clarendon Press, 1975), 116.

130 Ibid.; original emphasis.

131 Gasché, 'The Theory of Natural Beauty and Its Evil Star: Kant, Hegel, Adorno', 110; my emphasis.

132 For an illuminating account of Hegel's privileging of Greek sculpture, see Rebecca Comay, 'Defaced Statues: Idealism and Iconoclasm in Hegel's *Aesthetics*', *October*, no. 149 (Summer 2014): 123–42.

133 Cf. G. W. F. Hegel, *The Science of Logic*, trans. George Di Giovanni (Cambridge: Cambridge University Press: 2010), 677.
134 Hegel, *Aesthetics*, 120.
135 Ibid., 116.
136 Ibid., 108.
137 Ibid., 130.
138 Ibid., 116.
139 Ibid., 128; my emphasis.
140 Ibid., 130; my emphasis.
141 Ibid.
142 Ibid., 145–6.
143 Gasché, 'The Theory of Natural Beauty and Its Evil Star: Kant, Hegel, Adorno', 111.
144 Ibid.
145 Ibid., 109.
146 It exceeds the scope of the present chapter to provide a summary of Hegel's views on Judaism more generally. Suffice it to note that his attitude might politely be characterized as reserved. Cf. Nathan Rotenstreich, 'Hegel's Image of Judaism', *Jewish Social Studies* 15, no. 1 (January 1953): 33–52.
147 Hegel, *Aesthetics*, 175.
148 Ibid., 373. Indeed, according to Rancière, this Hegelian trope is precisely what Lyotard's identification of sublime art with 'the jews' tends towards. As he writes, 'What is assigning a people the task of representing a moment of thought, and identifying the extermination of this people with a law of the psychic apparatus, if not a hyperbolic version of the Hegelian operation that makes the moments of the development of spirit – and forms of art – correspond to the concrete historical figures of a people or a civilization?' Rancière, 'Are Some Things Unrepresentable?', 134.
149 For reasons of brevity, I am sidestepping Hegel's discussion of the individual arts – architecture, sculpture, painting, music and poetry – which follows the account of the three main forms of art.
150 Hegel, *Aesthetics*, 324.
151 I use 'maturity' here in contrast with Hegel's derisive (if typical for the time) description of 'nations' – for example, Persians, Indians, Egyptians – as persisting in a state of putative 'childhood'. Hegel, *Aesthetics*, 308.
152 David James, *Art, Myth and Society in Hegel's Aesthetics* (London: Continuum, 2009), 18.
153 Hegel, *Aesthetics*, 365.

154 James, *Art, Myth and Society in Hegel's Aesthetics*, 18.
155 Ibid., 21.
156 Cf. Peter C. Hodgson, *Hegel and Christian Theology: A Reading of the Lectures on the Philosophy of Religion* (Oxford: Oxford University Press, 2005).
157 Adorno, *Aesthetic Theory*, 73.
158 Ibid., 62.
159 Kant, *Critique of the Power of Judgement*, 185; my emphasis.
160 Adorno, *Aesthetic Theory*, 76.
161 Adorno, 'Progress', 153.
162 Ibid., 243.
163 Ibid., 41.
164 Adorno, *Negative Dialectics*, trans. E. B. Ashton (London: Routledge, 1973), 10; translation altered. See p. 35 of the present study. The view that there are more or less advanced works of art has earned Adorno the charge of progressivism from the likes of Peter Bürger. Cf. Peter Bürger, *Theory of the Avant-Garde*, trans. Michael Shaw (Minneapolis: Minnesota University Press, 1984).
165 Adorno, *Aesthetic Theory*, 78; my emphasis.
166 Ibid., 3.
167 Ibid., 1; my emphasis.
168 Ibid., 61; translation altered.
169 Ibid., 72.
170 See pp. 91–3 of the present study.
171 Ibid., 62.
172 Adorno, *Negative Dialectics*, 220. In addition to the 'Freedom' model from *Negative Dialectics*, see Adorno, *History and Freedom*.
173 Gasché, 'The Theory of Natural Beauty and Its Evil Star: Kant, Hegel, Adorno', 116.
174 Stewart Martin, 'The Absolute Artwork Meets the Absolute Commodity', *Radical Philosophy*, no. 146 (November/December 2007): 18.
175 Ibid. See also: Peter Uwe Hohendahl, 'Human Freedom and the Autonomy of Art: The Legacy of Kant', in *The Fleeting Promise of Art: Adorno's Aesthetic Theory Revisited* (Ithaca: Cornell University Press, 2013), 33–56.
176 Adorno, *Aesthetic Theory*, 63.
177 J. M. Bernstein, *The Fate of Art: Aesthetic Alienation from Kant to Derrida and Adorno* (University Park: Pennsylvania State University Press, 1991), 217.
178 Ibid.
179 Adorno, *Ästhetik (1958/59)*, 125; my translation.
180 Adorno, *Aesthetic Theory*, 62.

181 Ibid., 65.
182 Ibid., 74.
183 Cf. Joachim Ritter, *Landschaft: zur Funktion des Ästhetischen in der modernen Gesellschaft* (Münster: Aschendorff, 1963).
184 Heinz Paetzold, 'Adorno's Notion of Natural Beauty: A Reconsideration', in *The Semblance of Subjectivity: Essays on Adorno's Aesthetic Theory*, ed. Tom Huhn and Lambert Zuidervaart (Cambridge, MA: MIT Press, 1997), 219.
185 Adorno, *Aesthetic Theory*, 63; my emphasis.
186 Ibid., 66; original emphasis.
187 Adorno, 'The Idea of Natural History', 117.
188 Ibid., 118.
189 Adorno, *Aesthetic Theory*, 63.
190 Ibid., 73.
191 Schmidt, 'Der Begriff des Materialismus bei Adorno', 25; my translation.
192 Adorno, *Aesthetic Theory*, 65.
193 For an interesting account of Adorno's apparent misreading of Stendhal's dictum, see James Gordon Finlayson, 'The Work of Art and the Promise of Happiness in Adorno', *World Picture*, no. 3 (Summer 2009): 1–22.
194 Adorno, *Aesthetic Theory*, 65.
195 Adorno and Bloch, 'Something's Missing', 9.
196 Adorno, *Aesthetic Theory*, 61–2.
197 Ibid., 62.
198 Ibid., 46.
199 Adorno, *Ästhetik (1958/59)*, 79; my translation.
200 Ibid.; my translation.
201 Ibid.; my translation.
202 Adorno, *Aesthetic Theory*, 67.
203 Ibid., 66.
204 Jarvis, *Adorno*, 100.
205 Adorno, *Ästhetik (1958/59)*, 80; my translation and emphasis.
206 Adorno, *Negative Dialectics*, 362.
207 Adorno, *Aesthetic Theory*, 184; translation altered. Walter Benjamin's early essay 'On Language as such and on the Language of Man' (*c.* 1916) looms large in these passages. Cf. Walter Benjamin, 'On Language as Such and on the Language of Man', in *Selected Writings, Vol. 1: 1913–1926*, ed. Marcus Bullock and Michael W. Jennings (Cambridge, MA: The Belknap Press of Harvard University Press, 1996), 62–74. For a lucid account of Adorno's reception of Benjamin's philosophy of language, see Shierry Weber Nicholsen, 'Aesthetic

Theory's Mimesis of Walter Benjamin', in *The Semblance of Subjectivity*, ed. Tom Huhn and Lambert Zuidervaart (Cambridge, MA: MIT Press, 1997), 55–92.

208 Adorno, *Aesthetic Theory*, 136.
209 Ibid., 67.
210 Ibid.
211 Ibid., 112; my emphasis.
212 Ibid.
213 Benjamin, 'On Language as Such and on the Language of Man', 65.
214 Ibid., 74.
215 Once again, Adorno's thinking of the proper name comes into focus here. This dimension of his thought puts him in an unlikely correspondence with French Heideggerians, such as Jean-Luc Nancy. For an interesting exploration of this theme, see Alexander García Düttmann, 'The "Little Cold Breasts of an English Girl", or Art and Identity', in *International Politics and Performance: Critical Aesthetics and Creative Practice* (London: Routledge, 2013), 78–83.
216 In *Negative Dialectics*, Adorno contends that all thinking (and by extension all declarative speech) is of necessity conceptual. Accordingly, he defines his task as transcending the limitations of conceptual thought by means of the concept: 'Though doubtful as ever, a confidence that philosophy can make it after all – that the concept can transcend the concept, the preparatory and concluding element, and can thus reach the nonconceptual – is one of philosophy's inalienable features and part of the naïveté that ails it.' Adorno, *Negative Dialectics*, 9.
217 Ibid., 63.
218 Ibid., 74; translation altered; my emphasis.
219 Bernstein, *The Fate of Art*, 195.
220 Adorno, *Aesthetic Theory*, 233; translation altered.
221 Adorno, 'On Subject and Object', 247.
222 Gerhard Richter, *Thinking with Adorno: The Uncoercive Gaze* (New York: Fordham University Press, 2019), 96.
223 Adorno, *Aesthetic Theory*, 131.
224 Ibid., 78.
225 Adorno, *Minima Moralia*, 247.
226 For an analysis of the role played by mimesis in Adorno's thought, see Josef Früchtl, *Mimesis: Konstellation eines Zentralbegriffs bei Adorno* (Würzburg: Könighausen + Neumann, 1986). For an interesting account of Adorno and Horkheimer's citation of the image ban with reference to quasi-Freudian ideas of mimetic taboo, see Gertrud Koch, 'Mimesis & Bilderverbot', *Screen*, no. 34 (Autumn 1993): 211–22.

227 Ibid.
228 Ibid.
229 Adorno had, in fact, edited and introduced a collection of Borchardt's poems. Cf. Rudolf Borchardt, *Ausgewählte Gedichte,* ed. Theodor W. Adorno (Frankfurt am Main: Suhrkamp, 1968).
230 Adorno, *Aesthetic Theory*, 64.
231 Ibid., 65.
232 Adorno, *Ästhetik (1958/59)*, 52; my translation.

Reprise

1 'A sign we are, interpretationless / Painless we are and have almost / Lost our language in foreign lands'. Friedrich Hölderlin, 'Mnemosyne (2. Fassung)', in *Sämtliche Werke, Bd. 2,* ed. Friedrich Beißner (Stuttgart: Verlag W. Kohlhammer, 1951), 195; my translation.
2 Adorno, 'On Subject and Object', in *Critical Models: Interventions and Catchwords*, ed. Henry W. Pickford (New York: Columbia University Press, 1998), 247.
3 Schmidt, 'Der Begriff des Materialismus bei Adorno', 25; my translation.
4 Jarvis, 'Adorno, Marx, Materialism', 80.
5 Adorno, *Negative Dialectics*, 57.
6 Karl Marx and Friedrich Engels, *Marx & Engels Collected Works, Vol. 3: 1843–1844* (London: Lawrence & Wishart, 1975), 142.
7 Adorno, 'Parataxis', 142.
8 Ibid., 113.
9 Hans-Jürgen Krahl, 'The Political Contradiction in Adorno's Critical Theory', *The Sociological Review* 23, no. 4 (1975): 834.
10 Jürgen Habermas, *The Philosophical Discourse of Modernity*, trans. Frederick G. Lawrence (Cambridge, MA: MIT Press, 1990), 114.
11 Ibid., 119.
12 Ibid; original emphasis.
13 Giorgio Agamben, *The Times That Remain: A Commentary on the Letter to the Romans*, trans. Patricia Dailey (Stanford: Stanford University Press, 2005), 38.
14 Jacob Taubes, *The Political Theology of Paul*, trans. Dana Hollander (Stanford: Stanford University Press, 2003), 70.
15 Adorno, *Minima Moralia*, 247.

16 Derrida, 'Fichus: Frankfurt Address', 168.
17 Adorno, 'Parataxis', 136.
18 Adorno, 'Mélange', in *Minima Moralia: Reflections on a Damaged Life*, trans. Edmund Jephcott (London: Verso, 1974), 103.
19 Adorno, *Aesthetic Theory*, 63.
20 Adorno, 'The Handle, the Pot and Early Experience', in *Notes to Literature, Vol. 2*, trans. Shierry Weber Nicholsen (New York: Columbia University Press, 1992), 219.

Bibliography

Adorno, Theodor W. 'The Actuality of Philosophy', trans. Benjamin Snow, *Telos* 31 (Spring 1977): 120–33.

Adorno, Theodor W. *Aesthetic Theory*, eds. Rolf Tiedemann and Gretel Adorno, trans. Robert Hullot-Kentor. London: Continuum, 2002.

Adorno, Theodor W. *Against Epistemology – A Metacritique: Studies in Husserl and the Phenomenological Antinomies*, trans. Willis Domingo. Oxford: Blackwell Publishing, 1982.

Adorno, Theodor W. 'Brief an Leo Löwenthal, 22.08.1923'. In *Das Utopische soll Funken schlagen – zum 100. Geburtstag von Leo Löwenthal*, ed. Peter-Erwin Jansen, 45–8. Frankfurt am Main: Gesellschaft der Freunde der Stadt- und Universitätsbibliothek, Frankfurt am Main, 2000.

Adorno, Theodor W. *Critical Models: Interventions and Catchwords*, ed. Henry W. Pickford. New York: Columbia University Press, 1998.

Adorno, Theodor W. *Gesammelte Schriften, Bd. 2: Kierkegaard – Konstruktion des Ästhetischen*, ed. Rolf Tiedemann. Frankfurt am Main: Suhrkamp, 2003.

Adorno, Theodor W. *Gesammelte Schriften, Bd. 7: Ästhetische Theorie*, ed. Rolf Tiedemann, et al. Frankfurt am Main: Suhrkamp, 1970.

Adorno, Theodor W. *Gesammelte Schriften, Bd. 8: Soziologische Schriften I*, ed. Rolf Tiedemann, et al. Frankfurt am Main: Suhrkamp, 1972.

Adorno, Theodor W. *Gesammelte Schriften, Bd. 10: Kulturkritik und Gesellschaft*, ed. Rolf Tiedemann, et al. Frankfurt am Main: Suhrkamp, 1977.

Adorno, Theodor W. *Gesammelte Schriften, Bd. 11: Noten zur Literatur*, ed. Rolf Tiedemann, et al. Frankfurt am Main: Suhrkamp, 1974.

Adorno, Theodor W. *Gesammelte Schriften, Bd. 17: Musikalische Schriften IV*, ed. Rolf Tiedemann, et al. Frankfurt am Main: Suhrkamp, 2003.

Adorno, Theodor W. *Hegel: Three Studies*, trans. Shierry Weber Nicholsen. Cambridge, MA: MIT Press, 1993.

Adorno, Theodor W. *History and Freedom: Lectures 1964–1965*, ed. Rolf Tiedemann, trans. Rodney Livingstone. Cambridge: Polity Press, 2006.

Adorno, Theodor W. 'The Idea of Natural History', trans. Robert Hullot-Kentor, *Telos* 57 (Fall 1983): 111–24.

Adorno, Theodor W. *The Jargon of Authenticity*, trans. Knut Tarnowski and Fredric Will. London: Routledge, 1973.

Adorno, Theodor W. *Kant's Critique of Pure Reason*, ed. Rolf Tiedemann, trans. Rodney Livingstone. Cambridge: Polity Press, 2001.

Adorno, Theodor W. *Kierkegaard: Construction of the Aesthetic*, trans. Robert Hullot-Kentor. Minneapolis: University of Minnesota Press, 1989.

Adorno, Theodor W. *Metaphysics: Concept and Problems*, ed. Rolf Tiedemann, trans. Edmund Jephcott,. Cambridge: Polity Press, 2000.

Adorno, Theodor W. *Minima Moralia: Reflections on a Damaged Life*, trans. Edmund Jephcott. London: Verso, 1974.

Adorno, Theodor W. *Nachgelassene Schriften, Abteilung IV: Vorlesungen, Bd. 3: Ästhetik. 1958/59*, ed. Eberhard Ortland. Frankfurt am Main: Suhrkamp, 2009.

Adorno, Theodor W. *Negative Dialectics*, trans. E. B. Ashton. London: Routledge, 1973.

Adorno, Theodor W. *Notes to Literature, Vol. 2*, trans. Shierry Weber Nicholsen. New York: Columbia University Press, 1992.

Adorno, Theodor W. *Philosophische Terminologie, Bd. 2*. Frankfurt am Main: Suhrkamp, 1974.

Adorno, Theodor W. *Prisms*, trans. Samuel Weber and Shierry Weber. Cambridge, MA: MIT Press, 1981.

Adorno, Theodor W. *Problems of Moral Philosophy*, ed. Thomas Schröder, trans. Rodney Livingstone. Cambridge: Polity Press, 2000.

Adorno, Theodor W. *Quasi Una Fantasia: Essays on Modern Music*, trans. Rodney Livingstone. London: Verso, 1992.

Adorno, Theodor W. 'Theologie, Aufklärung und die Zukunft der Illusion'. In *Frankfurter Adorno Blätter VIII*, ed. Rolf Tiedemann, 235–7. Munich: Edition Text + Kritik, 2003.

Adorno, Theodor W. 'Theses on Need', trans. Keston Sutherland, *Quid* 16 (2005): 40–4.

Adorno, Theodor W. and Ernst Bloch. 'Something's Missing: A Discussion between Ernst Bloch and Theodor W. Adorno on the Contradictions of Utopian Longing. 1964'. In *The Utopian Function of Art and Literature*, trans. by Jack Zipes and Frank Mecklenburg, 1–17. Cambridge, MA: MIT Press, 1988.

Adorno, Theodor W. and Eugen Kogon. 'Offenbarung oder autonome Vernunft. i'. *Frankfurter Hefte: Zeitschrift für Kultur und Politik* 13, no. 6 (June 1958a): 392–402.

Adorno, Theodor W. and Eugen Kogon. 'Offenbarung oder autonome Vernunft. ii'. *Frankfurter Hefte: Zeitschrift für Kultur und Politik* 13, no. 7 (June 1958b): 484–98.

Adorno Theodor W. and Max Horkheimer. *Dialectic of Enlightenment*, trans. Edmund Jephcott, ed. Gunzelin Schmid Noerr. Stanford: Stanford University Press, 2002.

Agamben, Giorgio. *Homo Sacer: Sovereign Power and Bare Life*, trans. Daniel Heller-Roazen. Stanford: Stanford University Press, 1998.

Agamben, Giorgio. *The Kingdom and the Glory: For a Theological Genealogy of Economy and Government*, trans. Lorenzo Chiesa and Matteo Mandarini. Stanford: Stanford University Press, 2011.

Agamben, Giorgio. *Profanations*, trans. Jeff Fort. New York: Zone Books, 2007.

Agamben, Giorgio. *The State of Exception*, trans. Kevin Attell. Chicago: University of Chicago Press, 2004.

Agamben, Giorgio. *The Times that Remain: A Commentary on the Letter to the Romans*, trans. Patricia Dailey. Stanford: Stanford University Press, 2005.

Althusser, Louis. *Lenin and Philosophy and Other Essays*, trans. Ben Brewster. New York: Monthly Review Press, 2001.

Angermann, Asaf, ed. *Briefe und Briefwechsel, Band 8: "Der liebe Gott wohnt im Detail": Theodor W. Adorno & Gershom Scholem, 1939–1969*. Frankfurt am Main: Suhrkamp, 2015.

Ashfield, Andrew and de Bolla Peter, eds. *The Sublime: A Reader in British Eighteenth-Century Aesthetic Theory*. Cambridge: Cambridge University Press, 1996.

Bachmann, Ingeborg. *Werke, Bd. 2: Erzählungen*, eds. Christine Koschel, Inge von Weidenbaum, and Clemens Münster. Munich: Piper, 1980.

Banks, Erik C. *The Realistic Empiricism of Mach, James, and Russell: Neutral Monism Reconceived*. Cambridge: Cambridge University Press, 2014.

Benjamin, Walter. *The Arcades Project*, ed. Rolf Tiedemann, trans. Howard Eiland and Kevin McLaughlin. Cambridge, MA: The Belknap Press of Harvard University Press, 1996.

Benjamin, Walter. *The Correspondence of Walter Benjamin 1910–1940*, eds. Theodor W. Adorno and Gershom Scholem, trans. Manfred R. Jacobson and Evelyn M. Jacobson. Chicago: University of Chicago Press, 1994.

Benjamin, Walter. *Gesammelte Schriften VI: Fragmente Vermischten Inhalts / Autobiographische Schriften*, eds. Rolf Tiedemann and Hermann Schweppenhäuser. Frankfurt am Main: Suhrkamp, 1985.

Benjamin, Walter. *Origin of the German Trauerspiel*, trans. Howard Eiland. Cambridge, MA: Harvard University Press.

Benjamin, Walter. *Selected Writings, Vol 1: 1913–1926*, eds. Marcus Bullock and Michael W. Jennings. Cambridge, MA: The Belknap Press of Harvard University Press, 1996.

Benjamin, Walter. *Selected Writings, Vol. 2.2: 1931–1934*, eds. Michael W. Jennings, Howard Eiland and Gary Smith. Cambridge, MA: The Belknap Press of Harvard University Press, 1999.

Benjamin, Walter. *Selected Writings, Vol. 4: 1938–1940*, eds. Howard Eiland and Michael W. Jennings. Cambridge, MA: The Belknap Press of Harvard University Press, 2003.

Bernstein, J. M. *Adorno: Disenchantment and Ethics*. Cambridge: Cambridge University Press, 2001.

Bernstein, J. M. *The Fate of Art: Aesthetic Alienation from Kant to Derrida and Adorno*. University Park: University of Pennsylvania Press, 1991.

Besançon, Alain. *The Forbidden Image: An Intellectual History of Iconoclasm*, trans. Jane Marie Todd. Chicago: University of Chicago Press, 2000.

Bloch, Ernst. *Thomas Münzer als Theologe der Revolution*. Frankfurt am Main: Suhrkamp, 1962.

Blumenberg, Hans. *The Legitimacy of the Modern Age*, trans. Robert M. Wallace. Cambridge, MA: MIT Press, 1983.

Borchardt, Rudolf. *Ausgewählte Gedichte*, ed. Theodor W. Adorno. Frankfurt am Main: Suhrkamp, 1968.

Brassier, Ray. *Nihil Unbound: Enlightenment and Extinction*. New York: Palgrave MacMillan, 2007.

Bredekamp, Horst. *Image Acts: A Systematic Approach to Visual Agency*, trans. Elizabeth Clegg. Berlin: De Gruyter, 2018.

Brittain, Christopher Craig. *Adorno and Theology*. London: Continuum, 2010.

Brod, Max. *Franz Kafkas Glauben und Lehre*. Düsseldorf: Onomato, 2011.

Brod, Max and Hans-Joachim Schoeps. *Im Streit um Kafka und das Judentum*. Frankfurt am Main: Jüdischer Verlag, 1985.

Bromberg, Svenja. 'The Anti-Political Aesthetics of Object Worlds and Beyond'. *Mute Magazine*, last altered 25 July 2013, accessed 27 November 2015: http://www.metamute.org/editorial/articles/anti-political-aesthetics-objects-and-worlds-beyond

Brown, Nathan. 'The Speculative and the Specific: On Hallward and Meillassoux'. In *The Speculative Turn: Continental Materialism and Realism*, eds. Levi Bryant, Nick Srnicek and Graham Harman, 142–63. Melbourne: re.press, 2011.

Bryant, Levi, Nick Srnicek and Graham Harman. 'Towards a Speculative Philosophy'. In *The Speculative Turn: Continental Materialism and Realism*, eds. Levi Bryant, Nick Srnicek and Graham Harman, 1–18. Melbourne: re.press, 2011.

Bryg, Barton. *Landscapes of Resistance: The German Films of Danièle Huillet and Jean-Marie Straub*. Berkeley: University of California Press, 1995.

Buchholz, René. *Zwischen Mythos und Bilderverbot: Adornos Philosophie als Anstoß zu einer kritischen Fundamentaltheologie im Kontext der späten Moderne*. Frankfurt am Main: Peter Lang, 1991.

Buck-Morss, Susan. *The Origin of Negative Dialectics: Walter Benjamin, Theodor W. Adorno and the Frankfurt Institute*. New York: Free Press, 1977.

Bulhof, Ilse N. and Laurens ten Kate. 'Echoes of an Embarrassment – Philosophical Perspectives on Negative Theology'. In *Flight of the Gods: Philosophical Perspectives on Negative Theology*, eds. Ilse N. Bulhof and Laurens ten Kate, 1–57. New York City: Fordham University Press, 2000.

Bürger, Peter. *Theory of the Avant-Garde*, trans. Michael Shaw. Minneapolis: Minnesota University Press, 1984.

Caygill, Howard. *The Art of Judgement*. Oxford: Blackwell Publishing, 1989.

Caygill, Howard. *A Kant Dictionary*. Oxford: Blackwell Publishing, 2000.

Claussen, Detlev. *Theodor W. Adorno: One Last Genius*, trans. Rodney Livingstone. Cambridge, MA: Harvard University Press, 2010.

Cohen, Hermann. *Religion of Reason Out of the Sources of Judaism*, trans. Simon Kaplan. Oxford: Oxford University Press, 1995.

Cole, Andrew. 'Those Obscure Objects of Desire'. *Artforum*, accessed 07 January 2016: https://artforum.com/inprint/issue=201506&id=52280

Comay, Rebecca. 'Adorno's Siren Song'. *New German Critique* 81 (Autumn 2000): 21–48.

Comay, Rebecca. 'Defaced Statues: Idealism and Iconoclasm in Hegel's *Aesthetics*'. *OCTOBER* 149 (Summer 2014): 123–42.

Comay, Rebecca. 'Materialist Mutations of the *Bilderverbot*'. In *Sites of Vision*, ed. David Michael Levin. Cambridge, MA: MIT Press, 1997.

Connell, M. F. 'Through the Eyes of an Artificial Angel: Secular Theology in Theodor W. Adorno's Freudo-Marxist Reading of Kafka and Walter Benjamin'. In *Trajectories of Mysticism in Theory and Literature*, ed. P. Leonard, 198–218. London: Palgrave Macmillan, 2000.

De Vries, Hent. 'Inverse versus Dialectical Theology: The two Faces of Negativity and the Miracle of Faith'. *Cornellcast Video*, last altered September 2012, accessed 26 August 2014: https://www.cornell.edu/video/inverse-versus-dialectical-theology

De Vries, Hent. *Minimal Theologies: Critiques of Secular Reason in Adorno and Levinas*, trans. Geoffrey Hale. Baltimore: Johns Hopkins University Press, 2005.

Derrida, Jacques. 'Fichus: Frankfurt Address'. In *Paper Machine*, trans. Rachel Bowlby, 164–81. Stanford: Stanford University Press, 2005.

Derrida, Jacques. *Specters of Marx: The State of the Debt, the Work of Mourning and the New International*, trans. Peggy Kamuf. London: Verso, 1993.

Deuser, Hermann. *Dialektische Theologie: Studien zu Adornos Metaphysik und zum Spätwerk Kierkegaards*. Munich & Mainz: Kaiser Verlag, 1980.

Dierks, Sonja. 'Kafka-Lektüre'. In *Adorno Handbuch, Leben – Werk – Wirkung*, eds. Richard Klein, Johann Kreuzer and Stefan Müller-Doohm, 254–64. Stuttgart & Weimar: Verlag J. B. Metzler, 2011.

Düttmann, Alexander García. 'The "Little Cold Breasts of an English Girl", or Art and Identity'. In *International Politics and Performance: Critical Aesthetics and Creative Practice*, eds. Jenny Edkins and Adrian Kear, 78–83. London: Routledge, 2013.

Düttmann, Alexander García. *The Memory of Thought: An Essay on Heidegger and Adorno*, trans. Nicholas Walker. London: Continuum, 2002.

Eire, Carlos M. N. *War against the Idols: The Reformation of Worship from Erasmus to Calvin*. Cambridge: Cambridge University Press, 1986.

Elbe, Ingo. 'Between Marx, Marxism and Marxisms – Ways of Reading Marx's Theory'. *Viewpoint Mag*, last altered October 2013, accessed 20 October 2015: https://viewpointmag.com/2013/10/21/between-marx-marxism-and-marxisms-ways-of-reading-marxs-theory/#rf43-2941

Engels, Friedrich. *Dialectics of Nature*, trans. Clemens Dutt. London: Lawrence & Wishart, 1940.

Fenves, Peter. 'Image and Chatter: Adorno's Construction of Kierkegaard'. *Diacritics* 22, no. 1 (Spring 1992): 100–14.

Finlayson, James Gordon. 'On not Being Silent in the Darkness: Adorno's Singular Apophaticism'. *The Harvard Theological Review* 105, no. 01 (January 2012): 1–32.

Finlayson, James Gordon. 'The Work of Art and the Promise of Happiness in Adorno'. *World Picture* 3 (Summer 2009): 1–22.

Frank, Manfred and Kurz Gerhard. 'Ordo Inversus. Zu einer Reflexionsfigur bei Novalis, Hölderlin, Kleist und Kafka'. In *Geist und Zeichen: Festschrift für Arthur Henkel*, ed. Herbert Anton, 77–94. Heidelberg: Carl Winter, 1977.

Freud, Sigmund. *Moses and Monotheism*, trans. Katherine Jones. New York: Vintage Books, 1955.

Freud, Sigmund. *The Standard Edition of the Complete Psychological Works of Sigmund Freud, Vol. IV: The Interpretation of Dreams. First Part*, eds. James Strachey, Anna Freud, Alex Strachey and Alan Tyson, trans. James Strachey. London: Hogarth Press, 1953.

Freud, Sigmund. *Totem & Taboo: Some Points of Agreement between the Mental Lives of Savages and Neurotics*, trans. James Strachey. London: Routledge, 1966.

Fromm, Waldemar. 'Kafka Rezeption'. In *Kafka Handbuch*, ed. Bettina von Jagow and Oliver Jahraus, 250–72. Göttingen: Vanenhoeck & Ruprecht, 2008.

Früchtl, Josef. *Mimesis: Konstellation eines Zentralbegriffs bei Adorno*. Würzburg: Königshausen + Neumann, 1986.

Gasché, Rodolphe. *The Idea of Form: Rethinking Kant's Philosophy*. Stanford: Stanford University Press, 2003.

Gasché, Rodolphe. 'The Theory of Natural Beauty and Its Evil Star: Kant, Hegel, Adorno'. *Research in Phenomenology* 321 (2002): 103–22.

Geisenhanslüke, Achim. 'Bilderverbot: Kant – Lyotard – Kafka'. In *Der Bildhunger der Literatur – Festschrift für Günter E. Grimm*, eds. Dieter Heimböckel and Uwe Werlein, 37–49. Würzburg: Königshausen + Neumann, 2005.

Gethmann-Siefert, Annemarie. *Einführung in Hegels Ästhetik*. Munich: Wilhelm Fink Verlag, 2005.

Gethmann-Siefert, Annemarie. 'Phänomen versus System'. In *Phänomen versus System: zum Verhältnis von philosophischer Systematik und Kunsturteil in Hegels Berliner Vorlesungen oder Philosophie der Kunst*, ed. A. Gethmann-Siefert, 9–40. Bonn: Bouvier, 1992.

Gödde, Christoph, ed. *Theodor W. Adorno & Alfred Sohn-Rethel: Briefwechsel, 1936–1969*. Munich: Edition Text + Kritik, 1991.

Gödde, Christoph and Henri Lonitz, eds. *Briefe und Briefwechsel, Band 1: Theodor W. Adorno & Max Horkheimer, 1927–1937*. Frankfurt am Main: Suhrkamp, 2003.

Gordon, Peter E. *Adorno and Existence*. Cambridge, MA: Harvard University Press, 2016.

Guyer, Paul. 'The Origin of Modern Aesthetics: 1711–35'. In *The Blackwell Guide to Aesthetics*, ed. Peter Kivy, 15–44. Oxford: Blackwell Publishing, 2004.

Habermas, Jürgen. *The Philosophical Discourse of Modernity*, trans. Frederick G. Lawrence. Cambridge, MA: MIT Press, 1990.

Habermas, Jürgen. *Philosophical-Political Profiles*, trans. Frederick G. Lawrence. Cambridge, MA: MIT Press, 1983.

Habermas, Jürgen. *The Theory of Communicative Action, Vol. 1: Reason and the Rationalization of Society*, trans. Thomas McCarthy. Boston, MA: Beachon Press, 1987.

Hallward, Peter. 'Anything Is Possible: A Reading of Quentin Meillassoux's *After Finitude*'. In *The Speculative Turn: Continental Materialism and Realism*, eds. Levi Bryant, Nick Srnicek and Graham Harman, 130–41. Melbourne: re.press, 2011.

Hamacher, Werner. 'Das Theologisch-Politische Fragment'. In *Benjamin Handbuch, Leben – Werk – Wirkung*, ed. Burkhardt Lindner, 175–92. Stuttgart & Weimar: Verlag J. B. Metzler, 2011.

Hamacher, Werner. 'Guilt History: Benjamin's Sketch "Capitalism as Religion"'. *Diacritics* 32, no. 3/4 (Autumn–Winter 2002): 81–106.

Hamacher, Werner. 'Now: Walter Benjamin and Historical Time'. In *Walter Benjamin and History*, ed. Andrew Benjamin, 38–68. London: Continuum, 2005.

Hamacher, Werner. *Premises: Essays on Philosophy and Literature from Kant to Celan*, trans. Peter Fenves. Cambridge, MA: Harvard University Press, 1996.

Hammer, Espen. *Adorno and the Political*. London: Routledge, 2006.

Hegel, G. W. F. *Aesthetics: Lectures on Fine Arts*, trans. T. M. Knox. Oxford: Clarendon Press, 1975.

Hegel, G. W. F. *Faith and Knowledge*, trans. Walter Cerf and C. H. Harris. Albany: State University of New York Press, 1977.

Hegel, G. W. F. *Lectures on the History of Philosophy, Vol. III*, ed. Robert F. Brown, trans. Robert F. Brown, J. M. Stewart and H. S. Harris. Berkeley: University of California Press, 1990.

Hegel, G. W. F. *Phenomenology of Spirit*, trans. A. V. Miller. Oxford: Oxford University Press, 1977.

Hegel, G. W. F. *Philosophie der Kunst. Vorlesung von 1826*, eds. A. Gethmann-Siefert, J.-I. Kwon and K. Berr. Frankfurt am Main: Suhrkamp, 2004.

Hegel, G. W. F. *Philosophie der Kunst oder Ästhetik. Nach Hegel. Im Sommer 1826. Mitschrift Carl Hermann Victor von Kehler*, eds. A. Gethmann-Siefert and B. Collenberg-Plotnikov. Munich: Wilhelm Fink Verlag, 2004.

Hegel, G. W. F. *Philosophy of Mind: Being Part Three of the Encyclopaedia of Philosophical Sciences*, trans. William Wallace. Oxford: Clarendon Press, 1971.

Hegel, G. W. F. *Philosophy of Nature*, trans. A. V. Miller. Oxford: Oxford University Press, 2004.

Hegel, G. W. F. *The Science of Logic*, trans. George Di Giovanni. Cambridge: Cambridge University Press, 2010.

Hegel, G. W. F. *Vorlesung über Ästhetik. Berlin 1820–21. Eine Nachschrift*, ed. H. Schneider. Frankfurt am Main: Peter Lang, 1995.

Hegel, G. W. F. *Vorlesungen über die Philosophie der Kunst*, ed. A. Gethmann-Siefert. Hamburg: Felix Meiner Verlag, 2003.

Heidegger, Martin. 'The Age of the World Picture'. In *Off the Beaten Track*, trans. Julian Young and Kenneth Haynes, 57–85. Cambridge: Cambridge University Press, 2002.

Heidegger, Martin. *Nietzsche, Vol. 1: The Will to Power as Art*, trans. D. F. Krell. London: Routledge & Kegan Paul, 1981.

Henrich, Dieter. *Aesthetic Judgement and the Moral Image of the World*. Stanford: Stanford University Press, 1992.

Hodgson, Peter C. *Hegel and Christian Theology: A Reading of the Lectures on the Philosophy of Religion*. Oxford: Oxford University Press, 2005.

Hohendahl, Peter Uwe. *The Fleeting Promise of Art: Adorno's Aesthetic Theory Revisited*. Ithaca: Cornell University Press, 2013.

Hölderlin, Friedrich. *Sämtliche Werke, Bd. 2*, ed. Friedrich Beißner. Stuttgart: Verlag W. Kohlhammer, 1951.

Honneth, Axel. *Pathologies of Reason: On the Legacy of Critical Theory*, trans. James Ingram. New York: Columbia University Press, 2009.

Horkheimer, Max. *Critique of Instrumental Reason*, trans. Matthew J. O'Connell. New York: Seabury Press, 1974.

Horkheimer, Max. 'Was wir Sinn nennen wird verschwinden – Spiegel Gespräch mit dem Philosophen Max Horkheimer'. *Der Spiegel*, 05 January 1970: 79–84.

Hullot-Kentor, Robert. *Things beyond Resemblance: Collected Essays on Theodor W. Adorno*. New York: Columbia University Press, 2008.

James, David. *Art, Myth and Society in Hegel's Aesthetics*. London: Continuum. 2009.

Jameson, Fredric. *Late Marxism: Adorno or the Persistence of the Dialectic*. London: Verso, 1990.

Jameson, Fredric. 'The Vanishing Mediator: Narrative Structure in Max Weber'. *New German Critique* 1 (Winter 1973): 52–89.

Jarvis, Simon. *Adorno: A Critical Introduction*. Cambridge: Polity Press, 1998.

Jarvis, Simon. 'Adorno, Marx, Materialism'. In *The Cambridge Companion to Adorno*, ed. Tom Huhn, 79–100. Cambridge: Cambridge University Press, 2004.

Jay, Martin. *Downcast Eyes: The Denigration of Vision in Twentieth-Century French Thought*. Berkeley: University of California Press, 1993.

Johnston, Adrian. 'Empiricism'. In *The Meillassoux Dictionary*, ed. Peter Gratton and Paul J. Ennis, 61–3. Edinburgh: Edinburgh University Press, 2015.

Kafka, Franz. *Nachgelassene Schriften und Fragmente II*, ed. Jost Schillemeit. Frankfurt am Main: Fischer Verlag, 2002.

Kaiser, Hellmuth. *Kafkas Inferno: Eine psychologische Deutung seiner Strafphantasie*. Vienna: Psychoanalytischer Verlag, 1931.

Kant, Immanuel. *Critique of the Power of Judgement*, ed. Paul Guyer, trans. Paul Guyer and Eric Matthews. Cambridge: Cambridge University Press, 2000.

Kant, Immanuel. *Critique of Pure Reason*, trans. Paul Guyer and Allen W. Wood. Cambridge: Cambridge University Press, 1998.

Kant, Immanuel. *The Metaphysics of Morals*, trans. Mary J. Gregor. Cambridge: Cambridge University Press, 1996.

Kaufmann, Irene. *Die Hochschule für die Wissenschaft des Judentums: 1872–1942*. Berlin: Hentrich & Hentrich, 2006.

Khatib, Sami. *'Teleologie Ohne Endzweck': Walter Benjamins Ent-Stellung des Messianischen*. Marburg: Tectum, 2013.

Khatib, Sami. 'Towards a Politics of "Pure Means": Walter Benjamin and the Question of Violence'. *Anthropological Materialism*, last altered March 2014, accessed 18 July 2014: http://anthropologicalmaterialism.hypotheses.org/1040

Kierkegaard, Søren. *Either/Or, Pt. I*, trans. Howard V. Hong and Edna H. Hong. Princeton: Princeton University Press, 1987.

Koch, Gertrud. 'Mimesis and Bilderverbot'. *Screen* 34 (Autumn 1993): 211–22.

Kohlenbach, Margarete. 'Kafka, Critical Theory, Dialectical Theology: Adorno's Case against Hans Joachim Schoeps'. *German Life and Letters* 63, no. 2 (April 2010): 146–65.

Krahl, Hans-Jürgen. 'The Political Contradiction in Adorno's Critical Theory'. *The Sociological Review* 23, no. 4 (1975): 831–4.

Kraushaar, Wolfgang, ed. *Frankfurter Schule und Studentenbewegung: Von der Flaschenpost zum Molotowcocktail, 1946–1995*, 3 Vols. Hamburg: Rogner & Bernhard, 1998–2004.

Külpe, Oswald. *Outlines of Psychology, Based Upon the Result of Experimental Investigation*, trans. Edward Bradford Titchener. London: Swann, Sonnenschein & Co., 1901.

Lange, Frederick Albert. *History of Materialism and Criticism of its Present Importance*, trans. Ernest Chester Thomas. London: Trübner & Co., 1877.

Lenin, Vladimir Ilyich. *Collected Works, Vol. 14: Materialism and Empirio-Criticism*. Moscow: Foreign Languages Publishing House, 1961.

Lohmann, Ingrid. 'Das Motiv des Bilderverbots bei Moses Mendelssohn'. *Das Achtzehtne Jahrhundert – Zeitschrift der Deutschen Gesellschaft für die Erforschung des achtzehnten Jahrhunderts* 36, no. 1 (2012): 33–42.

Lonitz, Henri, ed. *Theodor W. Adorno & Walter Benjamin: The Complete Correspondence, 1928–1940*, trans. Nicholas Walker. Cambridge, MA: Harvard University Press, 2001.

Löwith, Karl. *Meaning in History: The Theological Implications of the Philosophy of History*. Chicago: University of Chicago Press, 1949.

Löwy, Michael. *Redemption & Utopia: Jewish Libertarian Thought in Central Europe*, trans. Hope Heaney. London: Athlone Press, 1992.

Lukács, Georg. *History and Class Consciousness: Studies in Marxist Dialectics*, trans. Rodney Livingstone. London: Merlin Press, 1971.

Lukács, Georg. *Realism in Our Time: Literature and the Class Struggle*, trans. John Mander and Necke Mander. New York: Harper and Row, 1964.

Lukács, Georg. *Theory of the Novel: A Historico-Philosophical Essay on the Forms of Great Epic Literature*, trans. Anna Bostock. London: Merlin Press, 1988.

Lyotard, Jean François. 'Adorno as the Devil'. *Telos* 19 (Spring 1974): 123–37.

Lyotard, Jean François. *The Differend: Phrases in Dispute*, trans. Georges Van Den Abbeele. Manchester: Manchester University Press, 1988.

Lyotard, Jean François. *Heidegger and 'the jews'*, trans. Andreas Michel and Mark Roberts. Minneapolis: University of Minnesota Press, 1990.

Lyotard, Jean François. *The Inhuman: Reflections on Time*, trans. Geoffrey Bennington and Rachel Bowlby. Cambridge: Polity Press, 1991.

Lyotard, Jean François. *The Lyotard Reader*, ed. Andrew Benjamin, trans. Geoffrey Bennington and Marian Hobson. Oxford: Blackwell Publishing, 1989.

Lyotard, Jean François. *Postmodern Fables*, trans. Georges van den Abbeele. Minneapolis: University of Minnesota Press, 1999.

Mach, Ernst. *The Analysis of Sensations and the Relation of the Physical to the Psychical*, trans. C. M. Williams and Sydney Waterlow. New York: Dover, 1959.

Martin, Stewart. 'The Absolute Artwork Meets the Absolute Commodity'. *Radical Philosophy* 146 (November/December 2007): 15–25.
Marx, Karl. *Capital, Vol. 3: Critique of Political Economy*, trans. David Fernbach. London: Penguin Classics, 1991.
Marx, Karl and Friedrich Engels. *Marx & Engels Collected Works, Vol. 1: 1835–1843*. London: Lawrence & Wishart, 1974.
Marx, Karl and Friedrich Engels. *Marx & Engels Collected Works, Vol. 3: 1843–1844*. London: Lawrence & Wishart, 1975.
Marx, Karl and Friedrich Engels. *Marx & Engels Collected Works, Vol. 5: 1845–1847*. London: Lawrence & Wishart, 1976.
Marx, Karl and Friedrich Engels. *Marx & Engels Collected Works, Vol. 35: Capital, Vol. 1*. London: Lawrence & Wishart, 1996.
Marx, Karl and Friedrich Engels. *Selected Correspondence*. Moscow: Progress Publishers, 1975.
McKnight, Stephen A. 'The Legitimacy of the Modern Age: The Löwith-Blumenberg Debate in Light of Recent Scholarship'. *The Political Science Reviewer*, accessed 26 August 2014: http://www.mmisi.org/pr/19_01/mcknight.pdf
Meillassoux, Quentin. *After Finitude: An Essay on the Necessity of Contingency*, trans. Ray Brassier. London: Continuum, 2008.
Meillassoux, Quentin. 'Spectral Dilemma'. *Collapse: Philosophical Research and Development* 4 (2008): 261–76.
Mondzain, Marie-Jose. *Image, Icon, Economy: The Byzantine Origins of the Contemporary Imaginary*. Stanford: Stanford University Press, 2004.
Moran, Dermot. 'Neoplatonism and Christianity in the West'. In *The Routledge Handbook of Neoplatonism*, eds. Svetla Slaveva-Griffin and Paulina Remes, 508–24. London: Routledge, 2014.
Müller-Doohm, Stefan. *Adorno: A Biography*, trans. Rodney Livingstone. Cambridge: Polity Press, 2009.
Nancy, Jean-Luc 'Ré-fa-mi-ré-do-si-do-ré-si-sol-sol. le peuple souverain s'avance'. In *La démocratie à venir: Autour de Jacques Derrida*, ed. Marie-Louise Mallet. Paris: Galilée, 2004.
Nietzsche, Friedrich. *On the Genealogy of Morals*, trans. Walter Kaufmann and R. J. Hollingdale. New York: Vintage Books, 1989.
Nietzsche, Friedrich. *Thus Spoke Zarathustra* trans. R. J. Hollingdale. London: Penguin Classics, 1969.
Nietzsche, Friedrich. *Twilight of the Idols & the Anti-Christ*, trans. R. J. Hollingdale. London: Penguin Classics, 1989.
Oberman, Heiko A. *Man between God and the Devil*. New Haven: Yale University Press, 2006.

Osborne, Peter. 'Adorno and the Metaphysics of Modernism: The Problem of a "Postmodern" Art'. In *The Problems of Modernity: Adorno and Benjamin*, ed. Andrew Benjamin, 23–48. London: Routledge, 1989.

Paetzold, Heinz. 'Adorno's Notion of Natural Beauty: A Reconsideration'. In *The Semblance of Subjectivity: Essays on Adorno's Aesthetic Theory*, eds. Tom Huhn and Lambert Zuidervaart, 213–36. Cambridge, MA: MIT Press, 1997.

Pannekoek, Anton. *Lenin as Philosopher: A Critical Examination of the Philosophical Basis of Leninism*. Milwaukee: Marquette University Press, 2003.

Pessin, Sarah. 'Islamic and Jewish Neoplatonism'. In *The Routledge Handbook of Neoplatonism*, eds. Svetla Slaveva-Griffin and Paulina Remes, 541–58. London: Routledge, 2014.

Plato. *The Republic*, trans. Allan Bloom. New York: Basic Books, 1968.

Pritchard, Elizabeth. 'Bilderverbot Meets Body in Theodor W. Adorno's Inverse Theology'. *The Harvard Theological Review* 95, no. 3 (July 2002): 291–318.

Rancière, Jacques. 'The Sublime from Lyotard to Schiller – Two Readings of Kant and their Political Significance'. *Radical Philosophy* 126 (July–August 2004): 8–15.

Rancière, Jacques. *The Future of the Image*, trans. Gregory Elliott. London: Verso, 2007.

Richter, Gerhard. *Thinking with Adorno: The Uncoercive Gaze*. New York: Fordham University Press, 2019.

Ritter, Joachim. *Landschaft: zur Funktion des Ästhetischen in der modernen Gesellschaft*. Münster: Aschendorff, 1963.

Rogge, Wolfgang, ed. *Theodor W Adorno. & Ernst Krenek: Briefwechsel*. Frankfurt am Main: Suhrkamp, 1974.

Rotenstreich, Nathan. 'Hegel's Image of Judaism'. *Jewish Social Studies* 15, no. 1 (January 1953): 33–52.

Rowley, David G. 'Bogdanov and Lenin: Epistemology and Revolution'. *Studies in East European Thought* 48 (1996): 1–19.

Rowley, David G. 'Introduction'. In *The Philosophy of Living Experience*, eds. Alexander Alexandrovich Bogdanov and David G. Rowley, 1–41. Leiden: Brill, 2016.

Schaper, Eva. 'The Kantian "As If" and Its Relevance for Aesthetics'. *Proceedings of the Aristotelian Society, New Series* 65 (1964–1965): 219–34.

Schivelbusch, Wolfgang. *Intellektuellendämmerung: Zur Lage der Frankfurter Intelligenz in den zwanziger Jahren*. Frankfurt am Main: Suhrkamp, 1985.

Schmidt, Alfred. *The Concept of Nature in Marx*, trans. Ben Fowkes. London: New Left Books, 1971.

Schmidt, Alfred. 'Der Begriff des Materialismus bei Adorno'. In *Adorno Konferenz 1983*, ed. Ludwig v. Friedenburg and Jürgen Habermas, 14–31. Frankfurt am Main: Suhrkamp, 1984.

Schmitt, Carl. *Political Theology*, trans. Georg Schwab. Chicago: University of Chicago Press, 1985.

Schoenberg, Arnold. *Schoenberg's 'Moses and Aaron', with the Complete Libretto in German and English*, ed. Karl Wörner, trans. Paul Hamburger. London: Faber & Faber, 1963.

Scholem, Gershom, ed. *The Correspondence of Walter Benjamin and Gershom Scholem 1932-1940*, trans. Gary Smith and Andre Lefevere. New York: Schocken Books, 1989.

Scholem, Gershom. *Major Trends in Jewish Mysticism*. Jerusalem: Schocken Books, 1941.

Scholem, Gershom. *The Messianic Idea in Judaism*. New York: Schocken Books, 1995.

Scholem, Gershom. *Walter Benjamin: The Story of a Friendship*, trans. Harry Zohn. London: Faber & Faber, 1982.

Shaw, Allen. *Arnold Schoenberg's Journey*. Cambridge, MA: Harvard University Press, 2002.

Simmel, Georg. 'The Philosophy of Landscape'. *Theory, Culture & Society* 24, nos. 7–8 (December 2007): 20–9.

Sohn-Rethel, Alfred. *Intellectual and Manual Labour: A Critique of Epistemology*, trans. Martin Sohn-Rethel. London: Macmillan, 1978.

Spaulding, Daniel. 'Inside Out'. *Mute Magazine*, last altered 20 October 2015, accessed 27 November 2015: http://www.metamute.org/editorial/articles/inside-out-0

Spinoza, Benedict. *On the Improvement of the Understanding/The Ethics/Correspondence*, trans. R. H. M. Elwes. London: Dover Books, 1955.

Steiner, Uwe. 'Kapitalismus als Religion'. In *Benjamin Handbuch, Leben – Werk – Wirkung*, ed. Burkhardt Lindner, 167–74. Stuttgart & Weimar: Verlag J. B. Metzler, 2011.

Taubes, Jacob. 'Ästhetisierung der Wahrheit im Posthistoire'. In *Alexandre Kojève: Überlebungsformen*, ed. Andreas Hiepki, 39–57. Berlin: Merve Verlag, 2007.

Taubes, Jacob. *The Political Theology of Paul*, trans. Dana Hollander. Stanford: Stanford University Press, 2003.

Toscano, Alberto. 'Against Speculation, or, a Critique of Critique: A Remark on Quentin Meillassoux's *After Finitude*. After Colletti'. In *The Speculative Turn: Continental Materialism and Realism*, eds. Levi Bryant, Nick Srnicek and Graham Harma, 84–91. Melbourne: re.press, 2011.

Toscano, Alberto. 'Divine Management: Critical Remarks on Giorgio Agamben's *The Kingdom and the Glory*'. *Angelaki: Journal of the Theoretical Humanities* 3, no. 16 (November 2011): 125–36.

Vaihinger, Hans. *The Philosophy of 'As If'*, trans. C. K. Ogden. London: Kegan Paul, Tench, Trubner & Co., 1935.

Valéry, Paul. *Valéry's Oeuvres, Vol. II*, ed. Jean Hytier. Paris: Gallimard, 1960.

Voller, Christian. 'Kommunikation verweigert. Schwierige Beziehungen zwischen Blumenberg und Adorno'. *Zeitschrift für Kulturphilosophie* 2 (2013): 151–75.

Wallace, Robert M. 'Secularisation and Modernity: The Löwith-Blumenberg Debate'. *New German Critique* 22 (Winter 1981): 63–79.

Weber, Max. *The Protestant Ethic and the Spirit of Capitalism*, trans. Talcott Parsons. London: Routledge, 1992.

Weber, Samuel. *Benjamin's Abilities*. Cambridge, MA: Harvard University Press, 2010.

Weber, Samuel. 'Guilt, Debt and the Turn to the Future: Walter Benjamin and Hermann Levin Goldschmidt. A Foray into Economic Theology'. *Dialogik*, last altered December 2012, accessed 18 July 2014: http://www.dialogik.org/wp/wp-content/uploads/2010/12/Sam-Weber-Turn-to-the-Future1.pdf

Weber, Samuel. *Return to Freud: Jacques Lacan's Dislocation of Psychoanalysis*, trans. Michael Levine. Cambridge: Cambridge University Press, 1991.

Weber Nicholsen, Shierry. 'Aesthetic Theory's Mimesis of Walter Benjamin'. In *The Semblance of Subjectivity*, ed. Tom Huhn and Lambert Zuidervaart, 55–92. Cambridge, MA: MIT Press, 1997.

Weigel, Sigrid. 'Zu Franz Kafka'. In *Benjamin Handbuch, Leben – Werk – Wirkung*, ed. Burkhardt Lindner, 543–57. Stuttgart and Weimar: Verlag J. B. Metzler, 2011.

White, Graham. *Luther as Nominalist: A Study of the Logical Methods Used in Martin Luther's Disputations in the Light of their Medieval Background*. Helsinki: Luther-Agricola-Society, 1994.

White, James. *Red Hamlet: The Life and Ideas of Alexander Bogdanov*. Leiden: Brill, 2019.

Wilcock, Evelyn. 'Negative Identity: Mixed German Jewish Descent as a Factor in the Reception of Theodor Adorno'. *New German Critique* 81 (Autumn 2000): 169–87.

Wolfgang Schopf, ed. *Theodor W. Adorno & Siegfried Kracauer: Correspondence, 1923–1966*, trans. Susan Halstead. Cambridge: Polity, 2020.

Zeller, Eduard. *A History of Greek Philosophy, from the Earliest Period to the Time of Socrates*, trans. Sarah Frances Alleyne. London: Longmans, Green, and Co., 1881.

Žižek, Slavoj. *Less than Nothing: Hegel and the Shadow of Dialectical Materialism*. London: Verso, 2012.

Index

Adorno, Gretel   105
Adorno, Theodor W.; *See also* materialism; metaphysics; negative universal history
   'Aberglaube aus zweiter Hand' 176 n.113
   'Actuality of Philosophy, The'   59
   'After Auschwitz'   80
      art   108, 122, 124
      poetry   118, 122
   Aesthetic Theory   49, 99, 105, 107, 118, 133, 135–8
   Against Epistemology   161 n.65
   on Aquinas   70
   Ästhetik (1958/59)   158 n.49, 168 n.204, 194 n.179, 195 nn.199, 205, 197 n.232
   on atomism   22–5
   on Borchardt   139, 146 (*see also* Borchardt, Rudolf)
   on Buber   58
   on Corot   139, 146, 147 (*see also* Corot, Jean-Baptiste-Camille)
   correspondence with Benjamin   35, 37, 55–6 (*see also* Benjamin, Walter)
   correspondence with Horkheimer   4, 59, 62–3, 87 (*see also* Horkheimer, Max)
   correspondence with Kracauer   58
   correspondence with Löwenthal   58
   correspondence with Scholem   7, 37, 95, 171 n.34, 173 n.62 (*see also* Scholem, Gershom)
   correspondence with Sohn-Rethel   47, 167 n.181 (*see also* Sohn-Rethel, Alfred)
   on Democritus   10, 22–5
   Dialectic of Enlightenment (with Horkheimer)   4, 7, 10, 33, 40, 44, 45, 59, 61–6, 73, 84, 87, 90, 92, 123, 133, 136
   on Epicurus   22–5
   'Extorted Reconciliation'   158 n.8
   on Franz Rosenzweig   58
   'The Handle, the Pot and Early Experience'   198 n.20
   on Hegel (*see* Hegel, Friedrich)
   Hegel: Three Studies   161 n.52
   on Heidegger   38, 65, 67–8, 71, 173 n.70 (*see also* Heidegger, Martin)
   History and Freedom   172 nn.39, 41, 43, 46, 194 n.172
   on Hölderlin   139, 150 (*see also* Hölderlin, Friedrich)
   'Idea of Natural History, The'   59, 139
   on identity thinking   12, 35, 44, 73, 79, 153
   on inversion   36–40, 47
   Jargon of Authenticity, The   58, 65, 67
   on Kafka   56, 101–3, 182–3 n.208, 183 n.211 (*see also* Kafka, Franz)
   on Kant (*see* Kant, Immanuel)
   Kant's Critique of Pure Reason 185 n.250, 188 n.53
   on Kierkegaard   38–40, 58, 69, 78, 102, 182–3 n.208 (*see also* Kierkegaard, Søren)
   Kierkegaard: Construction of the Aesthetic   37–8, 166 nn.150, 155, 171 n.37, 172 n.55, 183 n.208
   on language (of art)   99, 142, 143
   on Lenin   11, 14, 16–18 (*see also* Lenin; materialism)
   on Luther   70–1 (*see also* Luther, Martin)
   'Mahagonny'   170 n.20
   'Mahler'   186 n.2
   'Marginalia on Theory and Praxis'   33, 42
   on Marx   6, 23, 53, 165 n.144, 167 n.181, 184 n.235 (*see also* Marx, Karl)
   'Meditations on Metaphysics'   61
   on 'messianic light'   95, 102

Metaphysics 158 n.51, 176 nn.106, 108, 110, 177 nn.120, 122, 126, 186 n.270
Minima Moralia 75
   'Finale' 56, 95–7, 100
   'Mélange' 198 n.18
   'Picture Book Without Pictures' 50
on natural history 59, 61, 146
on nature
   first 46
   domination of 66, 71, 133, 134, 139, 141, 142, 168 n.194
   second 45–6, 139
on negation 40–3, 135, 177 n.120
   determinate 40–2, 49, 73, 74
   indeterminate 73
Negative Dialectics 7, 9, 10, 12, 23, 42, 48, 53, 59, 61, 76–8, 98, 105, 184 n.235
on nominalism 67–8, 70–1, 174 n.73
on non-identity 37, 48, 113, 140
'Notes on Kafka' 56, 95, 102, 165 n.144, 183 n.208, 185 nn.258, 261, 263
'Offenbarung oder autonome Vernunft' 173 nn.66, 71, 174 n.74
'On Subject and Object' 45, 46
'Parataxis' 186 n.3, 197 n.7, 198 n.17
Philosophische Terminologie 23, 158 n.12, 160 n.34, 161 nn.57, 64, 68, 162 n.71, 74, 83, 168 n.203, 169 n.215
on politics 6, 8, 11, 19–20, 26–7, 33–5, 44, 47, 150–3, 164–5 n.133
'Progress' 101
'Protokolle vom Seminar über Benjamins *Ursprung des deutschen Trauerspiels*' 165 n.134
'Reason and Revelation' 67–9, 72, 77, 94
on reflection theory (*see* reflection theory)
on religion 5, 58–9, 65–9, 72, 87 (*see also* Judaism)
on remembrance 107, 140–2, 150
on representational thinking (*see* representational thinking)
'Resignation' 165 n.133
'Sacred Fragment' 1, 53, 102
on Schelling 136
on Schiller 136
'Something's Missing' 157 n.45, 159 n.18, 165 n.144, 195 n.195
on standpoint of redemption 56, 95, 97, 98, 101, 102
on suffering 14, 33, 43, 48–9, 61, 67, 80, 142, 146, 177 n.119
'Theologie, Aufklärung und die Zukunft der Illusion' 157 n.40, 169 n.4
on theology (*see* theology)
'Theses on Need' 49
'Theses Upon Art and Religion Today' 157 n.39, 169 n.3
'Towards a Portrait of Thomas Mann' 169 n.212
'Über Tradition' 173 n.59
on 'Utopia of cognition' 11, 35, 44, 47–8, 51, 101, 135
on Vaihinger 100–1
aesthetic judgement 99, 109–11, 113, 115, 119
aesthetics. *See individual entries*
   Adorno on (*see* Adorno, Theodor W.)
   Hegel on 124–33, 192 nn.128, 132 (*see also* Hegel, Friedrich)
   Kant on 108–17, 186 nn.13, 17, 187 nn.21, 28, 31, 33, 187–8 n.37, 188 n.54 (*see also* Kant, Immanuel)
Agamben, Giorgio 97–100, 102, 151, 179 n.170, 184 n.235
   critique of Adorno 56, 97–8, 152 (*see also* Adorno, Theodor W.)
   'In Praise of Profanation' (Agamben) 88, 90
   on profanation 88, 90–1
   on religion 90–2
   on repression 91–2
   on secularization 90–2
Althusser, Louis 161 n.51
Anaximander 85
Anderson, Perry 158 n.3
apophatic theology 72, 174–5 n.90. *See also* negative theology
Aquinas, Thomas 70
   Summa Theologica 70

Index

Aristotle 70, 77
Aron 1
art 8, 111, 193 n.149, 194 n.164
   Adorno on 105–7, 133–47 (*see also* Adorno, Theodor W.)
   'as if' logic and 99
   autonomous 49, 137, 150
   beauty of 112, 125, 126, 128, 134–6, 138, 188 n.37
   as custodian of Other 124
   Hegel on 125–6, 128–32 (*see also* Hegel, Friedrich)
   Jewish 129, 130, 132–3
   Kant on 110–13 (*see also* Kant, Immanuel)
   language-like character of 99, 142
   as last vestige of metaphysics 105
   Lyotard on 118–124 (*see also* Lyotard, Jean-François)
   nature and 106, 107, 138, 139, 145, 146
   sacred 53–4
   sublime 119, 122, 123, 190 n.88, 193 n.148
   symbolic 130–3
   Utopia and 124, 135, 140, 141, 143
Ashfield, Andrew 189 n.54
'as if', logic of
   Agamben on 100 (*see also* Agamben, Giorgio)
   Kant on 98–9 (*see also* Kant, Immanuel)
   Taubes on 98 (*see also* Taubes, Jacob)
   Vaihinger on 100 (*see also* Vaihinger, Hans)
atomism 13
   Adorno on 22–5 (*see also* Adorno, Theodor W.)
   clinamen 25
   Democritus on 22
   Epicurus on 22–5
Auschwitz
   Adorno on 79, 80, 108, 118, 122 (*see also* Adorno, Theodor W.)
   art after 122

Bachmann, Ingeborg 155 n.1
Bacon, Francis 46
Badiou, Alain 163 n.97
bare life, notion of 179 n.170

Barth, Karl 71, 102, 182–3 n.208
   dialectical theology 182 n.208
Baudelaire, Charles 105, 178 n.147
Benjamin, Andrew 156 n.21
Benjamin, Walter 9, 35, 37, 43, 54–6, 59, 103, 142, 158 n.4, 178 n.142, 179 n.163, 180 n.182, 195 n.207
   Arcades Project, The 178 n.142
   'Capitalism as Religion' 81, 83, 93, 177 n.130, 178 nn.139, 147
   on constellation 165 n.134
   'Critique of Violence' 86, 178 n.135, 179 n.173
   'Dialogue on the Religiosity of the Present' 57
   'Fate and Character' 86
   'Franz Kafka: On the Tenth Anniversary of His Death' 55, 94
   on Freud 85 (*see also* Freud, Sigmund)
   image of theology 57
   on Kafka 102–3 (*see also* Kafka, Franz)
   on Marx 85, 178 n.142 (*see also* Marx, Karl)
   One Way Street 82
   'On Language as Such and on the Language of Man' 195 n.207
   on Nietzsche 85, 179 n.163 (*see also* Nietzsche, Friedrich)
   'On the Concept of History' 57, 101
   Origin of the German Trauerspiel 35, 139, 164 n.132, 165 n.134
   on *Schicksal* (fate) 84
   on *Schuld* (guilt/debt) 83, 84
   on *Schuldgeschichte* (guilt history) 84–5
   on thinking in images 164 n.132
   on truth 36
   'Untitled (Fragment 65)' 179 n.165
   on violence 35–6, 86
   'Wahre Politik, Die' 82
   'Wahre Politiker, Der' 82
Berkeley, George 17, 18
Bernstein, Eduard 14
Bernstein, J. M. 137, 142
Besançon, Alain 5
Biel, Gabriel 174 n.83
Bloch, Ernst 9, 56, 82, 83, 158 n.4
   'Something's Missing' 157 n.45, 159 n.18, 165 n.144, 195 n.195

Index

Spirit of Utopia 83
Thomas Münzer als Theologe der Revolution 82
Blumenberg, Hans 180 n.182
  Legitimacy of the Modern Age, The 88, 93, 180 n.177
  on secularization 88–91, 93, 180 n.177
Bogdanov, Alexander 16–17, 160 n.46
  Empirio-Monism 16
Book of Exodus 1–2
Borchardt, Rudolf 139, 146
  'Verse bei Betrachtung von Landschaft-Zeichnungen geschrieben' 106, 145
bourgeois interior 38–40
Brecht, Bertolt 56
  Mahagonny 56, 95
Bredekamp, Horst 5
Brittain, Christopher Craig 72
Brod, Max 102, 182 n.208
Bromberg, Svenja 163 n.97
Bryant, Levi 162 n.91
Buber, Martin 58
  I–Thou relation 58
Buchholz, René 50
Buck-Morss, Susan 38, 170 n.26
Burckhardt, Jacob 63
Bürger, Peter 194 n.164
Burgh, Albert 37
Burke, Edmund 188 n.54

Calvelli-Adorno, Maria 58
Caygill, Howard 98, 109, 187 n.21, 188 n.37
classical art 130
Claussen, Detlev 58
clinamen 25
cognition 96, 100, 176 n.117
  Utopia of 11, 35, 44, 47–8, 51, 101, 135
Cohen, Hermann 4, 66
  Religion of Reason out of the Sources of Judaism, The 156 n.30
Cole, Andrew 163 n.109
Comay, Rebecca 3, 5, 9, 11, 156 n.25, 172 n.56, 192 n.132
commodification and autonomous art 137
common sense, notion of 111

communication
  Adorno on 142 (*see also* Adorno, Theodor W.)
  Geuss on 75–6, 175–6 n.102 (*see also* Geuss, Raymond)
  Habermas on 74–5 (*see also* Habermas, Jürgen)
Corot, Jean-Baptiste-Camille 105, 139, 146, 147
correlationism 27, 29
Critical Theory 74–6, 175 n.94, 190 n.98

Darstellung (presentation) 117, 120, 121
  Adorno on 35, 80, 169 n.2, 180 n.177 (*see also* Adorno, Theodor W.)
  Benjamin on 35 (*see also* Benjamin, Walter)
Da Vinci, Leonardo 37
Derrida, Jacques 159 n.13
  on Adorno 152, 167 n.179 (*see also* Adorno, Theodor W.)
Descartes, René 31
Deuser, Hermann 58, 171 n.34
De Vries, Hent 59, 81, 183 n.208
dialectical materialism. (*See* Diamat))
Dialectic of Enlightenment (Adorno and Horkheimer) 4, 7, 10, 33, 40, 44, 45, 59, 61–6, 73, 84, 87, 90, 92, 123, 133, 136
Diamat (dialectical materialism) 31
  Adorno on 11, 16, 22, 25, 26, 33, 34, 37, 43 (*see also* Adorno, Theodor W.)
Dierks, Sonja 183 n.211
dislocation, concept of 103
  Freud on 92, 93, 181 n.200, 182 n.207 (*see also* Freud, Sigmund)
  Khatib on 88, 93 (*see also* Khatib, Sami)
domination
  Adorno and Horkheimer on 63
  Horkheimer on 63, 190 n.98 (*see also* Horkheimer, Max)
  of nature 66, 71, 133, 134, 139, 141, 142, 168 n.194
  principle of 33, 34
  self- 7, 46, 61
Düttmann, Alexander García 156 n.33, 177 n.119, 195 n.215
dynamical sublime 113

and mathematical sublime compared 115–16
  significance of 116–17

Eichendorff, Joseph von 105
Elbe, Ingo 14, 159 n.20
Engels, Friedrich 13, 14
  Anti-Dühring 13
  on dialectics 14–15
  Dialectics of Nature 13, 14
  on history 16
  'Letter to Conrad Schmidt, 1.11.1891' 14–15
  Ludwig Feuerbach and the End of Classical German Philosophy 13
enlightenment 7, 141, 147
  Adorno and Horkheimer on 4, 45, 46, 62, 63
Entstellung. *See* dislocation, concept of
Epicurus 22–5
epistemology 10, 11, 78, 80, 100, 161 n.65
ethics 2, 99, 141, 149, 151, 168 n.207, 189 n.80, . *See also* morality
  aesthetics and 118, 120, 122, 124, 132
  theology and 80, 83, 86, 89

fate 3, 63–4, 66
  Adorno and Horkheimer on 63–4, 66
  Benjamin on 84, 86–7 (*see also* Benjamin, Walter)
  guilt and 86, 87
  significance of 84
'feeling of resistance' 48, 147
Fenves, Peter 185 n.267
  on Adorno's relationship to Kierkegaard and Benjamin 164 n.132
fideism 30
Finlayson, James Gordon 195 n.193
  on Habermas's critique of Adorno 73
'first nature', concept of 46
form, Kant's notion of 119
Frank, Manfred 165 n.140
Freud, Sigmund 4, 6, 53, 156 n.25
  on *Entstellung* (dislocation) 92, 93, 181 n.200, 182 n.207
  Interpretation of Dreams, The 181 n.200
  Moses & Monotheism 4

on repression 85, 91–3, 136
Totem & Taboo 65
Früchtl, Josef 196 n.226
Fukuyama, Francis 159 n.13

Gasché, Rodolphe 106–7, 111–13, 125, 127, 128, 136
  on Adorno's reading of Kant and Hegel's aesthetics 107
Geisenhanslüke, Achim 117
Gethmann-Siefert, Annemarie 192 n.128
Geuss, Raymond 176 n.105
  on Habermas 75–6, 175–6 n.102
  (*see also* Habermas, Jürgen)
Gordon, Peter E. 103, 170 n.17
Grant, Iain Hamilton 162 n.91
guilt (*Schuld*) 182 n.208
  fate and 86, 87
  pervasiveness of 80, 84, 87
  significance of 83–5
  universal 85, 86, 87
guilt history 84–5
Guyer, Paul 110

Habermas, Jürgen 73, 80, 151, 175 n.94, 175–6 n.102
  on communication 74–6
  critique of Adorno 73–5 (*see also* Adorno, Theodor W.)
  on ideal speech situation 75, 176 n.102
  Philosophical Discourse of Modernity, The 197 n.10
  'Primal History of Subjectivity, The' 73
  public sphere 152
  Theory of Communicative Action, The 74
Halbertal, Moshe 2, 3
Hallward, Peter 29
  critique of Meillasoux 30, 32
Hamacher, Werner
  on Benjamin 84–5, 179 n.173
  (*see also* Benjamin, Walter)
  on Kafka 103 (*see also* Kafka, Franz)
Hammer, Espen 167 n.184
Harman, Graham 162 n.91
Hegel, Friedrich 20–2, 29, 106, 161 n.52, 172 n.40, 186–7 n.17, 193 n.151
  on absolute knowledge 29
  on aesthetics 124–32, 192 nn.128, 132

Aesthetics 129–30
on beauty
  of art 125, 126, 128, 134–6, 138
  of nature 126, 128, 134–6, 138
on dialectic 14–15, 22, 60, 136
Encyclopaedia of the Philosophical Sciences 124, 132
on forms of art
  classical 130
  romantic 130
  symbolic 130–3
on freedom 127
on Jewish art 129, 130, 132–3
on Judaism 132–2, 193 n.146
  ban on images 124, 125, 129, 131, 133, 167 n.171
  Psalms 131–3
on Kant 21, 41, 130–1 (*see also* Kant, Immanuel)
Lectures on the History of Philosophy 161 n.61, 187 n.17
on life 126–30
on negation
  determinate 40–2
  indeterminate 127, 128, 130
Phenomenology of Spirit, The 20, 21, 40, 41
Science of Logic, The 41
on soul 127, 128
on sublimity 130–2
Heidegger, Martin 23, 27, 38, 65, 67–8, 71, 156 n.33, 173 n.70
  similarity to Adorno 68
Hellenic Atomism 22
Henrich, Dieter 187 n.28
historical determinism 16, 25, 139
historical materialism 9, 10, 14, 34, 43, 50
history. *See* guilt history; natural history; negative universal history; universal history
Hodgson, Peter C. 194 n.156
Hohendahl. Peter Uwe 194 n.175
Hölderlin, Friedrich 105, 139, 150
  Mnemosyne 150
Homer 62
  Odyssey, The 46, 62
Honneth, Axel 165 n.139
  critique of first-generation Critical Theory 36

Horkheimer, Max 4, 59, 62–3, 87, 166 n.147, 172 n.54, 190 n.98
  wholly other 76, 175 n.94 (*see also* 'wholly other', idea of)
Hotho, Heinrich Gustav 125, 192 n.128
Huillet, Danièle 1
Hullot-Kentor, Robert 174 n.73
Hume, David 188 n.54
  Enquiry Concerning Human Understanding 29–30
Husserl, Edmund 45, 160 n.37

idealism 73, 78, 136, 152, 177 n.117, 187 n.33.
  and materialism, opposition of 10, 17, 44
ideal speech situation 75, 76, 176 n.102
identity thinking 12, 35, 44, 73, 79, 153
image ban. *See also individual entries*
  Adorno on 107–8 (*see also* Adorno, Theodor W.)
  Hamacher on 103 (*see also* Hamacher, Werner)
  Hegel on 124, 125, 129, 131, 133, 167 n.171 (*see also* Hegel, Friedrich)
  Kafka on 103 (*see also* Kafka, Franz)
  Kant on 108, 113, 117 (*see also* Kant, Immanuel)
  Lyotard on 107–8 (*see also* Lyotard, Jean-François)
  theological 10, 12, 13, 35, 43, 150
imageless materialism 9–13. *See also* imagelessness; materialism
  reflection theory and 13–19
    Adorno's critique of 19–26
  Speculative Realism and 26–33
immanence 4, 21, 54, 101, 149, 151, 161 n.65
intellectus archetypus 96–8, 103
intuition 30, 54, 68, 131
  intellectual 97
  sensible 97
inverse theology 52–7, 67, 68, 71, 78, 92–102; *See also* theology
inversion, significance of 36–40, 47
inwardness, philosophy of 38–9
irrationality 38, 67, 69–70, 73, 75, 87, 141

James, David   130, 131
Jameson, Fredric   174 n.73, 180 n.181
Jarvis, Simon   44, 141
Jaspers, Karl   65
Jay, Martin   189 n.80
Jewish art   129, 130, 132-3
Johannes the Seducer   39
Judaism   3-4, 58, 59, 122, 123, 129,
    155 n.2, 173 n.62, 174-5 n.90
judgement   27, 41, 82, 96, 103,
    134, 182 n.208
  aesthetic   99, 109-11, 113, 115, 119
  agreeable   110
  art and   142-3
  of beautiful   114
  determinate   108
  of good   110
  indeterminate   108
  'judgementless'   99
  Kant on   96-9, 108, 110-11 (*see also*
      Kant, Immanuel)
  practical   109
  reflective   109, 187 n.21
  regulative   98, 101, 108, 152
  of sublime   114
  of taste   109-11, 119
  teleological   96, 109
  theoretical   109

Kabbalah   56, 95, 171 n.34, 173 n.62
Kafka, Franz   56, 101-3, 182-3 n.208,
    183 n.211
  'Cares of a Family Man, The'   103
  Castle, The   101-2
  'Thou Shalt no Image –'   103, 169 n.1
Kaiser, Hellmuth   182 n.208
Kant, Immanuel   17, 18, 30, 70,
    136, 163 nn.109-10,
    167 n.181, 176 n.117
  on aesthetics   108-9, 186 nn.13, 17,
      187 nn.21, 28, 31, 33, 187-8
      n.37, 188 n.54
    analytic of beautiful   109-13
    analytic of sublime   113-17
  'Analytic of Aesthetic Judgement'   109
  on 'as if'   98-9
  on ban on images   108, 113, 117
  on beauty
    of art   110, 112, 113
    of nature   111-13, 133-6, 140

  as symbol for morality   112
  on common sense (*Gemeinsinn*)
      111, 187 n.21
  Copernican revolution   46-7
  Critique of Practical Reason   108
  Critique of Pure Reason   21, 28, 96,
      101, 108, 109
  Critique of the Power of Judgement   96,
      97, 99, 107-9, 134
  on disinterestedness   110
  on form   109, 111, 112, 114, 117
  on God   96
  *Groundwork of the Metaphysics of
      Morals*   184 n.237
  Hegel on   21, 41, 130-1 (*see also*
      Hegel, Friedrich)
  on *intellectus archetypus*   96-8
  on *intellectus ectypus*   96
  on judgement   96-9, 108, 110-11
      (*see also* judgement)
  Meillassoux on   28-9 (*see also*
      Meillassoux, Quentin)
  Metaphysics of Morals, The   188 n.44
  Prolegomena to any Future Metaphysics
      45
  on purposiveness without an end
      99, 111
  on reason   98
  *Religion Within the Limits of
      Reason Alone*   70
  sublime notion of, Lyotard on
      117-24 (*see also* Lyotard,
      Jean-François; sublime)
Kautsky, Karl   14
Khatib, Sami   88, 92-3
  Teleologie ohne Endzweck   88
Kierkegaard, Søren   58, 69, 78, 102,
    182-3 n.208
  on aesthetic sphere   38-9
  Either/Or   38-9
  on interiority (bourgeois *intérieur*)
      38, 40
  on window mirrors   38-40
Koch, Gertrud   197 n.226
Kogon, Eugen   173 nn.66, 70
Kohlenbach, Margarete   183 n.208
Kojève, Alexandre   184 n.228
Korsch, Karl   9
  Marxism and Philosophy   9
Kracauer, Siegfried   58

Krahl, Hans-Jürgen 152
  critique of Adorno's politics 151
Kraushaar, Wolfgang 165 n.133
Krenek, Ernst 171 n.28
Külpe, Oswald 160 n.37
Kulturlandschaft (cultural landscape) 138, 146
Kurz, Gerhard 165 n.140

Landauer, Gustav 56, 82
Lange, Friedrich Albert 23–5
  History of Materialism 23
Lanzmann, Claude 191 n.123
Law (Ten Commandments) 1–3, 5, 65, 108, 117, 118, 156 n.21
Lenin 11, 14, 159 n.19, 161 n.51. See also materialism
  on Bogdanov 16–17, 160 n.46
  on Mach 17–18, 160 n.46
    (*see also* Mach, Ernst)
  Materialism and Empirio-Criticism 11, 16, 20, 26
  and Meillassoux compared 30
    (*see also* Meillassoux, Quentin)
  reading of Engels 14, 16, 20, 32
  on reflection theory 13, 14, 16–19, 22, 25
  on representational thinking 13, 16, 20, 22, 23, 26
Löwenthal, Leo 58
Löwith, Karl 181 n.183
  Meaning in History 89
Löwy, Michael 56, 158 n.4
Lukács, Georg 9, 45–6, 56, 59, 63, 78, 138, 158 n.8
  History and Class-Consciousness 9
  on second nature 45–6, 113, 139
  Theory of the Novel 63, 139
Luther, Martin
  on faith 71
  relationship to nominalism 70–1, 174 n.83
  view of reason 71
Lyotard, Jean-François 107, 141, 189 n.80, 190 nn.84, 88, 191 nn.119, 123, 193 n.148
  'Adorno as the Devil' 190 n.83
  and Adorno compared 124 (*see also* Adorno, Theodor W.)
  Heidegger and 'the jews' 122

Inhuman, The 5, 189 n.80
  on Kant's notion of sublime 117–24
    (*see also* Kant, Immanuel; sublime)
  'Newman: The Instant' 118
  Postmodern Fables 191 n.114

Mach, Ernst 17, 160 nn.37, 46
Mahler, Gustav 6, 105
Malevich, Kasimir 5
Margalit, Avishai 3
Martin, Stewart 137
Marx, Karl 6, 53, 85, 165 n.144, 167 n.181, 178 n.142. *See also* materialism
  Anti-Dühring 13
  Capital, Vol 1 162 n.89
  Capital, Vol 3 165 n.141
  Difference between the Democritean and Epicurean Philosophy of Nature, The 23
  Ludwig Feuerbach and the End of Classical German Philosophy 13
  on materialism 15, 23, 184 n.235
  'Theses on Feuerbach' 15
Marxism 9, 11, 82
  materialism and 14, 16, 17, 19, 22, 26
  Soviet 13, 43, (*see also* Lenin; Materialism)
  Western 9, 158 n.3
materialism 7, 23, 80. *See also individual entries*
  dialectical 16, 22, 25, 26, 33, 34, 37, 43
  historical 9, 10, 14, 34, 43, 50
  and idealism, opposition of 10, 17, 44
  imageless (*see* imageless materialism)
  scientific 161 n.51
  significance of 11–12
  Soviet 11, 13, 20, 23, 35, 43
mathematical sublime 113
  and dynamical sublime compared 115–16
Meillassoux, Quentin 12, 26–8, 163 nn.97, 109–10, 164 n.124
  After Finitude 12, 26, 27, 31
  on ancestrality 28
  on Copernican revolution 28
  on correlationism 29

on Hume 29–30 (*see also*
    Hume, David)
on Kant 28–9 (*see also*
    Kant, Immanuel)
and Lenin compared 30
    (*see also* Lenin)
on non-necessity 29
Mendelssohn, Moses 186 n.13
messianic/messianism 51, 56, 97, 141
'messianic light' 95, 102
metaphysics 3, 5, 55, 62, 87,
        105, 135, 142
    fall of 7, 78, 79, 105
    materialism and 7, 23, 26,
        29, 31–3, 80
    negative universal history and
        76–81
    solidarity with 7, 78, 105
    and theology
        difference between 77
        similarity between 78
Mnemosyne (Hölderlin) 150
morality 99, 119. *See also* ethics
    and beauty, parallels between 112
moral law 116–19, 122, 187 n.33
Moses 3, 65
    on idolatry 1–3, 5
Moses und Aron (Schoenberg)
    (opera) 1, 53
Müller-Doohm, Stefan 171 n.28
myth 20, 65, 66, 84–7, 90
    Adorno and Horkheimer on 62–4

Nancy, Jean-Luc 92, 195 n.215
natural beauty 105–7, 128
    Adorno on 133–47 (*see also* Adorno,
        Theodor W.)
    Gasché on 111–13 (*see also*
        Gasché, Rodolphe)
    Hegel on 125, 127 (*see also* Hegel,
        Friedrich)
    Kant on 111–13, 133–6, 140 (*see also*
        Kant, Immanuel)
    promise of 140–7
    repression of 136
nature
    Adorno on 66, 71, 133, 134, 139, 141,
        142, 168 n.194 (*see also* Adorno,
        Theodor W.)
    first 46

Lukács on 45–6, 113, 139 (*see also*
    Lukács, Georg)
    second 45–6, 113, 139
negation 135, 177 n.120.
    Adorno on 41–3 (*see also* Adorno,
        Theodor W.)
    determinate 40–2, 49, 73, 74
    Habermas on 73, 74 (*see also*
        Habermas, Jürgen)
    Hegel on 40–1 (*see also* Hegel,
        Friedrich)
    indeterminate 73
    knowledge of God through 72
negative dialectics 36, 42. *See also*
    individual entries
    similarity with negative theology 74
negative theology 54, 67, 72–4, 76, 80–1.
    See also apophatic theology
    Habermas on 73 (*see also*
        Habermas, Jürgen)
negative universal history 90, 168 n.206
    metaphysics and 76–81
    religion and 64–6
    significance of 59–62
    theology and 66–76
Neo-Platonism 5
Newman, Barnett 119, 123
Nicholsen, Shierry Weber 195 n.207
Nietzsche, Friedrich 5, 6, 53,
        85, 179 n.163
    On the Genealogy of Morals 85
nihilism, Adorno on 79, 177 n.120
nominalism 67–8, 70–1, 174 nn.73, 83
non-identity 140
    Adorno on 37, 48, 113 (*see also*
        Adorno, Theodor W.)

Oberman, Heiko A. 174 n.83
object. *See* subject and object
Ockham, William of 174 n.83
Odyssey (Homer) 62, 64
original sin, Christian doctrine of 85
Osborne, Peter 80

Paetzold, Heinz 195 n.184
Pascal, Blaise 69
Plato 5
praxis 14–16, 43, 44
    affirmation of 15
    political 17, 18, 30

pseudo- 151
transformative 37, 49
revolutionary 25, 32
Pritchard, Elizabeth 40
profanation 57, 94, 135
  Agamben on 88, 90–1 (*see also*
    Agamben, Giorgio)
  and secularization, compared 91
  of theology 67, 68, 71, 72, 81,
    88, 90–1, 93
progress, concept of 60, 71, 85, 89,
  100–1, 180 n.177
*Protestant Ethic and the Spirit of
  Capitalism, The* (Weber) 81

Rancière, Jacques 193 n.148
  critique of Lyotard 119, 121–3
    (*see also* Lyotard, Jean-François)
realism 23, 67–8, 70, 71, 158 n.8. *See also*
  Speculative Realism
reason
  and faith 67–71
  secular modernity and 72
reconciliation 107, 138–40, 142
  of differences 152
  false 42
redemption 58, 118, 182 n.208
  standpoint of 56, 95, 97, 98, 101, 102
reflection theory 10, 106,
  158 n.8, 164 n.132
  concept and significance of 13–19
    Adorno's critique of 19–26
    (*see also* Adorno, Theodor W.)
  Leninist 35, 37, 42, 43
religion 59, 62, 64–6, 72, 78, 80,
  131–2, 177 n.130. *See also
  individual entries*
  Adorno and Horkheimer on 65
  Agamben on 90–2 (*see also*
    Agamben, Giorgio)
  capitalism as 81–7, 93
  Christianity 5, 68, 85 (*see also
    individual entries*)
  Islam 5, 129
  Judaism (*see* Judaism)
  positive 6, 53, 65, 67, 69, 76,
    87, 173 n.70
  revealed 65, 68–71
Reinhardt, Ad 5
remembrance 107, 123, 140–2, 150

representational thinking, Adorno's
  critique of 10–13, 20, 21–3,
    25, 26, 33, 42, 51
repression, significance of 50, 55, 63, 85,
  91–3, 113, 136, 138
'resurrection of the flesh' 10, 34, 43, 48
revelation 37, 65, 117
  Adorno on 67–9, 72, 77 (*see also
    Adorno, Theodor W.)
Richey, Lance Byron 18
Richter, Gerhard 143
Ritter, Joachim 195 n.183
romantic art 130
Rosenzweig, Franz 58
  Star of Redemption, The 58
Rotenstreich, Nathan 193 n.146
Rowley, David G. 160 n.46

sacred art, significance of 53–4
Scharper, Eva 99
Scheerbart, Paul 83
  Lesabéndio 82
Schelling, Friedrich Wilhelm Joseph 136
  Philosophy of Art, The 136
Schiller, Friedrich 136
Schmidt, Alfred 23, 140
  On Adorno's concept of materialism
    12, 159 n.19 (*see also* Adorno,
    Theodor W.)
  Concept of Nature in Marx, The
    159 n.19
Schmidt, Conrad 14, 15
Schmitt, Carl 55
  Political Theology 180 n.182
  on secularization 89, 91
Schoenberg, Arnold 1, 2, 53, 105,
  155 n.2, 170 n.10
Schoeps, Hans Joachim 102,
  182–3 n.208
Scholasticism, Adorno on 69, 70
Scholem, Gershom 7, 83, 95, 102,
  173 n.62, 183 n.208
  on Adorno 37, 171 n.34 (*see also
    Adorno, Theodor W.)
  Major Trends in Jewish Mysticism 95
  *Walter Benjamin: The Story of a
    Friendship* 171 n.34
Schuld. *See* guilt (*Schuld*)
'second nature', concept of 45–6,
  113, 139

secularization 55, 88–94, 180 n.177
  Adorno on 88–9, 93–4 (*see also* Adorno, Theodor W.)
  Agamben on 90–1 (*see also* Agamben, Giorgio)
  Blumenberg on 88–9 (*see also* Blumenberg, Hans)
  Khatib on 92–3 (*see also* Khatib, Sami)
  Löwith on 89 (*see also* Löwith, Karl)
  Schmitt on 89, 91 (*see also* Schmitt, Carl)
  Weber on 89 (*see also* Weber, Max)
semblance 39, 49105, 124, 135, 143–5, 184 n.235
Sohn-Rethel, Alfred 47, 167 n.181, 168 n.194
  correspondence with Adorno 47, 167 n.181 (*see also* Adorno, Theodor W.)
  Intellectual and Manual Labour 167 n.181
Sorel, Georges 82
Speculative Realism 26–33, 162 n.91
Spinoza, Baruch 37, 165 n.143
Srnicek, Nick 162 n.91
Stalin, Joseph 14
Steiner, Uwe 82, 83, 178 nn.135, 147
Stendhal 140, 195 n.193
Straub, Jean-Marie 1
subject and object 15, 27, 42, 44–9, 79, 135
  alienation of 39
  division of 33
  non-identity between 140
  rapprochement between 37, 40, 49
subjectivity 10, 14, 151, 168 n.194, 172 n.54, 176 n.117
sublime/sublimity 5, 106, 109, 188–9 n.54
  analytic of 113–17
  and beautiful
    commonalities between 114
    differences between 114, 133
  dynamical 113, 115–17
  Hegel on 130–2 (*see also* Hegel, Friedrich)
  Judaism and 130–2
  Lyotard on Kant's notion of 117–24 (*see also* Lyotard, Jean-François)
  mathematical 113, 115–16

suffering 14, 33, 43, 48–9, 61, 67, 80, 142, 146, 177 n.119
symbolic art 130–3

Taubes, Jacob 151, 184 n.228
  critique of Adorno 56, 97–9, 102, 152 (*see also* Adorno, Theodor W.)
teleological judgment 96–7, 109
telos 49, 151
  of history 16
  of Marxist materialism 50
  providential 172 n.40
theology 66
  apophatic 72, 174–5 n.90
  dialectical 48, 134, 182 n.208
  inverse 52–7, 67, 68, 71, 78, 92–102
  and metaphysics 77–8
  negative 54, 67, 72–6, 76, 80–1
  positive 6, 12, 35, 48, 50, 53, 65, 67, 69, 75, 76, 81, 87, 96
  and religion 66–72
  of the trace 81
Tiedemann, Rolf 105
Tikkun (restoration), idea of 56
Tillich, Paul 54, 58
Toscano, Alberto 91
transcendence 6, 47, 70–3, 78–80, 97, 100, 145, 167 n.181, 196 n.216
Trebatius 90
truth 25, 37, 41, 77, 100, 135, 143
  Benjamin on 36 (*see also* Benjamin, Walter)

Unger, Erich 82
universal history 60. *See also* negative universal history
  Adorno on 60–1 (*see also* Adorno, Theodor W.)
Utopia 6, 42, 159 n.13, 124, 143, 149–50
  of cognition 11, 35, 44, 47–8, 51, 101, 135
  of communication 75
  imageless image of 146, 147

Vaihinger, Hans
  Philosophy of 'As If', The 100, 101
Valéry, Paul 158 n.1
Voller, Christian 180 n.177
Voltaire 89

Weber, Max   81, 85, 89,
    177 n.130, 180 n.181
Weber, Samuel   83, 165 n.144,
    179 n.168, 182 n.207
Weber Nicholsen, Shierry   196 n.207
Weigel, Sigrid   182 n.208
Weill, Kurt   56
   Mahagonny   56, 95
Western Marxism   9, 158 n.3
White, Graham   174 n.83
White, James   160 n.46

'wholly other', idea of   72, 73, 75, 76, 79,
    103, 106, 175 n.94
Wiesengrund, Oskar   58
Wilamowitz-Moellendorff,
    Ulrich von   63
window mirror (*Reflexionsspiegel*)   38–40
Wolff, Christian   119

Zeller, Eduard   161 n.70
   History of Greek Philosophy, A   23
Žižek, Slavoj   162 n.93

www.ingramcontent.com/pod-product-compliance
Lightning Source LLC
Chambersburg PA
CBHW072231290426
44111CB00012B/2053